MOTHER
DAUGHTER
REVOLUTION

MOTHER DAUGHTER REVOLUTION

FROM GOOD GIRLS TO GREAT WOMEN

Elizabeth Debold

Marie Wilson

Idelisse Malavé

 Bantam Books

New York Toronto London Sydney Auckland

MOTHER DAUGHTER REVOLUTION

A Bantam Book / published by arrangement with Addison-Wesley
PUBLISHING HISTORY
Addison-Wesley edition published September 1993
Bantam trade paperback edition / October 1994

All acknowledgments for permission to reprint previously published material can be found on pages 376–377

Book design by Beth Tondreau Design/Robin Bentz.
Library of Congress Cataloging-in-Publication Data
Debold, Elizabeth.
    Mother daughter revolution : from good girls to great women / Elizabeth Debold, Marie Wilson, Idelisse Malavé.
       p.   cm.
    Includes bibliographical references and index.
    ISBN 0-553-37418-4
    1. Mothers and daughters—United States.   2. Feminists—United
States—Family relationships.   I. Wilson, Marie (Marie C.)
II. Malavé, Idelisse.   III. Title.
HQ755.85.D4   1994
306.874'3—dc20   94-14608
                                                         CIP

Published simultaneously in the United States and Canada

Bantam Books are published by Bantam Books, a division of Bantam Doubleday Dell Publishing Group, Inc. Its trademark, consisting of the words "Bantam Books" and the portrayal of a rooster, is Registered in U.S. Patent and Trademark Office and in other countries. Marca Registrada. Bantam Books, 1540 Broadway, New York, New York 10036.

PRINTED IN THE UNITED STATES OF AMERICA

BVG   0 9 8 7 6 5 4 3

To our mothers:
Martha, Collie, Emma.

To Idelisse's children:
Celeste and Gabriel.

To Marie's children:
Renée, Kirsten, Gene, David, and Martin.

(And to Elizabeth's future children.)

Contents

Introduction

ELIZABETH:

The heat that summer in Pittsburgh made tar roads sticky and burned through the soles of my mother's shoes. She tried to stay at home as much as she could. During her final trimester of pregnancy with me, her first child, the heat almost took her breath away. She would drag a stool into the shower and sit under the running water to cool off. She had read in a magazine that if, during your pregnancy, you did all of the things that you wanted your child to do, the child would grow up to do those things. So she listened to classical music and read; she wanted her child to appreciate "the finer things in life," the things to which she had so little access. (To this day, she's convinced that it worked.) My mother wanted a boy.

She knew how hard girls' lives were, particularly for the oldest daughter. Born to a smart and sassy working-class woman who was battered by her husband, my mother spent her adolescence going to school, cooking meals while her mother worked, taking care of her mentally retarded brother, and working part-time. Her mother felt she had a right—and certainly the need—to call on her daughter to lighten her own heavy load. They fought constantly.

My mother yearned to marry and be able to stay at home and raise her children. She bought the tantalizing promise of romance and family life held out to women in the 1950s. My mother's Prince Charming was a tall, handsome, bright, and, yes, charming man who was a lot of fun. They talked about how different they wanted their lives and the lives of their children to be. They married and within two years, she was carrying a child.

She didn't have a boy. She had me. And she promised herself that I would never have to do what she had had to do as an eldest daughter. She has kept her promise. My mother had the courage to break a cycle of generations.

Instead of her hoped-for family life, she found herself hanging by her fingernails to the bottom of the middle class. My father, out of a pain he never named, wasted his remarkable mind figuring out creative ways to avoid his responsibilities (and we were some of them) and devising torments and humiliations for all of us. And, as if to keep us on our toes, he *was* also smart and funny and charming and, unpredictably, loving.

My mother stayed with this man because she knew of no other way to provide us with a decent education. While an extraordinarily talented seamstress, cook, plumber—you name it, she could make it or fix it—she felt that she had no skills worth a paycheck and had no way of envisioning her life without his support. She sacrificed herself in a marriage with a man who seemed bent on her submission and destruction. But she made available to me teachers who would save me as she couldn't save herself.

Henry Duda and Jan Mellinger saved my mind and soul. Mr. Duda, my sixth-grade teacher, made me feel smart and funny and loved. Once in anger he said, "You know what's going to happen to you? You're going to find out about boys and then you'll flush your mind down the toilet." I didn't know exactly what he meant, but his dark words struck someplace deep inside me. They sounded very scary, very real. I took him my nearly straight A report card the next year, just to let him know I wasn't flushed yet.

But I was fairly flushed by eleventh grade. In Miss Mellinger's late-morning English class, I could barely croak out words because somewhere between the sixth and eleventh grades, I had silenced myself. She heard my voice, though, in a much hated poetry-writing assignment. Miss Mellinger encouraged me and gave me permission to speak out of places in myself that I no longer knew existed.

My mother's gift of an education born of her self-sacrifice has been heavy for me to bear. Her betrayal by my father and by a culture that left her feeling powerless without him has, in some ways, been felt by each of us at different times as betrayal of each other. "I know," she said to me during a difficult conversation, "that the reason why you do the work you do is because of me, because of my life."

She is absolutely right. The work that I do *is* because of her life, her brave and painful struggle to provide me, and my brothers and sister, with a life that she never had. One of the most moving moments of my life was when she, at the age of sixty-two, told me that she finally was going to leave my father. She was going to spend the rest of her life figuring out what made her happy. Oh, yes, she is right. I don't want another generation of mothers to have to wait that long.

MARIE:

"Mother, I'm going to write a book."
"What about?"
"Mothers and daughters."
Silence.
"Mom?"
Silence.
"What's wrong?"
"You know."
"You don't have to be afraid."

My mother grew up tough. She was the third of three generations of women who had abandoned their children because of poverty. Shuttled between foster homes, living with families who moved from one abandoned building to the next during the Great Depression, she was industrious. As a girl, she took in laundry and delivered it in her red wagon. She was creative. She swears she invented covering Easter baskets with cellophane as a teenage employee of Woolworth's. And she was and is beautiful.

She dealt with sexual abuse by ignoring it, and she survived poverty by knowing how to work hard. For the rest, she had to count on her creativity and beauty. During my growing up, she worked as a dental hygienist (she changed fields at fifty-two). If she had been a man, she would have been Steve Ross and built Time-Warner. They both grew up tough and smart. As it is, she has supported the careers of many successful men.

Her chaotic growing up made her a hurt and angry woman. She had never been really mothered, and I thank God she had to work outside the home, because she had a temper. But whatever flew from her hands and her lips, I knew she loved me fiercely. And I remember always knowing that the anger came from something else that was completely outside of her and me.

She taught me beauty was essential—hadn't it helped her survive? She taught me men were essential—having a father for her child had allowed her to break the cycle of her past and keep me. She schooled me to be the perfect woman and never to hurt anybody. God knows she had seen enough hurt. She taught me all the survival skills that had worked for her.

When I went to a counselor as an adult, he told me that I should understand that because of how my mother grew up, she just couldn't love me. I took in all the helpful things he told me and junked this one. In my mid-thirties, I was able to go back for my mother, to help her be a better ally for herself and for me, and she continuously gives me credit for that.

From her I learned about the integrity of work; I learned to work hard and long, and to view no task as "beneath" me. She personified "Bread and Roses" by showing me the value of beauty and order as nourishment. I think it was my mother who was at the Sermon on the Mount:

Making a loaf of bread and a fish feed a crowd would be nothing to her. No one can make food stretch so far and look so elegant. She showed me you could create beauty and have fun with scarce resources. All of these values and skills have sustained me through thirty years of long hours, drudgery mixed with gratification, stretching of scarce resources, and dancing. This is the work of social change.

She taught me well. I, too, am a mother of daughters who teach me as well. When I feel sorry for myself about having to take tough stands and receive bruises, my daughters remind me I grew up as a resister. When I am afraid that my work will be misunderstood, they laugh and assure me it will. Then they pull out ten resources I can use to soften the blow. I am sure they have struggled with and learned from the ways I taught them based on my own survival. The good news is that we have a lifetime, that I am writing this book, and that my mother has nothing to fear.

IDELISSE:

My mother sews. She made my clothes when I was growing up, mostly dresses and skirts. She loved circle skirts, those wide, flared skirts that open up and spin like phonograph records when you turn. I loved them, too, and I danced when I wore them.

She made me beautiful pastel dresses, in pale pinks, yellows, and blues. Simple little-girl dresses, they tied in the back with a big bow. But they weren't ordinary dresses. Around the bottom of the skirt my mother embroidered and painted pictures. On one dress, couples of boys and girls dressed in Mexican peasant garb danced around *sombreros*. On another, ducklings and chicks pecked at the ground.

For Easter Sunday, she would work weeks in advance to make my outfit. Together we would pick patterns for the dress and the spring coat or jacket. With an eye for color and a love of textures, she would lead me through aisles of bolts of fabrics with pretty names: silk georgette, batiste, wool crepe, chambray, handkerchief linen. She would explain what fabrics suited which designs, and she subtly guided me to just the right fabric for my dress or my jacket—at a price we could afford. One year she even made my hat and purse. Her skills with needle and thread were magical to me, and I thought she could make almost anything with a piece of cloth. My mother helped me, a poor child in a middle-class neighborhood, fit in by making sure that I looked right.

As I got older, I began to long for store-bought clothes. At thirteen I was invited to my first teenage party with boys and dancing, and my mother generously took me shopping for a dress. I tried on dress after dress under my mother's expert eye. Each was rejected in turn. One wasn't slimming. Another didn't make me look taller. I looked too flat-chested in the blue. My waist didn't look small enough in the red, green, or gray. I began to realize that we weren't looking for a dress, not really. We were looking for a disguise, a costume that would mask my many flaws and fool boys into believing I was attractive, when I wasn't. I came to understand that there was something wrong with me, not the dresses. Finally, we found the perfect dress, the best disguise. It was black, of course.

My mother understood the realities of the world. To make it, to be safe, a woman has to be attractive to men. The more attractive you are, the more things you will have and the safer you will be. Loving me, she wanted the best for me. She was trying to help me to be a successful woman, and this was the strategy she knew worked. Everyone knew that, surely? Like most of us, I don't think she let herself think about what the costs were to her and would be to me. What was the point when there were no options.

But my mother made sure I had insurance. She took pleasure in my intelligence, taught me English in a few short months before I started school, encouraged me from kindergarten to law school, and defended me from the fourth-grade teacher who doubted my capacity. She showered me with praise for my achievements and lit candles to make sure I was graced with good fortune.

I want to support my daughter, too. Celeste, my "Esti," is nine now, bright and strong and lively. Her mind is as agile as her body, and both are as lively as her sense of humor. She likes how she looks. When I asked her why, what was it about her looks that she liked, she answered, "Just the way I am is fine with me . . . because it's me." It is one of the most important lessons she has taught me, although I still have to struggle to hold on to it. She is there to make sure I do. And I am here to make sure, with all my strength and courage, that she does not lose her sureness and easy confidence, her strong sense of herself. No "unnecessary losses" for my girl.

OUR STORY

"I don't want another generation of mothers to have to wait that long."

"The good news is that we have a lifetime, that I am writing this book, and that my mother has nothing to fear."

"No 'unnecessary losses' for my girl."

We came together, we three women, because we smelled a revolutionary idea. The findings had just come out from the Harvard Project on Women's Psychology and Girls' Development under psychologist Carol Gilligan's leadership. Girls' self-esteem plummets at adolescence, marking the profound intersection of the personal and political in women's development. While younger girls are strong, outspoken, and clear about themselves, at the edge of adolescence they begin taking in what they are told about how girls *should* be and come to see how women are treated in this society. At first, they resist, continuing to trust themselves. They question the accommodations to goodness and niceness increasingly demanded of them. But they become overwhelmed by how little they feel valued and trusted by adults, by the idealization and exploitation of their budding sexuality, by violence, and by increasing injunctions to be silent. Too often, they give up their resistance and give in to what society wants them to be. Girls' intelligence and strength is betrayed by a culture that doesn't really want either.

The voices of girls that we heard in this research began to resound in us. They shattered our surface calm as we remembered our own early resistance to losing bits and pieces of our strength and courage. Not only did this research identify adolescence as a time of risk, but it also cast a light on what might be done to foster girls' strength and courage. Girls' relationships with women, particularly their mothers, are key to their ability to resist self-negating changes and to thrive.

We began to realize that raising a daughter is an extremely political act in this culture. Mothers have been placed in a no-win situation with their daughters: if they teach their daughters simply how to get along in a world that has been shaped by men and male desires, then they betray their daughters' potential. But, if they do not, they leave their daughters adrift in a hostile world without survival strategies. Being stubborn and/or hopeful and/or naive, we persisted: What if mothers and daughters were to join as powerful allies in withstanding the pressures on girls to give up and give in? We smelled the potential for revolution.

Carol Gilligan called to each of us to join her, to join in resisting girls' suffering by linking our struggles with theirs. The three of us found the possibilities irresistible. Idelisse couldn't resist changing the world for her daughter with the brilliant eyes. Marie couldn't resist plotting social change through our most intimate relationships. Elizabeth couldn't resist jumping out of the ivory tower back into the streets.

We met at the Ms. Foundation for Women, where Marie and Idelisse are, respectively, president and vice-president. Elizabeth, a member of the Harvard Project, joined as a consultant in the summer of 1991. As a part of the Ms. Foundation's campaign to get the word out about what's happening to girls and to fund program development based on this new information, we presented the research to groups of women and asked them to respond. Women were excited and began to reclaim the memories of their own girlhood courage. Based on their responses, we began to ask: What if girls were to keep their psychological strength, courage, and voice? What would the world be like if women said what they knew and said it with authority? What if women paid attention to what they wanted and moved with confidence and joy toward their deepest desires? What if we really said the truth? We wondered where to begin.

"You should commission someone to write a book about this—maybe like Deborah Tannen," Margie Booth, the president of her own public relations firm, explained as we pondered this problem around the conference table at the Ms. Foundation offices. Elizabeth's eyebrows shot up. "Let's do it," she mouthed the words across the table to Ide and Marie.

We wanted to write a book for mothers. To a great extent, the feminist enterprise has avoided discussing motherhood. While child care, health services, and other social services are seen as "women's issues" upon which feminists have thoughtfully argued policy, motherhood has been relatively ignored or viewed, in its stay-at-home 1950s version, as a powerful aspect of women's oppression. But mothering is powerful. We wanted to suggest that mothers recognize the role that they have been asked to play as conduits and, thus, perpetuators of the dominant culture. We wanted to provide a new way of seeing how mothers *can* transmit a different culture—heritage more than history.

WHAT ON EARTH WE THINK WE ARE DOING

The information and approach presented in this book explore how mothers can have more power by bringing more of themselves into mothering their daughters. We present ways to transform what has been experienced as a cycle of betrayal between mothers and daughters into a powerful catalyst for social change. We see girls betrayed by a culture that diminishes women. The journey from betrayal to power traces how mothers can support girls in resisting the unnecessary losses they experience in growing into womanhood: losses of voice, of freedom, of power to do and to be in the world. This journey begins as women reclaim their powerful preadolescent voices as a prerequisite to voice lessons with their daughters. Then, mothers and daughters join to take action.

A primary theme of the book is resistance. We share with mothers and daughters diverse strategies to resist, that is, to fight against the silencing messages that girls receive from the culture. We question our society's and developmental psychology's focus on rugged individualism and an independence that denies interdependence. Research conducted both with women and in communities of color validates the importance of human connection to human growth. We question traditional theories of development that assume separation from mothers is normal and necessary. We think mothers will be relieved to hear that while their relationships with their daughters in adolescence will change, separation is not necessary to their daughters' self-esteem.

As adult daughters, we need new relationships with our own mothers. The tools we propose for mothering a daughter are also useful in changing our relationships with our own mothers. Too many women spend time either endlessly fighting against becoming like their mothers or unwittingly repeating their mothers' lives. Both are reactive efforts that consume life energies and power.

We women need to join together in order to liberate our daughters. Most women carry the enormous responsibility for mothering alone. We want to free mothers, to help them claim the power that should be granted to those who carry and bring life into the world, raise and care for each new generation. We ask all women to join in the political act of raising children. Concern for girls connects women across lines of race, class, sexual orientation, and disability. We have yet to experience the real healing power of taking action on behalf of girls in a community of women.

To be effective, a mother daughter revolution has to face the fact of violence in girls' and women's lives. Fear of emotional and physical violence systematically silences girls and limits their healthy entrance into womanhood. We address this in every chapter of the book, just as it is in every chapter of women's lives. Daughters' physical safety is the first concern of the mothers we spoke with. For women and girls to be able to thrive, they first must be safe from harassment, violence, and abuse. Violence will stop only when women join first with each other and then with men.

To create a society where girls can be safe and whole, we must erase the boundary between work and family, between public and private life. The assignment of men to the work world and women to the world of nurturance and love precludes women's full participation in public life and men's full participation in private life. This separation, deemed necessary to the culture, keeps women's voices from being heard.

In writing this book we relied on Elizabeth's expansion of Carol Gilligan's trailblazing theory of women's development. Carol Gilligan's working theory rests on Lyn Mikel Brown's insightful study of girls at a private school in Cleveland, Ohio. Elizabeth's expansion of this working theory frames development more explicitly in terms of the power relations that structure our culture along gender, race, and class lines. She has integrated the work of other colleagues—Annie Rogers, Deborah Tolman, Janie Victoria Ward, Dana Crowley Jack, Catherine Steiner-Adair, and Jill McLean Taylor—as well as research on trauma and cognitive development. Elizabeth explores the psychological dynamics of power, knowledge, and desire that come into play as girls begin to understand that they are becoming women in this culture.

Most importantly, we sought out a cadre of "specialists" of our own choosing: mothers who have been thinking and creating new ways of mothering that were congruent with this research. We spoke with a diverse group of women, individually and in groups, gleaning every possible strategy that moved them and their daughters along. We have learned immensely from these authorities. Their experience has brought us inspiration as well as greater proof that, in fact, what we are suggesting is feasible.

CAVEATS

We chose to write this book now because we believe that offering women this information, along with our best thinking, could lead to profound change. Our intent is to inspire *your* best thinking, to generate ideas, to engage you. This is an inquiry that is closer to the beginning than the end, a work-in-progress. This is not a recipe for perfect mothering. We do have some provocative ideas. We believe these ideas, and the questions we raise, have relevance for many women and girls. We are, however, describing patterns—of development, of relationships between mothers and daughters—that are useful constructs, not the absolute truth of any woman's or girl's experience. Your experience may not fall directly within these parameters. If it doesn't, look beyond the details to the overall theme, and don't discount our ideas or your experience prematurely. Our ideas are shaped by our experience. You are the authority, the expert on yours.

Writing a book together meant that no single one of our voices would speak. With such a personal and moving subject as mothers and daughters, we found resorting to a less-than-personal voice was sad—and distancing. But for the sake of clarity, we (the authors) generally use *we* to define ourselves as authors and *women* and *mothers* to define the community of which we, too, are a part.

Too little information has been collected on the entire community of women. The research community has neglected girls and women of color; too few women of color get to join that elite community. Young lesbians and girls with disabilities have been virtually ignored. This lack of information, which has hampered our efforts, is frustrating and unfair to us all. That which does exist we incorporated into our analysis, including the most recent Harvard Project studies with an inner-city population of ado-lescent girls considered to be "at risk," and with preadolescent girls at both a public and a private school. These studies and the American Association of University Women nationwide study on girls' self-esteem begin to con-firm that adolescence is also a time of crisis and loss for girls of color. We know that, ultimately, this is not a book about all women and girls. When we speak of "women" and "girls" we do not mean to imply a false homo-geneity. We aimed for a balance between respect for difference and effec-tive, concise communication. We strived for this balance, but we know we did not fully reach it.

Throughout the book, we have chosen to specify the race, class, ethnicity, sexual orientation, or disability of persons cited when directly relevant to the point we are making. Whether these characteristics are or are not relevant is a question of discretion, and reasonable women may differ. Further, when we write of "culture" or "society" or "Western civili-zation," we refer to the dominant culture that has largely been created and enforced by privileged white men as a group.

Now we want to invite you to enter into this inquiry. We have brought our information and ideas. Bring your experience and knowledge and enthusiasm. We believe that a mother daughter revolution unlocks the doors to the possibility of a very different world. We have gone as far as we can. We need you to join with us. This research has created the powerful germ of a new revolution, one that could change the lives of women and girls, men and boys for the better and for good. We welcome you to see— and read—for yourself.

ONE

Unnecessary Losses

IDELISSE:

"Just before dying, the Little Mermaid turns to the Prince and says with her dying breath, 'Fool!' It was the only word she—"

"You made that up!"

"No, I didn't. Look." I offer the book to my nine-year-old daughter, Esti, pointing to the passage I've just read to her. Her eyes widen as she sees that in this version of the fairy tale the Little Mermaid does, indeed, call the prince a fool. I smile at her, knowing that, familiar with my bedtime reading style, she suspected that I had manufactured and inserted this bit of dialogue. I ask her what she thinks, and she tells me, "It's . . . surprising. You don't expect to see that in stories."

Of course, she is right. This alternative version of the Hans Christian Andersen fairy tale takes many liberties with the original. The Little Mermaid never loses the greenish cast to her complexion and has a slightly, but not unattractive, fishy look to her features. The prince and she marry just a week after "she appeared out of the night" in a "romantically mysterious way," but they don't live happily ever after. They never really hit it off or feel comfortable with each other, and they end up spending less and less time with each other. In the end, the prince inadvertently kills her.

Certainly, this is not the story girls usually hear. They are raised on romantic fantasies that fit better with cultural expectations. I tried reading Esti some of the other stories from the anthology of feminist fairy tales that offered this very different version of the Little Mermaid, but most of them weren't as good. They bored us. What to do?

We decided to write our own story. I wasn't sure about how to do this with her. I started by asking her who the heroine should be. She quickly answered, "Heavenly." (I have been making up bedtime stories for Esti for years. I created a surrogate Esti to be the heroine for these stories and named her with the English-language translation of "Celeste.") "All right," I told Esti, "but let's give her a nickname." She thought a while, grinned, and said, "Steamroller." When I stopped laughing, I asked her who the other characters in this story were. "Her mother and father, and a brother."

"What are their names?" Esti decided that she shouldn't have to do all the work, so she gave me the job of coming up with their proper names and offered to provide the nicknames. Agreeing, we decided to name the mother first. I called her "Mercedes"—I've always liked that name. Esti thought for a brief moment and then, looking at me intently, said, "Lifeforce."

1

The Crossroads

We will mark this place as a crossroads in women's development: a meeting between girl and woman.

Lyn Mikel Brown & Carol Gilligan
MEETING AT THE CROSSROADS

Suddenly, through birthing a daughter, a woman finds herself face to face not only with an infant, a little girl, a woman-to-be, but also with her own unresolved conflicts from the past and her hopes and dreams for the future. Severing the umbilical cord to give a daughter breath joins a woman with generation after generation of women who came before, who birthed our foremothers. And, perhaps more importantly, this act of bodily separation connects each mother of a daughter with the next generation of women. As though experiencing an earthquake, mothers of daughters may find their lives shifted, their deep feelings unearthed, the balance struck in all their relationships once again off kilter.

Some new mothers of daughters find themselves confronting their relationships with their own mothers. "As soon as I saw my daughter," remembers Zena, "and felt how much I wanted for her, I knew that whatever my mother had done in her relationship with me, she did it out of love." Holding her daughter in her arms for the first time after the struggle of labor, Emily was struck: "What do I do? If the estrangement in my own relationship with my mother happens with her, I don't think I could bear it." Other women find themselves envisioning the future. Teresa recalls holding her daughter, looking into her wrinkly face and thinking, "Someday I will see her back as she walks away from me. You know, we hardly ever think of our babies' backs. But that's what I'll see as she begins to explore the world. There are things that I want her to know. I know some things I can teach her that can help her make her way." There are also women who never wanted a daughter because they couldn't be sure that her life would be different from their own.

Many women want something different for their daughters no matter how good the relationship with their own mothers. When the Ms. Foundation for Women and the Center for Policy Alternatives conducted a nationwide survey in 1992 to determine the concerns and priorities of women, they found that the hope that sustains women through long hours of work, school, and caring for their families is the hope of a better future for their daughters. In fact, when women who participated in the study's focus groups were asked to write a letter to their daughters, these women expressed hopes for a very different future for their daughters—one with less stress, one with more joy. Mothers hope for a different world and a different relationship for daughters, and in many cases, so did their mothers before them. Generation after generation of women have pledged to raise their daughters differently, only to find that their daughters grow up and fervently pledge the same thing.

Of all the crossroads in the life of a woman, becoming a mother of a daughter is one of the most powerful and the most political. Raising a daughter in a society that has been largely constructed by white men and is still, for the most part, run by them and by their desires is a political act. The desire to raise our daughters differently from the way we were raised may come from the anger and trouble in our relationships with our own mothers. Or it might arise simply from the recognition that our daughters' horizon of opportunity will be different. Regardless, only an understanding of the political context surrounding mother daughter relationships will begin to heal the wounds between and within generations of women.

By mothering differently we confront the status quo, which in our culture is patriarchy (a synonym for "civilization" in Western culture), or the according of higher status and greater privileges to men as a group than to women. Educated white men's views guide the beliefs and structures that cement the dominant culture. Thus, for example, the world of work is considered more noble and more real than the world of home and hearth because paid work has been men's sphere. Women can begin changing mother daughter relationships only if they look beyond the relationship and see how it is shaped by the demands and threats of the dominant patriarchy of the white middle class, as well as by the other patriarchies in which women live.

PARADOXES OF PROGRESS

The next generation of women will enter a world in which they are perceived to have more opportunities for creating fulfilling lives than women have ever had before. According to several national polls, a majority of women believe that the women's movement has changed their lives for the better. More women are working more and earning more in more occupations than ever before (although they still earn less than men). The Dick-and-Jane family of the 1950s is no longer the norm, so women have greater freedom to create new families and lives. As our visions for our own lives change, so do our visions for our daughters. For them, we believe, life should be even better.

Yet, here's the paradox: adolescent girls, as a group, are suffering deeply. Just as the world opens to them, many girls find themselves psychologically distressed. Recent large-scale studies of adolescent health indicate that adolescent girls suffer more from depression, disturbances about their appearance, eating disorders (from anorexia to obesity), stress, and other manifestations of psychological distress than adolescent boys do. Eating disorders and teenage pregnancy, once associated with opposite ends of the social class spectrum, are more prevalent among girls of all classes and all races than ever before. Each year brings the news that the percentage of girls and women who have been victims of violence and abuse, typically perpetrated by intimates, has been underreported.

Researchers have described what is happening to girls as "a picture of quiet disturbance" because adolescent girls and boys differ in their ways of experiencing distress. Boys tend to act out, to throw their distress onto the world around them through delinquency and aggressive acting out. Girls, however, tend to take their distress into themselves, to internalize it and become anxious or depressed. Girls seemingly blame themselves for their pain and self-destruct under its weight. Weighted down by hopelessness, girls attempt to kill themselves between four and five times more than boys do. While boys' greater violence makes them more successful in annihilating themselves, girls' deep pain leads them to try over and over again in utter despair.

Reports indicate that girls lose ground in school beginning at adolescence as well. While girls' academic performance surpasses boys' through grade school, this trend begins to reverse at early adolescence. Many girls consider mathematics to be their favorite subject in elementary school, only to lose interest in adolescence—and more importantly, they come to believe that they are no good at it. Detailed evidence from schools indicates that girls are treated considerably differently from boys. Girls are silenced in schools by not being called on as often, and teachers encourage boys more and take them more seriously.

Girls' silencing and their internalization of pain and distress make "girls' cries for help . . . harder to hear and easier to ignore." But larger reasons explain why girls' distress may be easier to ignore. First, we live in the country that created a neutron bomb, which would kill people and not damage property. Our society obviously shows alarm when property is damaged. Our society also recoils when violence and danger are directed against innocent people. In Oregon, for example, state budgeting procedures require a determination that public safety is threatened before granting funding for services to troubled children. A statewide coalition has challenged this focus as discriminatory to girls because girls are far less threatening to others, and thus to public safety, than are boys. Although girls are beginning to participate more in violent acts, boys remain the primary perpetrators. Thus, from a societal perspective, because girls aren't acting out aggressively and disturbing society, nothing much of consequence seems to be happening to or with them.

Second, the differences in patterns of distress that adolescent girls and boys experience mirror differences between adult women and men. From a very traditional perspective on female psychology (one that is echoed in stereotypes about women), women's tendencies toward depression, anxiety, and other forms of self-destructive, silent distress are considered simply "woman's nature." The supposed "riddle" of femininity has plagued psychology since Sigmund Freud asked in exasperation, "What do women want?" Women within male culture pose a puzzle to understandings of human life that have been built on men's experience. Unfortunately, virtually every psychological theory has been constructed with men as the model. If it is assumed that women's nature is emotional, depressive, and anxious, then why should anything be done for adolescent girls who appear to be just like women? From this perspective, these differences between adolescent girls and boys only confirm women's inherent psychological weakness. What sense does it make to attempt to "cure" adolescent girls when the "disease" is their femaleness?

Solid evidence disproving these traditional views of "woman's nature" has emerged only recently. In studies of psychological health in childhood (ages four to ten), boys outnumber girls in the prevalence of psychological and behavioral problems. As the prominent research psychologists Kimberly Schonert-Reichl and Daniel Offer state, "Prior to the onset of adolescence, girls are mentally healthier than boys, whereas, after adolescence, this state of affairs is reversed." Adolescence, too, is when girls' slide in academic performance begins. Whatever it is that creates the supposed weakness of women's nature does not seem to be a part of girls' constitution in childhood.

Girls and boys both seem to understand that life for boys and girls, men and women is very different. The Michigan Board of Education recently published a statewide study of students' perceptions of what it means to be male or female in this society. When asked how their lives would be different if they were the opposite sex, nearly 50 percent of the girls spoke of advantages to being a boy, while only 7 percent of the boys saw advantages to being a girl. While the girls found it interesting or exciting to think of life as a boy, nearly 20 percent of the boys gave extremely hostile, derogatory responses. A surprising number of boys said that they would commit suicide if they were girls. One boy wrote, "I would *kill* myself *right away* by starting myself on fire so no one knew."

In 1990, the American Association of University Women (AAUW) conducted a nationwide survey to determine, in part, whether something happens to girls' sense of or belief in themselves at adolescence. Intrigued and alarmed by early findings of the Harvard Project that pointed to the onset of adolescence as a crisis in girls' lives, the AAUW wanted to know more. The survey contained basic questions on how boys and girls think about themselves and their abilities. Sixty percent of elementary school-aged girls and 67 percent of boys felt happy with themselves. In high school, only 29 percent of the girls still felt that way, while nearly half of the boys held themselves in high esteem. While adolescence is difficult for both boys and girls, girls consistently seem to feel worse about themselves. The most precipitous drop in girls' feelings about themselves occurs between grade school and junior high.

The drop in the way girls think about themselves is bad enough, but in some ways, this finding was not the worst news from the AAUW study. A person's way of thinking about herself has real ramifications for what she will do and think of her abilities. As the AAUW report states: "The survey finds that adolescent girls are more likely than are boys to have their declining sense of themselves inhibit their actions and abilities." Adolescent boys have a greater sense of confidence in their ability to do things in their lives than girls do. Twice as many boys as girls consider their unique talents to be what they like best about themselves. Sadly, twice as many girls as boys consider what they like best about themselves to be some aspect of their appearance. Further, adolescent boys dream bigger dreams than girls do—and they are more likely to believe that their dreams can become reality.

Something happens for girls between the ages of nine and ten and early adolescence, age twelve. Some traditionalists have wondered whether the women's movement has created this distress in adolescent girls. This makes no sense when adolescent girls' distress paints an exact psychological portrait of classic womanhood. The anxiety, self-doubt, and depression that characterize girls in trouble are other ways that society identifies the traditionally feminine woman's emotionality, intellectual weakness, and demureness. Whatever has been classically, and derogatorily, called woman's nature can't be natural, as it clearly develops at adolescence, not at the beginning of a girl's life. Furthermore, not all girls in these studies develop this nature that leads to depression and anxiety. A negotiation takes place where girls trade in parts of themselves in order to become women within this culture.

Certainly, the kinds of change that we have experienced as a culture cause upheaval and confusion for generations. Increased freedom allows previously unnamed and closeted distress to move into the light of day. When Betty Friedan wrote *The Feminine Mystique,* for example, she named a problem in the lives of white American home-makers in the 1950s and 1960s. She placed the depression and malaise that these women were feeling in a larger context so that women could see it. Naming the previously unnamed allowed many women to see that they were neither sick nor crazy; "the feminine mystique" made sense out of their feelings. The openings and opportunities in girls' lives may give girls the freedom to question—often at an unconscious and psychological level—the bargains that women are still asked to make. Different girls seem to know different strategies for holding on to different parts of themselves as they make their way into womanhood. What is this struggle about? What are the forces that pull at adolescent girls and diminish them?

THE WALL

Carol Gilligan has spoken about girls' adolescence as a "crisis of connection," a time when girls experience themselves as coming up against "a wall." The "wall" is our patriarchal culture that values women less than men, that sees women largely in sexual or reproductive terms. To get through the wall, girls have to give up parts of themselves to be safe and accepted within society. Once through the wall, it becomes hard to recognize its structure as anything but "reality." As Gilligan puts it, girls give up relationship—with themselves and their own knowledge, desires, and needs—to secure relationships as prescribed in patriarchal culture.

The approach to the wall happens slowly, over a period of years. Because it happens slowly, girls and their closest companions on the journey often get used to the changes that happen. When girls are shown the differences in their voices and in themselves over time, they often balk. "When we were little," said one girl to Lyn Brown and Carol Gilligan, "we were stupid." Stupid? "Not stupid, honest," she replied. The honesty of childhood becomes stupidity in adolescence.

"What sort of scares me," says Alyshea, a twelve-year-old, "is that sometimes I'm on the phone with friends and I hear it happening. It's not the sort of thing that comes out right in front of your face and you say, 'Oh, I see this.' It's the sort of thing that sneaks up on you more and more, and you don't realize it. So it's sort of scary that it could be happening to you and you don't know it. I watch kids at school and I see—I mean I don't sit and take notes—but I look around and it seems more obvious than it did before."

Alyshea read about the AAUW study and thought that it was so ridiculous that she would prove it wrong by doing the study in her school. She got the same results. Shocked, she began to look around, to notice what was happening with her and her friends. The following year, at age thirteen, she did the study again with the same girls—girls who had seen the questions and had heard about the results. Shocked again, she saw that these girls were continuing to slide deeper into negative feelings about themselves.

In childhood, girls have confidence in what they know, think, and feel. Straight talkers, they are able to speak their minds directly. As psychologist Annie Rogers puts it (and as we explain further in chapter 4), girls have courage in an old sense of the word—they are able to speak their minds with all of their hearts. Talking seriously with a young girl is like staring into the sun: an intense eyeball-to-eyeball interaction. They are very serious people, but they don't let that stop them from being crazy and silly. Even shy and quiet girls have a presence, an authority about them as simply themselves. Girls live completely (and often squirmily) in their bodies: they are fully themselves but not full of themselves. Young girls are extremely sensitive to and articulate about unfair and uncaring treatment. For many, their call to arms is "Mo-om! That's not fair!"

But by late childhood, girls' minds and bodies have begun to change rapidly. Mentally, girls develop the intellectual ability to understand that the dynamics and arrangements of power in the world have implications for who they are and can be. Acutely sensitive to these power and relational dynamics, girls between the ages of eight and ten comment on the ways that the world prioritizes men over women. While they don't have full-blown ideas about society or politics, they know what the evidence of their years of living in patriarchal contexts has shown them.

Rebecca, age eight, and her parents were going to a prochoice march in Washington, D.C. She wanted to know more about it. Hila, her mother, explained that the march was for women to be able to have more opportunities and more control over their lives. She told Rebecca that the march would be like the one Martin Luther King, Jr., had led, which Rebecca had seen clips about on television. Rebecca paused and then turned to her mother with a question: "How come white men have all the stuff?"

Rebecca's observation of who holds "the stuff" in this cultural system marks the beginning of her capacity to reason abstractly. Within a few years, Rebecca will have to confront for herself what it means to be a girl in a world where "white men have all the stuff." At that point, she will be able to use her newfound capacity for abstract thinking to understand, often on an unspoken level, what it means to be a woman in the world that is organized as it is. Every girl's family, school, and community show her different dynamics to which she must respond.

In early adolescence, girls begin developing into women. By twelve, more than two-thirds of girls will have begun menstruating. Their breasts usually have budded, and the very contours of their bodies have changed. Desire for explicitly sexual contact spreads through their bodies for the first time. Changes in girls' bodies visually disconnect them from the world of childhood and identify them with women, and thus with images of women. Girls become looked at, objects of beauty (or not), models for idealized or fantasized relationships.

These enormous changes are difficult for girls, and for those most close to girls, to get used to. Through their own greater awareness of the world and of how others' awareness is focused on them, girls become extremely self-conscious and vulnerable. By paying close attention to what girls say and how they say it, Lyn Mikel Brown describes a distinction that she hears emerge between what girls can know and authorize out of their own relationships and experiences, and what they come to believe is acceptable to know and say publicly as young women. At this time the phrase "I don't know" enters girls' speech, indicating girls' confusion about what they believe, what they know.

Girls poised at the edge of adolescence, standing at the crossroads to womanhood, actively struggle to authorize themselves—that is, to trust, value, and speak from their experience—as they begin to move psychologically into a culture populated by ideals of perfect girls and pure women. Incorporating images from magazines, books, and television, from other girls, and from the adults in their lives, girls come to label their vitality, desires, and thoughts as "selfish," "bad," or "wrong." They lose the ability to hold on to the truth of their experience in the face of conflict. They begin to see themselves as others see them, and they orient their thinking and themselves toward others. "Like this year I've changed a lot," seventh-grader Michele announces with pride. "I think of, um, more of what to do to be nice than, um, what I want to do."

Girls at this crossroads face an excruciating dilemma. As Carol Gilligan explains, girls have to give up their relationship with the world of girls and women, the world that they have lived and loved in, and also give up relationship with parts of themselves that are too dangerous to keep in the adult world of male desire. Girls give up these relationships for the sake of the relationships that have been prescribed for them in male led societies. The wall of patriarchy expects girls to separate from what they know, from each other, and from the women who care for them. Like sunflowers, they turn their faces into the glare of men's dominance of women.

OTHER BRICKS IN THE WALL

At the edge of adolescence every girl collides with the wall of the culture. But this wall is not simply made of the power relations between women and men. There are other bricks in the wall: racism, classism, homophobia, and bias against persons with disabilities. As Violette, a young woman with spina bifida, remarked: "When I was little, everything was normal. I played with my friends and my brothers and sisters. I was who I was and they were who they were. I was teased a lot because of my canes and leg braces but that didn't seem to matter so much. Then, at about eleven, everything changed. I saw that I wasn't normal. I became so ashamed of myself."

As each girl, from her particular community and experience, comes to take in the beliefs upon which the wall of the culture is constructed, she realizes that parts of herself are no longer just "normal" but abnormal, bad, not good enough, sick, or dangerous. The differing impact of these bricks in the wall not only leaves girls with different losses but nearly shatters the hope for a community of all women.

A healthy response to such blame and potential shame is to fight, to resist: *No, you are wrong about me!* Girls struggle to resist devaluation by a cultural system that unfairly divides and defines people on the circumstances of their birth. For individual girls, this knowledge creates deep losses and, perhaps paradoxically, can also tap deep wells of strength as girls find their families and communities rallying to their aid. Every situation of domination holds the possibility for resistance. As the social critic bell hooks reminds us, the wall has "margins, gaps, and locations" that create powerful opportunities for agency. Each community of women holds different bits of wisdom about affirming life in the face of oppression. While this wisdom is learned at enormous cost, it points to possibilities of resistance for all women, to gaps and margins in the wall of cultural reality.

Many African-American girls manage to hold on to their voices and their belief in themselves in adolescence, more so than white or Latina girls. To do so, they draw on strong family connections and communities, and on the role that women play in those families and communities (although these communities have suffered in the last decade or so as fewer resources have come their way). In a protective but costly maneuver, they distance themselves from schools and other institutions in the culture that tell them they are worthless.

This strategy makes for effective resistance in the short term, but in the long run it leaves these girls dangerously outside paths to economic security. Racism and sexism, as interconnected oppressions within the wall, rob girls of their power to act and be fully in the world. Psychologist Janie Victoria Ward often tells a story from the poet Audre Lorde's life to illustrate how painful and enraging this is—both for these girls and for all who love them.

Audre, in the sixth grade, hears that elections will be held for two class presidents, a boy and a girl. Voting, the students are told, should be on the basis of merit, primarily grades. Audre is the best student in the class. Filled with anticipation, she runs home and tells her mother. Her mother is furious, knowing that they never will elect a black girl president, and yells at Audre to give up this "foolishness." Seeing the confusion and hope in her daughter's face, the mother warns, "Don't come in here . . . with a long face, and any 'I didn't win, Mommy,' because I don't want to hear that either."

Audre is still certain—after all, the rules said that the election would be based on who had the best grades. But, on the day of the election, Audre learns that there will be only one president, and it has to be a boy. Girls can only run for vice-president. Despite this first "rude awakening," Audre runs for vice-president and has a second "awakening" when she receives only four votes (including her own). Humiliated and confused, she runs home to cry.

When her mother gets home from work, she finds Audre sobbing and guesses what happened. After her mother's anger passes, Audre timidly complains about the unfairness of it all. Her mother places her hand on

Audre's head, looks at her daughter with sad and tired eyes, and tells her, "Fair, fair, what's fair, you think? Is fair you want, look in God's face. . . . Child, why you worry your head so much over fair or not fair. Just do what is for you to do and let the rest take care of themselves."

Audre Lorde credited her mother with teaching her "all manner of wily and diversionary defenses learned from the white man's tongue." Her mother's rage at a world where she knew that her daughter would not be treated fairly became a protective rage warning her daughter away from humiliation. The righteous anger of mothers of girls who face multiple oppressions keeps their daughters from a head-on collision with the wall.

Janie Ward calls African-American girls' loss at the foot of the wall a loss of innocence. No longer can they hold the hope that they will be known within the wider world for their intelligence, their verve, their uniqueness. No longer can they fully expect to achieve their heart's desire. Of no account to white men because they will not bear them heirs, African-American girls become outsiders to and witnesses of the paths to power in dominant culture. Hence, from this loss of innocence can arise a powerful gift of knowledge through the double vision of the outsider.

Audre Lorde's life is an extraordinary tribute to the knowledge born out of loss. She died in 1992 as the poet laureate of New York State. Her brilliance as a poet and essayist was created from the weight of her oppression as a woman, an African-American, and a lesbian. A clarity of vision led Lorde throughout her life to encourage women to join with each other instead of being divided by these other bricks in the wall.

Girls' varied experiences of the wall give all women a deeper understanding of the wall's construction and of the places where cracks, gaps, and margins exist. Differing expectations and experiences arise among girls and women of different classes and races, but the power of culture shapes them all. Middle-class white girls develop a romantic innocence by losing their self-assertion and knowledge of sexism. Latina girls lose confidence in themselves later in adolescence than white girls do. African-American girls and Latinas tend to discount the importance of school and drop out more often.

Apparently, these differences in girls' experiences are related to the differing importance given to women's roles in their families and communities. As they move through adolescence, both Latina and white girls are less likely than African-American girls to respond positively to statements that they are "an important member of my family" or that they "feel good about myself with my family," just as they are less likely to feel good about themselves. While Latinas may enjoy stronger family and community connections than white girls, neither group highly values the role of women. Latina mothers are least likely of the three groups to work outside of the home, and their contribution to the family and community is commonly minimized in comparison to men's economic support. These attitudes are reflected in Latina high school girls' views of the homemaker role: 83 percent would not like or enjoy being a homemaker, yet over a third expect that this is the role they will have to assume. Girls learn about being a woman in families that reflect their heritage.

Little information exists on how Asian girls confront racism and sexism, or on how they deal with the pressures and advantages of being the so-called model minority. Nor does research exist on how Native American girls, lesbian girls, or girls with disabilities face multiple oppressions. In fact, within a culture in which the paths to power, success, and even human development are based in men's experience, any research that pays attention to the voices of even white *girls* is in itself groundbreaking. But we have so much more to learn.

Perhaps women can learn from girls with disabilities how to negotiate freedom within extraordinary constraints. From young lesbians they might learn how to keep the flame of desire burning when it is doubly dangerous to do so, or how to pursue a fulfilling life without men at the center. What do Native American girls bring from a culture that has learned to trust life in the face of annihilation? Despite the ways in which the dominant culture seeks to trivialize Native American spiritual traditions, those tradi-tions are powerful sources of resistance. Simply raising such possibilities and questions hints at what could be if women lived free from patriarchy. After colliding with the wall, our being is deeply changed. Bringing to-gether our different strengths as women can only hint at what could be.

Relationships between women, especially different women, are dis-torted within the culture, too. The dominance hierarchies that structure the wall warp women's interactions with each other because, living within the wall's reality, women divide by race, class, and sexual orientation, rather than recognizing the enriching possibilities of "the notion of differ-ence as a dynamic human force." Women's different experiences of op-pression make connection difficult. White women enjoy the privileges of racial dominance, and out of that privilege springs a persistent ignorance of other women's struggles. Patriarchy thrives by keeping women divided, setting them up to compete with each other. These separations between women mirror the separation between mother and daughter, a lie basic to developmental psychology and to patriarchy.

THE LIES OF SEPARATION

Mothers are set up in patriarchal culture by lies told about separation. Separations between races and classes are not the only separations the culture depends on: we must separate from our mothers, as conventional wisdom has it, to become strong, independent individuals. Scientific ex-perts tell mothers that each child should separate to achieve autonomy. This is a lie. This distorted view of good mothering places a mother's feelings at odds with cultural perceptions of what is necessary for her child's growth and well-being. Moreover, this lie of separation leads moth-ers into an unintentional betrayal of daughters.

Scientists (most notably, doctors and psychologists), the priests of patriarchy, have "wooed their female constituency," as authors Barbara

Ehrenreich and Deirdre English describe in *For Her Own Good: 150 Years of the Experts' Advice to Women,* "promising the 'right' and scientific way to live, and women responded—most eagerly in the upper and middle classes, more slowly among the poor—with dependency and trust." Mothers in suburbia found themselves more and more removed from intergenerational networks of women and thus from opportunities to learn the skills of mothering. In this isolated world of mothering, write Ehrenreich and English, "the expert looms larger and more authoritative than ever before," thus creating a new tableau of "the Mother, the Child, and the Expert." What concerned mother would dare to ignore the kindly advice of well-meaning experts on how to raise a healthy, happy child?

But for the last hundred years experts have based their advice on theories of psychological development defined by male experience. Separation became a developmental necessity, because of boys' early struggle to understand the meaning of sex differences. In early childhood, boys develop the intellectual awareness that they are male and different from females. As they learn how boys and men are supposed to behave, they distinguish themselves as little men, different from girls and from their moms. At this young age, they don't understand that no matter what they do, they won't become a girl or a mom, so they separate from all of what *mom* meant to them—the nurturing intimacy of infancy.

This radical emotional separation from "the mother" became *the* critical task in theories of child development, rather than a dilemma posed for certain male children by the culture. To theorists of child development, such as Sigmund Freud, Erik Erikson, and Margaret Mahler, pulling away and distancing emotionally from mother was necessary for a boy to feel capable of being on his own. This mandated separation produces "tough guys" who seek glory and honor away from the influence of women. For boys this is a dubious goal, and for girls, a betrayal.

The lies about separation are now deeply held cultural beliefs about the way life goes. Emotional separation is confused with autonomy, the ability to care for oneself, to be self-ruling. Separation and autonomy are not equivalent: a person need not separate from others emotionally to be autonomous. Under the dominion of experts, mothers are urged to create a separation and disconnection from daughters that their daughters do not want. Early childhood and adolescence are the two stages of life where separation has been decreed as imperative to the independence and autonomy of children. To mother "right," women disconnect from their daughters and begin to see them as society will. Rather than strengthening girls, this breach of trust leaves girls weakened and adrift.

Only recently, as the field of psychology has finally begun to include girls and women in its theory-building research, has the whole notion of separation as the true model of development been questioned. Women's voices revealed the difference between emotional separation and autonomy. Until women were included in research on human development, the human need for connection and intimacy was obscured by the quest for individual achievement. For many psychologists, including women who were trained in white male ways of conceptualizing psychological health and development, girls' and women's strong articulation of connection and relationships as central to their lives came almost as a surprise. When women's voices were taken seriously, rather than reinterpreted to fit theories that devalue connection, researchers, particularly feminists, began to notice that women themselves characterized the relationship-based core of their lives as a strength, not as a failure in separating. This strength then becomes the basis, as Jean Baker Miller describes, for a "new psychology of women."

Within our culture, men and women have been molded to experience separation and connection in different ways. The human experience of "self" is at best a fluid balance between the experience of our physical separateness and our common, interdependent humanness. For infants and young children, the threat of separation, of being cut off from care, raises the traumatic specters of isolation, loneliness, ostracism, abandonment, and even death. But, in general, men are not encouraged to feel these connections. Both privileged and blinded by their dominant position in patriarchy, they are told that they are individual, independent actors who make unilateral decisions about themselves and their relationships with others. Despite the apparent freedom, emotional isolation is the cost. Women are shaped to experience others' feelings and needs rather than their own because, as subordinates with little power in patriarchy, we've been told to give up ourselves to ensure survival. Neither the behaviors traditionally prescribed for women nor those prescribed for men offer any real balance—in either case, parts of the self must be sacrificed.

Exposing the lies of separation profoundly affects mother daughter relationships, particularly at adolescence. Terri Apter, a psychologist who studied sixty-five mother and daughter pairs in England and America, writes how she, too, began her work under the false and overly simplistic assumption that "the 'task' of adolescence is separation from the parent" and set out "to understand how the daughter 'succeeds' or 'fails' to separate from the person to whom she has been closest." Upon listening to girls describing their relationships with their mothers, she realized that her questions were coming from the wrong direction. Rather than asking how the daughters became independent and separate, Terri Apter found that it was much more congruent with what the girls were saying to ask, instead, how the daughters retained their attachment to their mothers.

"In the context of the other information that I was getting from adolescent daughters," she observes, "I felt that the traditional balance— that of seeing the rejection of the mother's advice, perception, interference as a bid for separation—was inaccurate, weighted by theory." She was forced to conclude that the struggle between adolescent girls and their mothers is one of redefining their connections to adjust to the daughter's growth, rather than an attempt to sever connection or create emotional distance.

"I doubt, however," writes Terri Apter, "that in speaking to mothers alone that I ever would have been persuaded to change the bias." Survivors themselves of the collision with the wall in early adolescence, mothers tended to misinterpret conflict with their daughters as separation. "The notion," she explains, "that the adolescent is trying to separate, and to become autonomous, to break with childhood ties, to tear out the childhood loves and ideals, is firmly rooted in parents' and professionals' expectations and interpretations."

There's the rub: if mothers accept the story of development as it has been presented to them, they subtly create a disconnection that their daughters do not want. Mothers are the ones within the culture who have traditionally been charged with enforcing the separations that are necessary for this culture to perpetuate itself. In so doing, we mothers end up losing or distorting the love and connection with daughters that have meant so much to us.

The dilemmas that girls face as they enter adolescence are painful and traumatic, but the dilemma mothers face is perhaps more painful. For mothers who made their own painful compromises and self-amputations in order psychologically to enter patriarchy, bearing witness to a daughter's struggle not only causes pain but rekindles their own preadolescent anxiety, pain, and helplessness. The traditional experts' advice to separate can have some appeal in this messy situation, because it offers relief from the dilemma of what to do and prepares a daughter for her role as man's helpmate.

The kind of separation that experts urge mothers to make leads girls to feel that they cannot deeply trust connection with women. Turning to men looms as the logical alternative. As Thelma Jean Goodrich, a family therapist, notes: "The better you've done your job as prescribed for you as a mother, the more you've trained your daughter to fit into patriarchy—that's the saddest part of it. That's the squeeze play or the dilemma of it. The better you do it, the better you've done, the worse for your daughter —in one way." But to encourage a daughter not to separate and not to fit means just that—she doesn't fit in—and that is incredibly painful, too. In addition, mothers, being the most important and closest women in their daughters' lives, get blamed for their daughters' pain.

MOTHER BLAMING

In patriarchal culture, mothers are blamed for the pain their children experience in trying to fit the narrow roles that the culture demands. Mother blaming is a sleight-of-hand trick in patriarchal culture: just like in *The Wizard of Oz,* all of our attention is spent hunting down the Wicked Witch so that we "pay no attention to the man behind the curtain." The trouble is that the Wicked Witch that everyone is pointing to is our mother or—more horribly—our mother in ourselves.

In Alice Walker's *Possessing the Secret of Joy,* Tashi, the heroine, finds herself in a consulting room with a white male psychiatrist. "Negro women, said the doctor, are considered the most difficult of all people to be effectively analyzed. Do you know why?" Tashi says nothing. "Negro women, the doctor says into my silence, can never be analyzed effectively because they can never bring themselves to blame their mothers." The shared comradeship of mothers and daughters in the African-American community is turned into a source of sickness by experts. Even feminists have scapegoated mothers. We live in a world where blaming mothers is the yellow brick road to "health" and a "positive adjustment" to society.

Over the past hundred years, mothers almost universally have been seen as the cause of dynamics that lead to children's psychological distress. Barbara Ehrenreich and Deirdre English observe that an entire generation of psychoanalysts mounted an "effort to trace each childhood disorder to a specific disorder in the mother, just as the bacteriologists sought to trace each disease to a specific type of microbe."

This blanket blame of mothers persists. "Mothers," notes the feminist psychologist Janet Surrey about a recent review of the causes of children's problems, "were also blamed for children's problems ranging from sleepwalking, ulcerative colitis, hyperactivity, peer avoidance, delusions, poor language development, and inability to deal with color blindness." The terms used to describe mothers' behavior are also blaming: *controlling, intrusive, engulfing, enmeshed, seductive, overprotective, cold, critical, competitive, distant, depleted, narcissistic, abusive, crazy.* As one researcher writes: "The indictment of mothers in the psychological literature has historically been so nasty, so massive, so undifferentiated, and so oblivious of the actual limits of a mother's power or her context that it precludes a just assessment of real responsibility." The basic message is clear: Look no farther; the cause of what ails you is your mother.

Within many forms of psychotherapy, blaming one's mother is tantamount to being "cured." In *Don't Blame Mother*, Paula Caplan describes how women in therapy are led into blaming their mothers and feeling rage toward them, only to be left there. Apparently, raging at our mothers rather than working through our child-based feelings toward a more layered and subtle adult resolution is supposed to be a cure, but such a cure leaves the present relationship between a mother and daughter forever caught in the feelings of the past. While exploring the difficulties in our relationships with our mothers is critical to therapy, healing is about moving beyond the angers and hurt that were not expressed in childhood. Very little effort is made in traditional therapies to explore the complexities of a mother's behavior, place it in the appropriate socioeconomic or political context, or wonder about her partner's role (or lack of it).

When the institutions that define *health* and prescribe the practices for recovery encourage mother blaming, such blaming obviously has reached epidemic proportions. While the domain of psychotherapy is an often esoteric one, its standards and values identify what is "normal," "good," "healthy," and "valuable" within society—as well as what is "abnormal," "sick," "pathological," and "undesirable." Mother blaming is the automatic answer for too many social ills: it supposedly explains students' school failure, urban violence, and a range of other major problems in our civilization. In fact, after the Korean War, the crack-up of American servicemen under torture was attributed to mothers who had not raised sons tough enough to be "real" men.

Think how often a child's behavior is explained in terms of the mother's problems. Much of the recent discussion of "family values" is actually encoded mother blaming: families are in trouble not because of the inequities in our economic, child-care, and health-care systems but because mothers aren't doing their jobs right—often because they haven't been able to keep a man in the house. When the authorities in our culture easily turn to mother blaming, individuals feel more than justified in doing so. And in the media, as in conversations, anger and attention focus on individual mothers' inadequacies rather than on the inadequacy of our social systems.

Mother blaming is a fire that has been kindled by a spark of truth: our mothers were almost all powerful when we were totally dependent as infants. Growing up has meant that we have had to move from dependence to interdependence. Blaming mother can feel right: Wasn't she the one who was there or supposed to be there? Didn't each of us need her more than anyone or anything else when we were young and vulnerable? Feeling anger and assigning blame initially seem effective ways of being strong and independent when, in fact, such behavior often protects against feelings of powerlessness and dependence.

In truth, our mothers exerted (and often still exert) a deep and complex power in our lives. Too often, though, our own mother's ability to be with us emotionally was compromised by her struggles to provide for herself and for our well-being—whether this meant focusing on the man in her life or working both within and outside the home. In communities where mothers' survival struggle is most visible, there tends to be less mother blaming. When racism, poverty, and abuse shackle families and communities, there is less mother blaming because the realities are too obviously not of the mothers' making. However, some mothers within every context become so overwhelmed that they cannot provide for their children, and some mothers whose need for comfort and support have never been met adequately cannot effectively nurture their children. Because we are not taught to explore the connections between our own mother's struggles and her lack of status in the world, mother blaming becomes an easy rationalization.

While daughters may not be consciously aware of this antimother bias, girls grow up breathing this air. From mother to daughter, in the last few generations, mother blaming has become particularly rampant within the middle and upper classes. Historians have shown how the alienation between mothers and daughters has paralleled the devaluation and displacement of women's work. As women have had less of value to teach their daughters in the way of useful knowledge, such as how to care for the sick or how to produce food and clothing, more daughters have felt alienated from their mothers. Now mothers are just expected to teach daughters the deadening skills needed to fit well in patriarchal society. The skills of fitting in are learned by self-negation, not affirmation.

When mother blaming is offered as the cure for women's struggles, the feelings aroused can become more bewildering and frightening as women become mothers. Women who become mothers are asked to walk a razor's edge, bounded on either side by betrayal. Mothers are held accountable for being totally powerful in their children's lives, yet they often feel powerless to improve the quality of their children's lives. The first question asked about a girl who behaves in "unacceptable" ways is, "Where is her mother? Doesn't her mother know?" Mothers are judged by every behavior of their daughters. In order to maintain the status quo, which prioritizes men's authority and needs, mothers are encouraged to raise daughters who comply, who hold men's desires and needs as the center of their lives. Then, women are "good" mothers, but they betray their daughters' potential for self-realization. To reject this and raise daughters differently means to betray the culture, to risk ostracism for themselves and their daughters, to risk punishment, to be charged with heresy, to be cursed as "bad" mothers.

FAULT LINES ACROSS GENERATIONS

The unintentional betrayal of daughters by mothers is the root of matrophobia—the fear, as writer Adrienne Rich explains, of becoming one's own mother. Many women have "matrophobia." Psychotherapists report that while men often express the wish to be more like their fathers, women more commonly express the desire to be different from their mothers and struggle not to be like them in any way. Matrophobia creates fault lines between generations of women. How often is the desire for something different for our daughters fueled by the heat from a passion not to be like our own mothers?

As virtually every mother has found out, our own mothers live deep within us. "I couldn't believe it—my mother seemed to just leap out of my mouth." In countless phrases ("We'll see about that, young lady"), in tone, attitudes, and fears, our mothers leap out of us into our relationships with our daughters. And that often leads women to feel bad about themselves and about mothering—"Oh, god! I'm doing just what she did." Why, though, why does this feel so alarming to so many mothers? For some it may be the shock of losing control over who they are and what they say, a feeling of being psychologically highjacked.

But for many of us, being like our mother is almost terrifying. Even when each of us realizes how much we love our own mother, being *like* her is entirely another matter. In researcher Judith Arcana's study of mothers and daughters, she found that 49 percent of the women actively competed with their mothers "to bypass them, to best them, to succeed where they have failed—*we* will be exceptional women; *we* will not be this degraded creature, woman."

As she points out, we women learn that we are basically interchangeable, but there is room for only one woman because each man supposedly selects only one woman to love and protect. Each woman, particularly in the middle and upper classes, competes with other women for men's attention. The unspoken hope is that, in a culture where relationships are often seen as contests, we will prove ourselves special enough to be truly loved and thereby exempted from our oppression as women by being swept off our feet by a prince—a seductive, romantic illusion. Even if some women are treated as queens, many women are "one man away from Welfare," as lawyer and activist Flo Kennedy has put it.

Competition between women is usually first learned in mother daughter relationships. Competition may be learned in subtle battles between mothers and daughters. "Being attractive was my mother's power," says Ethel. "I remember being surprised upon coming home from school when I was twelve or thirteen and finding my mother trying on a frilly, full-skirted, girly yellow dress that I had. I was upset that she would just go into my closet like that. When I complained, she yelled at me for being selfish. I remember laying awake that night wondering why she'd do that. It seemed so inappropriate. But my mother has always been competitive and this competition was vital to her."

Or daughters may learn from mothers how to compete against other women outside the home by learning the ways of romance—how to be attractive and pleasing to men. But individual solutions through that one special man or relationship only keep women locked in their individual houses, perhaps more dependent and isolated than ever. Trying to exorcise the mother in ourselves is another doomed individual solution to mothering, for it involves a self-destructive hatred of and retreat from parts of ourselves.

"Matrophobia," as Adrienne Rich explains, "can be seen as a womanly splitting of the self, in the desire to become purged once and for all of our mothers' bondage, to become individuated and free. The mother stands for the victim in ourselves, the unfree woman, the martyr." When mothers do what the culture has prescribed—namely, teach daughters to fit in—daughters associate the pain and compromises of fitting in with their mothers. What is hateful is not so much our mothers but the part of ourselves that seems weak and compromising—many of us identify that part of ourselves with our mothers. Because we are urged to direct our own anger toward and hatred of women's oppression at our mothers, something like the San Andreas fault forms between each generation of women.

Matrophobia exists even in close relationships between mothers and daughters, so that under the seemingly solid ground of love and connection lies the possibility for a sudden shift and the opening of a chasm along the fault lines of blame. Having some hint at how painful such a confrontation would be, many women have become experts at negotiating closeness within a self-protective distance and covering mistrust with the appearance of openness. With such open faces and hearts, women show themselves as perfect women: loving, nurturing, and selfless, with no bad thoughts or feelings.

THE PERFECT MOTHER

The culture of mother blaming creates a psychological prison for mothers of daughters. Whether or not a mother is conscious of these forces within the culture, the desire to do right, to provide a daughter with new opportunities, makes mothering incredibly pressured. Messages about "good" mothering and the necessities of providing for children often conflict, leaving mothers guilty and torn. The enormous responsibility without full authority, the impossible ideals and required sacrifices, the self-doubt and confusion all lead to powerlessness and a deep, vague sense of loss. Mothers can't afford to fail; failure would damage their daughters. But being set up by impossible expectations, mothers are doomed to fail.

The psyche copes by pushing us into the prison of perfection. An internal dialogue springs up: *The whole world can't be wrong; it's simply that*

I'm not good enough, not perfect. If I were perfect, then everything would be okay. If our daughters are perfect, then we have mothered well. Women who work outside the home subtly blame themselves and get blamed by others for not caring enough about their families, so they push extra hard when they are with their daughters. Women who do not work feel incredible pressure to produce perfect daughters, otherwise, how can they justify not being productive (that is, employed) in the workplace? The comparisons and the competitiveness divide mothers from other mothers. We lose each other as a source of support and counsel; we only have the impossible ideals of the "good" mother left to turn to. The prison of perfection is wallpapered with patriarchal images of the good mother.

Who are the "good" mothers? While not the mother of a daughter, the Virgin Mary is the epitome of the good mother in Western culture. She is all-nurturing, all-loving, selfless. "Love, according to [male Christian] theologians, is completely self-giving, taking no thought for its own interests but seeking only the good of the other," writes theologian Valerie Saiving. Within this cultural framework, she explains, a mother "will believe that, having chosen marriage and children and thus being face to face with the needs of her family for love, refreshment, and forgiveness, she has no right to ask anything for herself but must submit without qualification." Through this selfless love, a mother raises good children. The Virgin Mary's child was not just good, but perfect. Since mothers' goodness is judged by their children's goodness, Mary represents the ultimate in good mothering. While the Virgin Mary is a cultural ideal, her perfection is not humanly possible.

Fairy tales hold stories of mothers who are either too good to be true or too bad to fathom. Sidestepping motherhood directly, fairy tales are populated with evil stepmothers and fiendish older women who are pitted against good fairy godmothers. Cinderella has the most famous of wicked stepmothers and fairy godmothers. Sleeping Beauty has a small flotilla of good fairy godmothers who are almost rendered powerless by one evil fairy who curses the girl in her crib (bad mothering has more force, more truly powerful magic). Beneath pieties about good mothers, fairy tales ensure that mothers stay in line by unsubtly disguising bad mothers as stepmothers. The slander against mothering, and particularly against mother daughter relationships, that these vile mothers represent serves as a warning to mothers and sends a message to daughters that they can't trust mothering women. Evil stepmothers are outright untrustworthy; good godmothers have too little power to protect daughters. Yet, both are unreal, inhuman. (The "real" mother is invariably dead in fairy tales.) Neither pure goodness nor pure evil is human mothering. We can't live in absolutes.

Woody Allen's Hannah, in Allen's film *Hannah and Her Sisters,* tries to embody a perfectly "good" mother. Hannah is long suffering and self-sacrificing. She is so perfect that her husband finds he can't relate to her and begins to have sex with her sister. While Hannah gets her man back (by giving him her vulnerability, which is what he now needs of her), the story hints at the empty promise of being the perfectly nurturing mother. Oddly enough, though, there aren't many images of perfectly "good" mothers in stories and movies. Even in fiction, they are fiction. But there are plenty of "bad" mothers who serve as sirens alerting us to avoid the danger of bad mothering (and, perhaps, the temptation of thinking for and about ourselves for a change).

More often films present lessons to those who might dare try to escape from the impossible confines of perfect mothering. In *A World Apart,* a daughter struggles to figure out whether her mother was bad or not. Does her mother's political activism against racist, apartheid South Africa define her as a bad mother when it takes her passion and time away from nurturing her daughter? The reviewers almost unanimously said yes.

The heroine of *The Good Mother* has her daughter taken away from her basically because, after her divorce, she begins a playful, sexual, caring relationship with another man. Finally, she gives up all hope for pleasure or fulfillment in her life and moves into a meager apartment near her ex-husband and his new wife, just to be in her daughter's neighborhood. In so doing, she becomes, ironically, "the good mother." "Bad" mothers, we all know, have their daughters taken from them.

One of the most potent and dangerous weapons used against mothers in films and in real life is the threat of losing their children. While there are mothers who, for complex emotional and economic reasons, do endanger their children's lives, these women are remarkably few and are over-represented in the popular imagination, fed by news reports and stories. As journalist Susan Faludi documented in *Backlash,* the threat of "bad" mothering was liberally sprinkled in magazine and newspaper stories throughout the 1980s. These media suggested that "good" mothers were leaving work and returning home, that "good" mothers didn't leave children in bad day care.

Sue, a working mother, says, "People say things indirectly. They won't say that you're being a terrible mother for working but they'll say that the reason they chose to stay at home is because they want to have a better life for their child and take care of them and that's important to them—as if it's not important to you!" Most mothers love their children, want the best for them, and feel enormously guilty when they are told that they are not meeting their children's needs. Too many mothers know that they are powerless to ensure the best. The threat of "bad" mothering is frightening not just because it is guilt producing (am I doing something bad for my kids?) but because it risks the very relationship between a mother and her children. The decade of backlash pitted women's economic viability against the well-being of their children, and this backlash made good women feel like bad mothers.

But cultural standards of good mothering are no protection. Psychologist Phyllis Chesler's research in *Mothers on Trial: The Battle for Children and Custody* shows that mothers have had their children taken from them both for caring too little and working *and* for not caring enough to work and provide greater financial support for their children. Women have also lost their children because they left a man who abused them or because they lived with a woman who loved them. While the 1980s backlash tried to send women back into the home under threats of "bad" mothering, women can be considered to be "bad" mothers when working only in the home, too. Straddling this fence, mothers are betrayed by a culture that offers guilt rather than resources for raising children.

In countless ways, mothers are locked into double binds. Western culture, so fond of dichotomies, divides the world into black and white, good and bad, perfect and evil. To be good according to these standards is not humanly possible. The complexity and difficulty of mothering in a culture that scapegoats mothers are washed over. Too often women are forced to make choices along the lines of these false, exaggerated dichotomies. Listening between the lines to some of the myths about mothering and mothering a daughter, one can hear the seductive whisper of perfection. The truths in these statements—because there is some truth to all of them—is whitened to the point that they obscure more than they make clear. As recipes for patriarchal perfection, they set up a mother's needs against her daughter's and give mothers the right to live out their lack of fulfillment through their daughters.

First, there are the myths of perfection and self-sacrifice:

If I do everything right, then my children will be all right.

A good mother would give her life for her children.

I can protect my daughter from the harsh realities of the world if I don't talk about such things or if I say everything will be okay or if I say just the right things.

Then, there are the myths that encourage mothers to seek their satisfactions through their daughters, not through themselves:

Your daughter is a reflection of who you are.

My daughter can have whatever I didn't have.

35

Competition is the way of the world; she needs to know how to compete in order to survive. Success is her only insurance.

Finally, there are the myths about adolescent separation that justify the creation of schisms between generations of women:

Adolescence is a time of separation when daughters are struggling to be independent, particularly from their mothers.

Daughters in adolescence don't want to listen to their mothers or be like them in any way.

If your daughter doesn't hate you in adolescence, then she's going to have serious problems.

Through fairy tales and myths of mothering, women learn to give up what they have loved best and want most for the sake of being a "good" mother. "Good" mothering, as it now exists for mothers and daughters, guarantees that a daughter is abandoned by the woman closest to her at the door to patriarchy.

MOTHERING AS TRUTH TELLING

As family therapist Thelma Jean Goodrich comments, "It's not like mothers have missed the high road, missed the road that would have made their daughters happy, healthy, wealthy and wise. There isn't one." The well-worn paths into patriarchy lead to treachery between mothers and daughters and among women across lines of race, class, and sexual orientation. Can we find another path through the wilderness? Can we mother a revolution for women and girls by telling the truths about our lives?

It doesn't have to be like this: a cycle of separation, loss, and betrayal, generation after generation. If mothers could step outside the stultifying order of patriarchal relationships by joining with the girls they once were, with the parts of themselves that they have lost, with their daughters, as well as with other women, then perhaps something radically new could happen. "When women and girls meet at the crossroads of adolescence," write Lyn Mikel Brown and Carol Gilligan, "the intergenerational seam of a patriarchal culture opens. If women and girls together resist giving up relationship for the sake of 'relationships,' then this meeting holds the potential for societal and cultural change."

Women meeting girls at this crossroads, at the foot of the wall, transforms the act of mothering from betrayal—which literally means "turning over to the enemy"—into power and connection. The lies of separation make walls out of the differences between women and threaten to divide each generation of women from the next. By naming the lies of separation, by telling the truths about those overlapping and sometimes contradictory experiences women have in a culture whose rules are created by men, women can find chinks, gaps, and margins—spaces for exercising power— in the seemingly impenetrable wall of interlocking dominance in this culture.

But the truths of women's lives often seem less than self-evident. Stories of development, fairy tales and romantic myths, and stories of what is good and worthwhile are all told from the perspective of patriarchy. Women's truths are often characterized as crazy, naive, or stupid because patriarchy holds the power to name what is and is not real. Truth telling becomes another double bind for women: to stay with patriarchal definitions of reality, we often are alienated from authenticity and power, but to name what women truly think and feel, we risk being called crazy. Given each woman's distorting confrontation as she enters society, truth telling becomes a continual process of re-vision. We need to recover the capacity for the vision of the outsider that many of us had as girls but lost when we learned to see as women. By seeing as outsiders and by meeting girls before their collision with the wall, all of us—women and girls—can more fully hear and share the truth of being female in this male culture.

The meeting between women and girls leads to the transformation of mothering into truth telling. Women, taking in girls' courage and questions, reclaim their authority to envision a future in which girls do not have to sacrifice their knowledge and authenticity. Girls, hearing the authority of truth from their mothers, find themselves joined in their resistance to losing voice, vision, and potential. Rather than protecting a daughter only through teaching her to fit into a culture that is deeply hostile to her integrity and power, a mother can fight against the oppressions that violate her own and her daughter's spirit, thus connecting with and protecting her daughter. Ignited by the truths of women's oppression, mothers' passion for daughters and daughters' passion for mothers can burn away the lies that have caused women to lose each other through the betrayals of separation. Moving out from the shadows of betrayal, women and girls together can claim the power of connection, community, and choice. And this power might just bring the wall down.

2

From Power to Betrayal

The oppressed condition of women is thus the ultimate, usually hidden, source of the daughter's disappointment in her mother, and it fuels the daughter's desire to separate and be different from her mother. The failure to discern the larger contexts in which the daughter's contempt arises can make it appear as if the mother-daughter conflict is inherent in their gender and thus almost impossible to resolve. This is the mistake that Freud made.

Judith Lewis Herman & Helen Block Lewis
"ANGER IN THE MOTHER-DAUGHTER RELATIONSHIP"

Women's relative lack of power in society creates a bitter complication in mother daughter relationships. One of the most painful ironies of mothering in patriarchal culture is that mothers, because they have to enforce the limits on their daughters to protect them, end up being betrayers in their daughters' eyes. Mothers take the rap for a situation that is neither their fault nor their creation. The schism, the San Andreas fault, dividing generations of women stems from the role assigned to mothers: the enforcers of ever more costly losses in girls' freedom to do and to be.

"When we think of loss we think of the loss, through death, of people we love," says writer Judith Viorst in *Necessary Losses*. "But loss is a far more encompassing theme in our life. For we lose not only through death, but also by leaving and being left, by changing and letting go and moving on." Viorst describes these losses, "necessary losses," as ranging from actual departures to "our conscious and unconscious losses of romantic dreams, impossible expectations, illusions of freedom and power, illusions of safety." Loss, she rightly points out, is a painful and necessary part of growth. Every ending is also a beginning. To grow and to realize our place in the world, we must leave our younger self behind.

But there are also *un*necessary losses in our development. In a culture where privileged white men have mapped the permissible longitude and latitude of mind, spirit, voice, and body, women have no place. Men's map of reality is a guide to power relations. Power-less, women struggle to be knowledgeable, to feel whole, to speak freely, or even to be considered normal.

"Power would be a fragile thing if its only function were to repress," argues the philosopher Michel Foucault, "if it only worked through the model of censorship, exclusion, blockage and repression, . . . exercising itself in a negative way. If, on the contrary, power is strong this is because, as we are beginning to realize, it produces effects at the level of desire— and also at the level of knowledge."

Women's physical contortions to embody men's desires, their persistent feelings of craziness, and their self-silencing expose "reality" as a dance, an interplay of power. Voicing perceptions and acting outside this reality threatens women, causing them to feel, if not experience, danger. Girls feel deep loss and betrayal as they grow into increasing awareness and experience of women's powerlessness.

Power is essential to growing up healthy and whole. The root of the word *power* has nothing to do with domination: *power* means "to be able." Desires *to be able* to exercise our intelligence, our strength, and our compassion—to know how to do so and to be recognized for our contributions —are motivating forces in human life. When our power, our ability to do, is consistently thwarted or considered too dangerous to explore, we take this knowledge deeply into our psyches. This knowledge leads us to lose part of our selves, a loss felt as betrayal. This experience is often overwhelming and traumatic, and our psyches protect us by pushing these feelings and knowledge out of conscious awareness. We create a firewall of fear around the feelings to prevent them from entering our awareness. Over time, women assimilate these losses as "just life" and end up feeling that something is wrong with them when they are uncomfortable.

Only when a political movement lifts what has become "just life" into public awareness do these losses appear unnecessary. Only then does society begin to demand change. Wife beating was seen for years as a part of marriage for women. The phrase "rule of thumb" derives from the allowable circumference of the stick that a husband could legally use to beat his wife under British common law. Though wife beating has not ended, the movement against domestic violence has at least lifted what was commonplace to the level of an unnecessary and illegal loss of safety for women.

Taking the journey with girls from power to betrayal permits a fresh look at growing into the culture from a girl's-eye view. While much of developmental theory justifies who and what women become, listening to and learning from girls allows women to hear and know what they themselves have given up and have slowly accepted as reality. There are two places where a girl's growth, understanding, and experience give her access to a wider social reality: early childhood and early adolescence. "At each stage," write psychiatrists Judith Herman and Helen Lewis, "the daughter comes to a fuller awareness of the relative place of males and females in society. At each stage, she reacts with shock, disappointment, and anger against her mother."

PRINCESS OF POWER

Between the ages of three and five, many girls discover She-Ra, Princess of Power, a doll licensed from a movie in the 1980s. With the body of a Barbie doll, but endowed with superpowers, She-Ra captures the hidden

41

self-image of many girls in early childhood. While girls are typically not mesmerized by the notion of invincibility the way many boys are, little girls are potent creatures, curious and eager to explore the world around them. They enjoy strutting their stuff and using their expansive language and intellectual abilities to figure out what's going on around them. "World," they seem to say, "look out—here I come." They start out with power and integrity, but they soon glimpse the compromises that entry into the larger world will demand.

From infancy, girls grow up experiencing power and powerlessness within Western culture. First, they become aware of their physical power-lessness. They are smaller than their caretakers and, so, are vulnerable to oppression and domination. Their size allows mothers to swoop down on them and carry them off—sometimes kicking and screaming. But little girls also experience psychological power through their emotional connec-tions. The fierce connection that a daughter feels for her mother is recipro-cated by a mother's fierce love for her child. The power balances here can sometimes offset the power differences felt as inequality. Children often say, "I hate you!" when they feel the brunt of their inequality with adults: they use the power of withdrawing their love to balance the inequity of their position.

To little girls, assurances that they are loved and have an impact are a great source of power, sometimes surprisingly so. "She's only three years old and she's manipulating me!" said one mother. Little girls want to know that they have an effect, that their mothers care enough even to be hurt by them. Through this, they come to know that they matter. Through relationships with their mothers and with the women who peo-ple their childhood world, girls begin to weave a powerful psychological safety net that supports them in their early exploration of the environ-ment.

Between the ages of three and five, girls' understanding of their small, familial world expands. Children are not born grasping the concepts "male" and "female." When asked questions like "Will you be a mommy or a daddy when you grow up?" children between two and three are likely to say that it depends on what they feel like. They haven't quite figured out that when one is born female, one stays female all of one's life. Between the ages of four and six, children have put it together: If I'm a boy, I'll grow up to be a dad; if I'm a girl, I'll grow up to be a mom.

Learning that gender is constant through life has an extraordinary impact on young children. At five, Sandra is mesmerized by her Barbie doll. "Why do you like playing with her so much?" Daniel, her father, asks her. "Because she looks just like Mommy," is Sandra's reply. To many five-year-old girls, the exaggerated breasts, the long hair, and the slender legs of a Barbie doll capture the differences that they are just sorting out. As though they've found the key to understanding everything, they create rules for themselves based on the most salient gender differences and use them to organize the world and guide their behavior: Girls have long hair and wear dresses; boys don't play with dolls.

As little girls begin to understand that being a girl means that they will also be women, they often fasten their attention on their mothers and on the differences between the men and women in their lives. Ming, at two, tells Willa, her mother, "I wanna watch" when Willa is doing just about anything. "Wow," says another mother of a three-year-old, "she sure is a mommy's girl." Little girls' early identification with their mothers and with their mothers' role as primary caretaker teaches little girls that caretaking and nurturance are particularly and essentially female work. Only under unusual circumstances—for example, when a mother is battered or frequently absent or very ill, or when older siblings take care of the young girl—will a girl not identify primarily with her mother.

Children's exuberant desire to know, to feel, to act, and to love—essential strands of their being—are woven tightly together in childhood. This is the basis of their integrity—their wholeness. They are all aspects of their desires, and none are particularly sexual, at least not as adults understand sexuality. However, as little girls learn the ways of heterosexual living and romantic loving, with the accompanying code for feminine behavior, they channel more of their power—their doing and ability—into this learning.

Faith, a single mother, is surprised to watch Ivy, at four, bat her eyes and flirt coquettishly with a handsome young waiter at their favorite Indian restaurant, because Faith doesn't flirt. Ivy wants both her mom and herself to marry him. Girls' growing understanding of romance adds another dimension to their power, but with it comes a vague awareness that this power is also dangerous. The little girl herself has no idea what adult sexual activity is about, nor does she want it. Her innocent power play can be dangerous in a culture where women and girls are so often sexually victimized. Virginia Demos, a psychologist specializing in work with young children, says that when she has asked little girls why they stopped being flirtatious, they have talked about feeling so powerful that such behavior seemed too risky.

The violence and danger that girls and women face in this culture place mothers at odds with their daughters' desires for physical freedom, self-assertion, and exploration. Girls' desire and self-love first grow out of their pleasure and confidence in their bodies. Our sense of freedom, power, and mastery are first tested and learned through our bodies. Daughters often experience their mothers' interference as a betrayal. Yet mothers face a dilemma because daughters who suffer abuse end up feeling an oceanic sense of betrayal.

A mother's tendency to be watchful of her daughter's interactions with males, including her stepfather and father, is perfectly understandable given the number of young girls who are victims of incest and sexual abuse. Approximately 5 percent of girls "are incestuously involved with their fathers or stepfathers." One girl out of three has an unwanted sexual encounter before the age of eighteen with an adult male, and roughly a quarter of the abuse occurs before puberty. Amazingly, before the early 1980s many psychiatrists and psychologists still argued that incest and sexual abuse of girls were not harmful as long as the actions were not violently coercive. However, a mother's "surveillance of the daughter's sexual activity often extends to a general interference with autonomy, adventurousness, and initiative."

Recalls Iris:

I couldn't have been more than three or four. It was my first experience at the ocean. I had on a pair of little shorts and was playing in the sand when a woman walked by and said something to my mother. Immediately, my mother whisked me to the nearest beachfront store and bought a little halter. It was such a dramatic experience that I can even remember the color, cut and feel of that ridiculous garment that covered God only knows what. I certainly didn't. But I remember being angry at my mother and confused and ashamed of something I didn't understand.

While coming to grips with the prospect of becoming a woman, a little girl senses another order of power in her life, that is, her mother's relative lack of power in relation to her father. "I don't want Daddy to stay with me; I only feel safe when you're home," six-year-old Janet tells her mother. Nell is surprised to find that she is the powerful protector in her daughter's eyes. Janet's father is not abusive, but neither is he very involved with his children on a daily basis. Over time, however, Nell's faith in her mother's power is compromised as she sees that no matter how little her father has to do with daily life, he rules whenever he returns.

Men's power over women is even more evident to a child if her mother continually defers to the men in her life or is repeatedly subjected to emotional or physical violence at the hands of men. "It is indeed a shock when the little girl first recognizes what it means to be female in a world where power and privilege are the province of males," explain Judith Herman and Helen Lewis. "At the same time she recognizes her own inferior status, she is forced to reevaluate her estimation of her mother. The woman who once appeared all-powerful to her is now revealed as subservient and weak."

Susan, who has suffered from an almost chronic depression, speaks of how her daughter, Jane, has come to see her role as pleasing her father: "A lot of times when [her father's] gone, we're all relaxed and happy, we're harmonious, things are so nice. He'll drive up the driveway and I see Jane start looking around the house thinking, 'Now what can we do to make sure Daddy does not get set off. Is the room picked up, what are we going to have for dinner tonight, Mommy, is dinner ready?' " Susan sees in her daughter an orientation to her husband's power and a silencing of the self that Susan now recognizes led to her depression. Recognizing her mother's inferiority in relation to her father, Jane has begun to be, as her mother puts it, "the kind of child that wants to please."

When a little girl realizes that her mother is not so powerful and may not always provide a safe haven, she experiences loss and betrayal. As she realizes that her mother's power-lessness is hers, too, because she is also female, her loss is compounded. A mother's inferiority angers her daughter because it strips the daughter of her power as well. The betrayal is even greater if girls see that their mothers favor the men in their lives over their daughters. When they begin to realize that the world is not a safe place for them, little girls fleetingly show their rage through early protestations and cries of unfairness. In their minds, much of the fault still lies with their mothers, who hold the keys to their daughters' survival and to their development as females.

Within this context of her mother's waning power, a young daughter may emulate her mother's choice and turn to her father for protection. In early childhood, this limited and individual strategy for solving the dilemma of women's inequality is one of the few options that a little girl has. For many women this becomes a lifelong strategy. Sadly enough, as Adrienne Rich says, the father is loved at the mother's expense, and the subsequent support that men give women and girls is "always stolen power, withheld from the mass of women in patriarchy."

While little girls can be angered and betrayed, the knowledge of women's inferiority relative to men is not quite clear to them. They do not

yet have the intellectual skills to understand the framework of power relations at a societal level. Because the implications of the framework are
obscure to girls, they are not devastated by what they do understand, so
they don't lose their emotional strength and resiliency. On an everyday
basis, each girl connects powerfully with her mother and other women
who do have enormous power in her world. Only in the context of abuse
by a parent, where a daughter is betrayed bodily, are a daughter's integrity
and trust in herself and the world truly compromised. Most little girls live
in a world of women that is the foundation for their sense of power.

IN THE SHADOW OF THE WALL

Girls shimmy, wiggle, move; they are eye-to-eye intense. "Guileless
and without vanity," writes Toni Morrison in *The Bluest Eye,* "we were still
in love with ourselves then. We felt comfortable in our skins, enjoyed the
news that our senses released to us, admired our dirt, cultivated our scars."
An eight-year-old girl walks down the street three steps behind and to the
right of her hurried mother. The daughter walks along doing the King
Tut, arms bent and pointing front and back, while humming to herself.
Vibrant, embodied, just herself. In a rush, the mother pays her daughter
no mind; after all, she's just a young girl.

Young girls, all but unnoticed by the adults around them, bring their
sense of power into school. Throughout the grade-school years, girls play
with their power in a world of their own making populated by girlfriends
and primarily women teachers and mothers. But as girls approach the wall
looming at the edge of adolescence, they find themselves more and more
in its shadow. Their power play becomes more brutal psychologically as
they absorb the ways of competition in school and between women.

Initially, the grade-school world with its priority on relationship feels
right to them. When asked, children of both sexes identify the things of
grade school as female, almost as an extension of their home environment,
where mothers preside. Within this world, girls often thrive. They learn

about being friends. In fourth grade, Judy hears her best friend in conversation with another girl who "goes away and starts talking to someone else," leaving the best friend "just talking into space, so I just came to her so she wouldn't feel bad." Judy knows that her friend "gets a little boring," but she doesn't "want her to feel bad." School is a place where she experiences connection and the possibility of rejection.

Differences fascinate young girls, differences between them that can lead to disagreement and hurt feelings. Margaret, a ten-year-old, observes that "different people have different opinions . . . because you have a different mother and a different family, and a different skin, different color, different color eyes, color hair and intelligence." Deb, another fourth-grader, says "all kids have different feelings about different people, so they might disagree." She says it's "good to be different." Difference is apparent, natural, and interesting to young girls. "Why are you *like* that?" Darleen, an African-American fourth-grader, says to a white classmate. "I mean you never say anything. What's wrong with you anyways?" Girls with disabilities recall being simultaneously teased and accepted by classmates in the schools where they were mainstreamed. Differences and likenesses, named and pointed out, are the coins in girls' relational economy, the things that make life interesting.

Relationship power plays are girls' primary game: Who's in and who's out? Jessie, an eight-year-old, describes how she was excluded by a friend who invited another girl over to play and then left Jessie out. Going to her friend, Jessie says, "This is really making me feel bad, for leaving me out. Can you please play with me, too?" And she adds, "I will go home if you don't, 'cause this isn't any fun for me, just sitting here." Her friend answers, "Just go home." As Jessie laments, "They don't really care, they don't really care. They just leave—they just don't talk to me. They whisper in each other's ear, saying things about me. I just don't like it." While this is painful to Jessie, she authorizes herself and her feelings by speaking directly. Jessie, intent on keeping her friendship, does later find a way to show her friend just how it feels to be excluded so that they can still be friends. Lyn Mikel Brown explains that self-authorization—an ability to know and to claim the rightness of one's feelings and thoughts, even in the face of disagreement, disappointment, and anger—is one of the most striking strengths of young girls.

At home and in school, girls monitor the emotional climate for the winds of exclusion, the threat of abandonment and loss. They voice their distress when they are excluded; they fight to be included. Lyn Mikel Brown and Carol Gilligan name these girls "whistle-blowers in the relational world," after the story told by Diana, who brought a whistle to the dinner table. When her brother and sister interrupted her and stole her mother's attention, Diana blew the whistle and stopped their conversation. "That's much nicer," she remarked calmly. Four researchers enter a fourth-grade classroom. Saundra, an African-American girl, wryly notes aloud to herself, "Hmmm, three white women and only one black woman. I guess that's okay." Saundra's school has only one person of color on the teaching staff for a very diverse population. Young girls are persistent about their observations; they know what they know. Many of these girls feel determined to make themselves heard, particularly by those to whom they are close.

As girls gain exposure to and experience in a world structured on competition, their power games become more deadly psychologically. Most grade schools begin to assign letter grades to students in the fourth or fifth grade. Despite words about cooperation or community, children understand that success in school is based on competition with one another. Not only do girls compete for grades, but they begin to compete with other girls for attention. The hormones that prepare a girl's body for reproduction begin to flow at this time. Girls are menstruating as early as age nine, and when a girl experiences the new feelings aroused by the changes in her body, she wants to know more about the dynamics between men and women, and among women.

Looking to women, girls observe and then act out the competition that they see. Five fifth-grade girls improvise a play about popularity in which they trash a new girl. "Would your mothers have trashed a new woman among her friends?" asks Lisa Sjostrom, their teacher. "Oh no," says Chloe, "our mothers would have been nice." "Yeah," agrees Evie, "and when she left they would have talked about her."

Carol Gilligan suggests that girls at this time are enacting a dumb show of women's place in men's world. While the world of white men excludes women from positions of real power and authority, white women gain access to a safe place through competition with each other for men's favors. Both women and men of color find themselves competing for access that is never forthcoming. Girls about to encounter the wall of the culture bear witness to these divisions and tensions. The fierce power girls feel in their close relationships with their mothers and in their families begins to give way. Slowly, they realize that the *world* decides who is in and who is out based on sex, skin color, class, and other differences that they have no power to change. Their competitive response fits into the world as they find it.

Girls learn from women's responses to girls' fights. Having collided with the wall at adolescence, many women, particularly middle- and upper-class ones, insist that their daughters "be nice," as if doing so would solve everything. Girls also notice that adults do "the thing where [they don't] listen to your half of the story." Not listened to and shut down by "niceness," many girls begin to find solutions to their problems that hide conflict and bury feeling. In stories of their own and others' conflicts, girls begin to paste on false resolutions, like ". . . and they lived happily ever after," as they struggle to resolve painful dilemmas in relationships. As Brown and Gilligan explain, "The 'happy endings' heard from other girls seem more like wishful thinking on their part, something heard in a fairy tale, a pleasing and acceptable cover for experiences of feeling left out and fears of being abandoned."

Ann Martin's best-selling "The Baby-Sitters Club" series and her companion series, "The Baby-Sitters Little Sisters," present girls with stories where girls "solve" problems through niceness. Martin's success (over

82 million books in print) speaks to girls' hunger for books about the relationship issues that most concern them—divorce, death, boys, each other. While educators have expressed concern over a limiting of girls' expectations through the books, with their focus on an upper-middle-class world of babysitting and with their pedestrian prose style, of greater concern is "the sugary buzz of goodness and niceness," as one journalist called it, and the unrealistically simplistic solution of relationship problems. Girls speak out in these books, saying what they feel and think, but as in the fairy tales, the endings are pat and idealized. The pull of "nice" and "good" leads to the artificially sweetened happy ending in this fictional world of privileged girls.

Lyn Brown and Carol Gilligan observe that the words "I'm sorry" take on a magical significance in the fourth and fifth grades. Girls come to believe that simply saying "sorry" has "the power to cover cruel or mean behavior or resolve ardent disagreements. Stories in which an apology is given have almost fairy-tale-like happy endings, so that strong feelings of pain or indignation end abruptly with this final act of contrition." The smooth endings to stories echo the cloaked feelings and conflict that girls observe in women's behavior. Girls observe their mothers change their behavior to keep the peace, and they see that many women either silence their feelings or speak and are punished.

Repeatedly warned by mothers and women teachers to be nice, girls begin to lose power in their most important relationships. They begin to suspect that their mothers would love them more if they were not who they are but instead were nicer and kinder, more nearly perfect. They are put in the impossible dilemma of giving up what they know and feel to keep from being abandoned or excluded by their mothers and the other women closest to them. Girls' haunting response leads them to envision the "Perfect Girl" who they are not.

For many middle-class girls, as Lyn Brown discovered, the Perfect Girl is created in response to disapproval and to the admonishments of women, usually mothers and teachers, to be nice, kind, quiet, and neat, and to get along with everyone else. Girls are told in subtle and not-so-subtle ways that their bad feelings, like anger, sadness, or impatience and, too often, their exuberance have no place in the world. The Perfect Girl is always someone else. Even the girls whom others consider to be perfect know, because they have bad feelings, that they are not her. The struggle is impossible; the loss of self is profound.

Girls begin to act out their loss of power to the Perfect Girl through competition and cruelty. Girls' cliques and backstabbing duplicate the rivalry and competition they see underlying women's relationships within a male-defined world. As girls take in more of the message that they are not "right," they experience loss, which leads many to try to live up to the impossible ideal of the Perfect Girl. They act out their anger covertly through increasingly painful games of inclusion and exclusion. Unlike eight-year-old Jessie, they have no way to authorize themselves as they enter a patriarchal society.

Women, unwittingly, collude in girls' gradual disempowerment in a variety of ways. When girls complain of unfairness in their lives, their mothers often respond, "Life's not fair." While true, the passivity and resignation of this response send girls a clear message that they cannot do anything about what they see. Victoria's mother agrees with her that it's unfair that she's paid less than the boys at the stable where she works. But her mother says nothing when Victoria complains to her father. He responds, "People are going to think you are dumb when you say that." Victoria's mother remains silent.

Girls often see that mothers favor the males in their lives. "I had to talk to my mom," says Flo. "I had to tell, because it was sort of important, so I just talked to her and then my dad started talking and she paid attention to him and not to me." "We talk to each other about how my father treats my brother better," JoHanna says, referring to her mother and sister, "but we don't talk to our father about it." "My brother always gets his way," notes another girl.

In the shadow of the wall, girls see the injustices in their worlds but have no recourse and few allies. The dawning realization of women's subordinate position within the culture becomes more and more clear to them. In traditional families, they see their mothers pay more attention to and collude with their fathers' authority. Boys and men often get more attention. As girls, as their mothers' daughters, they are asked to be silent, to be helpful, and to be nice so that there isn't trouble. Mothers and women teachers know that they can depend on girls' desire for connection to ask them to bear more than they would ever ask from boys. While asking for girls' cooperation and compliance, mothers and teachers also tell girls that silence, niceness, and kindness are what is expected from them. Middle-class girls are often asked to give up their strong feelings and loud voices in order to get along or to create an artificial harmony in the classroom or family. The unspoken threat is abandonment and exclusion. From this they learn that these aspects of themselves, as well as what they know, are bad, rude, and unwelcome. By shutting off what they know and feel, these girls buy continued closeness with their mothers and the other women in their lives. But as they do so, they know and feel that it is not fully real.

POLITICAL RESISTANCE

Poised on the edge of adolescence, at age eleven and twelve, girls have lived and experienced enough to develop the capacity to describe the world abstractly, to begin to move beyond the concrete world of the everyday to think about the "what ifs" that their experience poses for them. At the same time, they begin to see that the world they live in is highly categorized and structured: men over women, rich over poor, whites over people of color. While girls have experienced these power relations all their lives, it is only at this age, right before adolescence and at the very base of the wall, that they are capable of taking in this knowledge conceptually. In many ways, it is as if they are able to see the world around them clearly for the first time.

"Seeing the framework for the first time," write Lyn Mikel Brown and Carol Gilligan, "and also feeling the power with which this framework or construction is enforced or held in place, girls pose genuine questions about love and power, truth and relationship. And their questions, if taken seriously, disturb the framework and disrupt the prevailing order of relationships." The "framework" is the wall of the culture. Girls, glimpsing this apparently solid wall, resist having their power and authority compromised. Because what girls know has deeply political implications, Carol Gilligan has referred to girls' struggle as "political resistance."

Girls firsthand gain an extraordinarily political knowledge about men and women by observing how women are denied power in patriarchal culture. At eleven, Victoria begins an interview by stating that the way women take men's names when they get married is unfair. Later she clarifies what she meant: "Because it always says Mr. and Mrs. [Jim Hanson] and it's like, what about the woman? she's here, too. And then it says, Mrs. and then not her name but my dad's name, Mrs. [Jim Hanson]. But it never says Mrs. Elaine or Ms. Elaine something like that, her name, it just says Mrs. and then his name, and that's unfair because it makes it look like she's not even there."

When Victoria explains why this bothers her, she speaks of her mother: "She's good and she's smart and she's understanding, but like everything about these names and stuff is kind of draining her, draining her potential and stuff. . . . Because like everything always points to the man, like the man is most important and the woman is not even alive. It just always shows like that." From Victoria's observations of her mother and her women teachers, she concludes, "I think that this happens with a lot of women when they get married; the men always think they're better." "Like, God!" she exclaims, "this is not right!" The subordination of women, particularly her mother, is painful and outrageous to Victoria. But she is left not knowing what to do or who could join her in her knowledge.

Not only do girls see the toll that cultural conventions take on their mothers and other women in their lives, but they also see women, like

Perfect Girls, deny the reality of their feelings. Ritu, a twelve-year-old from a study run by Annie Rogers, Carol Gilligan, and Normi Noel, tells Carol how she knows that her mother is angry at her even when she is acting friendly: "I say, 'Mom, are you mad at me?' And she says, she goes, 'Nooo' (high, thin voice). . . . She just goes, 'Hhhhhaaaa' (exasperated sigh), So—" Ritu persists with her mother when her mother's voice and sighs show what her mother denies, she says, " '*Mom,* it seems like you're mad at me,' and then she goes (high voice), 'No. I'm not mad at you, okay?' So okay." Ritu is left with one avenue—she'll "just sort of forget about it."

Emma, age ten, is on a tour of the local fire station as part of a photography project. Noticing the male fire fighters' nude pinups of women, she crosses her arms over her chest. "What do you think about that?" she asks the female fire fighters who are her guides. They say that it doesn't bother them, that it's really okay, not a problem. The response shocks Emma. It seems almost unimaginable to her. "You know what I would do?" she says. "I'd wait until they were getting dressed and then take pictures of them without any clothes on and hang them up. See how they liked it then."

These girls find themselves pitted against a reality that is hurtful and false. Lyn Mikel Brown first wrote about how young girls engage in an active struggle to stay with themselves, their thoughts and feelings, in the face of what is increasingly called "reality" but does not jibe with what they have experienced as real. Becka, at twelve, speaks of her struggle as she feels her self slipping away in relationships: "I wasn't thinking of myself, I just wanted to have this group of friends. . . . I was losing confidence in myself. I was losing track of myself, really, and losing the kind of person I was." Victoria speaks of "building a little shield" to protect herself from this "reality." Other girls speak of coming up against a wall, of not knowing where to turn, whom to trust, or what to do. Girls lose what they have trusted most—their sense of power through connection with others, their ability to discern truth and falseness around them—as they learn the lies that hold the wall upright.

As they struggle to speak and, so, authorize what they have known from their experiences of sight and sound, thought and feeling, girls move from the light of knowledge into shadows of doubt marked by the phrase "I don't know," which is a sign of loss, a clue to powerlessness. Carol Gilligan heard the phrase "I don't know" marking the gateway to "the underground city of female adolescence—the place where powerful learning experiences were happening."

"I don't know," Katie says in seventh grade, "like parents have authority, or adults, and they like to be obeyed. As a matter of fact, they should be obeyed, by law, but—I don't know, they worked their way up to adulthood and they deserve something in return." Katie plots her strategy to protect what she knows from the greater power of the adults around her:

> Well, you really don't want to argue with an adult, because they have authority and all that, so you might just ignore it or like think "I'm right," or, you know, "He's wrong." So you could just think of the solution to yourself and just forget about it, or you might do it more and get in trouble or, I don't know.

Katie describes strategies that other girls also use to negotiate their way through disagreements when their experience as children doesn't match the ways of the powerful adults around them. First, Katie holds on to what she thinks and drops the issue with the adult; in effect, she goes underground with what she sees, hears, feels, and thinks. The second strategy is to forget all about it, to lose what she knows. The third alternative is to keep on and get in trouble. Katie doesn't have ways of negotiating what she feels and thinks without losing her own knowledge or risking the loss of her relationship with a powerful adult. At age twelve, she assumes that she will probably not be heard.

Even at this point, struggling against losing their power, girls still know what they know. The underground lies just below the surface.

Within the context of a supportive relationship, girls will articulate what they know even when that differs from what they are told they should know. Yet their experience has already taught them to be wary, to look for signals that it is safe to speak about what is happening in their families, what they see at school, and what they know about false relationship.

Girls' knowledge is political because it reveals that the "natural" order of social reality is a system of power relations, a system of privilege that values men over women, whites over people of color, rich over poor. These girls see women shoring up fragile men while denying male vulnerability. They see the ideas of people of color and of working people ignored because these people don't look or sound like members of the white middle class. They see the enormous energy invested in denial. Like political refugees, they read faces and situations, looking for safe houses, stations on the underground, where they can speak what they know and feel. They struggle to know; they resist losing the truth of their experience. But as Lyn Brown and Carol Gilligan note, "In the absence of safe-houses where girls can say what they feel and think, girls' healthy resistance may turn into a psychological resistance as girls become reluctant to know what they know and fear that their experience if spoken will endanger their relationships and threaten survival."

PSYCHOLOGICAL RESISTANCE

Girls, eventually and inevitably, collide head-on with the wall. The final, traumatic impact happens when girls realize the implications of their changing bodies. As girls' bodies change, they find themselves looked at by men and boys in ways that are new and strange—and exciting—to them. As girls' minds expand to take in the violence and objectification of women, they are overwhelmed. Girls learn that it is dangerous to be the girls they once were.

Like a net ripped away from under a novice trapeze artist, the web of relationships that has sustained girls is torn away. The early skills of relating that girls developed and the trust that they had in themselves and in those closest to them, stops working as girls move from a world of women to a culture made by men. Operating just outside of conscious awareness like a premonition, the knowledge that girls take in about being female in this culture subtly reshapes their sense of self—even as it is being reshaped by changes in mind and body. They adopt the false protection of *psychological resistance,* and take their knowledge and truth underground.

The collision rearranges memory as girls unconsciously distance and disconnect from the young women selves that they now become. In their collision with the wall, girls resist psychologically and reinterpret what they once knew. Psychological resistance is both a response to fear and a protection from it. To keep from being too frightened and overwhelmed, the psyche cuts off feeling from thinking, memory from consciousness, and experience from knowledge of "reality."

At an almost wordless level, girls come to realize that they are, in fact, threatened with annihilation—through punishment, violence, or ostracism —as the cost of not complying with patriarchal expectations. Trying to protect the young adolescent girl from harm, her psyche urges her to look around and live according to the expectations of the culture and to not know frightening thoughts and feelings. What she has cut off from, what she has resisted knowing, is still within a girl's psyche but is ignored, not known, because knowing is too threatening to the new "self" that girls develop to survive and to succeed in adolescence. They lose some aspect of themselves as the price of admission to civilized adult society. And they lose memory of their feelings as they first hit the wall.

Girls are powerless to stop themselves from entering the culture as women, and this experience is deeply traumatic. Trauma is the human psyche's response to extreme powerlessness, loss of control, and the threat of annihilation. In traumatic situations, ordinary psychological functioning changes, often permanently. Sometimes trauma occurs after one extreme instance of powerlessness, like rape. Sometimes, though, trauma happens over time, as a person finds herself captive and helpless. While adolescence is not typically thought of as traumatic (painful, yes; traumatic, no), the knowledge that girls take in about their social reality creates symptoms similar to those seen in trauma survivors. Like prisoners of war, girls are captive in a culture where men are dominant.

What an adolescent girl cuts off from speaks to the dangers in her life, the threats of loss. Some African-American girls who do well in school face a painful dilemma when their individual success pits them against the value that their communities place on joining together against oppression. Psychologist Signithia Fordham, studying research on African-American adolescents in a public school in Washington, D.C., shows that one strategy high-achieving girls adopt, wittingly or unwittingly, for success is "racelessness." As sixteen-year-old Rita says, "I identify with Blacks and Whites alike—I don't—see, that's one thing I don't go for: I don't like when people ask me do I identify with Black people or do I identify with white people? I identify with *people*. People are people, Black or white, Spanish, red, white or blue, we're all the same." Rita's sentiment would be lovely if the painful, organized inequalities between whites and African-Americans in this culture didn't exist. In their "raceless personae," these girls deny their affiliation with their "eternal and unbreakable bond and . . . obligation to the Black community" and defend against facing racism by adopting the dominant culture's values and beliefs.

Girls' most traumatic loss is the ability to live fully and powerfully in their bodies. Most girls view the physical changes—the complete alteration of the body's shape—not as an empowering experience but as a loss of control. The power that girls gain to reproduce life is typically viewed, by boys and girls, as a curse, not as an awesome mystery. Boys, generally, are excited by the changes in their bodies because these changes give them access to greater control and power in the world. While girls are bigger than boys throughout childhood, in adolescence, boys rapidly become bigger and stronger. The ongoing irritant of boys' sexual harassment of girls—from bra snapping to "titty twisters"—now becomes much more threatening. Jessica, a sixteen-year-old, mimicked the boys in her school:

"They stand around watching us go through changes. They say, 'Great, they're going through all of these changes just for us.' "

Yet, the key to adolescent girls' trauma is not simply their loss of control relative to boys' increased size: girls' trauma results from the peril of their sexuality in a culture shaped by men's desires. The integrity of girls' being in childhood—the unity of knowing, feeling, and acting—unravels when they absorb this knowledge into their psyches. Girls disintegrate by "losing" their bodies in a profound form of psychological resistance—one that alters how a girl experiences her very self.

The body is the root of our power and desire for living. As girls' bodies awaken to the powers and pleasures of adult sexual feeling, girls desire to experience something deeply moving, to be deeply moved. But the sexualized images of women around them, the stories of violence and rape, the difference between men's and women's physical power, and the comments and stares of boys and men all come together to make very different sense of the world. Lively, exuberant girls are told over and over again that they are sexually provocative. While Cyndi Lauper's pop favorite "Girls Just Want to Have Fun" put a sexual spin on the word "fun," girls who do have fun, who want fun, are "asking for it."

In a recent study of sexual harassment in schools, conducted by the Wellesley Center for Research on Women, eight girls out of ten who experienced harassment reported having been touched, pinched, or grabbed. Well over a third of the girls reported being harassed *every single day in school*—through looks and comments, as well as through touching or other more aggressive harassment.

While most girls report harassment to teachers and other authorities, nothing happened to the harasser in nearly half of the incidents. "I told my friends and they made me feel like a total slut!" wrote one thirteen-year-old girl in the study. "They said, *'You should tell him to stop.'* Don't they know I've tried! I told my counselor and he told me to get used to it because I was more mature than everybody else! PLEASE! It made me feel a little powerless, like it was out of my control."

Harassment happens to *all* girls, regardless of race or class or school setting. As one fourteen-year-old girl wrote, "I think schools need to pay more attention to what's going on around them because girls like me are just dying inside because no one will believe us." Many of the girls in the study spoke of being scared and of getting "scareder and scareder every day."

Girls come to understand that their expressions of desire—curiosity, outspokenness, pleasure—are seen as sexual or are sexualized by the adults around them. While this begins early in childhood, at early adolescence when girls begin to feel explicitly sexual impulses, they find their behavior misinterpreted and themselves in trouble or danger. Men's facility for splitting deep feeling from physical sensation has created a culture in which they see women's bodies as sources for pleasure and sensation. Sexuality poses a terrifying dilemma for girls—and for their mothers. This is an absolutely critical problem, one full of real dangers that girls face. They develop problematic strategies as they struggle to hold on to their desires and their sexuality.

Adolescent girls are simply not safe in their bodies, and most of the danger has to do with sex. For most girls, their awareness of and exposure to physical danger becomes acute in adolescence (although many girls have learned hard lessons about violence, particularly sexual violence, at a very young age). Of girls who have been sexually abused, the greatest number were eleven years old when such abuse first occurred. While one in three girls acknowledges an unwanted sexual contact before age eighteen with an adult male, three-fourths of that unwanted contact occurs in adolescence. Date rape and other forms of rape are most common in adolescence. In fact, psychiatrist Judith Herman writes that rape might be thought of as girls' "social rite . . . of initiation into the coercive violence at the foundation of adult society." As many as one-third of all high school– and college-age girls are involved in violence in an intimate or dating relationship. Within sex education courses, girls are also warned repeatedly of the dangers of AIDS, sexually transmitted diseases, and pregnancy.

Yet the threat of physical danger is not the only threat to girls. As psychologist Deborah Tolman discovered in studying girls' dilemmas with their sexual desire, girls face the difficult task of exploring their desire and remaining not only physically safe from violation and disease, but also socially safe from being ostracized as a slut, and psychologically safe from being seen as shamefully bad. Boys name "bitches," "whores," and "sluts," and they talk about who is "fly" or "cool." They label girls in the hallways of schools and on the streets.

As girls begin enforcing boys' rule among themselves, girls find themselves increasingly dependent on the social sanction of boys. The threat of losing a boyfriend if a girl doesn't act "right" or isn't pleasing enough is an often-present dynamic in adolescent girls' lives. For girls caught in the clutches of "goodness," owning and claiming their sexuality poses psychological dangers. "Good" girls' sexual feelings place them psychologically at risk because being bad—sexual—is overwhelmingly shameful and places the girl at risk of being abandoned by her family and peer group.

This leaves girls with a general sense of anxiety, a fearful alertness. "When I'm home alone I always make sure that all the doors and windows are locked because I'm always afraid that a stranger is coming," says four-teen-year-old Alicia. "I guess my imagination gets the best of me. But I know things can happen. And you hear things on the news, like about rape and stuff." Girls, much more than boys, experience greater "nervousness, hopelessness, restlessness, sadness and anxiety" as well as feelings of being out of control.

Girls' increased intellectual ability allows them to see themselves as if from the outside, from another's point of view. They lose their capacity to enjoy difference (as defined by their peers), particularly in themselves. With this new capacity, they monitor themselves incessantly—looking at their looks, witnessing their every movement from the perspective of the boys who have increasing power in their lives. This potential allows them to become self-conscious, to create a self that they can compare to the ideals they see. The struggle that many girls engage in with weight and eating—with both extreme thinness and obesity—is partially girls' attempt to use their new mental power to stop becoming a woman or to camouflage themselves as they enter a world that moves to men's desires. Self-consciousness becomes almost a curse as girls shamefully find that they don't measure up.

When girls dis-integrate, they paper new selves over their underground knowledge and feelings of their bodies. Out of this loss of integrity (or wholeness), girls' thoughts and feelings get out of sync with what they say and do. Many girls, particularly middle-class girls, "disembody" by distancing from the sexual knowledge and feelings in their bodies so that they feel safer and less vulnerable. Despite knowing the dangers around them, girls (and women) split off their knowledge and *act* as if rape couldn't happen to them. "Like rape is one of my biggest fears," Kim, age fourteen, says. Yet when asked about date rape, the most prevalent type of rape in her age group, she seems almost surprised: "I've never really thought about date rape, but I guess it's like what everyone says, like it couldn't happen to me."

"Disembodying" by disconnecting from sexual feeling is debilitating and blinding. The agony that many girls and young women go through about "going too far" often comes from this disjunction. By not being able to "own" their sexuality and integrate it within their ideas about who they are, girls find themselves taken by surprise by the urgency of their feelings, and they become confused into "love."

Some girls lose their integrity in another way entirely. They disconnect from the danger that surrounds them with a false bravado and aggressive sexuality. Don't worry, they seem to be saying, I can handle myself—I'm strong. This defended stance shields them from their vulnerability, the openness of intimacy, and their fear. Middle-class white society defines these girls as "bad," then shames them and denies them success in the dominant culture.

The trauma girls suffer on collision with the wall breaks their trust in their girlhood world of mother and friends, although evidence from the

African-American and Latina communities indicates that connection to a strong community of women can counter or delay girls' trauma. Many girls find themselves on rocky ground with each other after the inclusion-exclusion struggles of late childhood and, then, their failed efforts to be the Perfect Girl. As girls lose their way with each other and with the women in their lives, they become even more vulnerable to thinking that what they see on television and in magazines is real and holds the key to a successful future. Girls come to accept as possible the crazy-making perfection of the Superwoman and the surgically sculpted bodies of super models.

As girls' relationships change from centering around childhood play to centering around talk and a sharing of personal secrets, girls begin to speak of painful betrayals between them. The gossip and betrayals are about "like who likes who and who cheated with who and all that stuff," fourteen-year-old Kim explains. "And then it goes into the back-stabbing —like 'she stabbed me in the back because she knew I liked him' and that kind of thing."

Competition for boys becomes an additional test of girls' relationships with each other. Heather, another fourteen-year-old, argues that "girls will do anything to get ahead, even if it's their friend—girls will do anything—like be a back-stabber to get ahead." "Get ahead" means "to get that one guy." Having lost faith in girls on a level of basic trust, they increasingly turn to men for the answers to how to get along in the world. Betrayed by their girlfriends, they sometimes find that their relationships with boys are a relief, as Melody says, "because they don't get all worked up about every little thing."

Girls' dis-integration creates a profound loss of resilience and voice, the keys to mental health, and produces a deep shame at being other than they "should" be to be loved and safe. By denying or walling off part of their psyches, girls become vulnerable to depression, self-mutilation, eating disorders, anxiety, and the horde of distresses that plague adolescent girls. Their integrity is severely impaired. The internal conflict between denial and knowledge consumes tremendous psychic energy. As a short-term survival strategy, this loss of integrity keeps girls from feeling endangered. But in the long term the trauma of these losses is etched into girls' psyches and actually starts shaping what they know about the world and what they desire. Girls' loss of being able to be themselves in the world leads them either into longing for self-perfection or, increasingly, into the self-loathing of becoming "one of the guys." Most painfully, it leaves them mistrustful of the love that they knew as girls.

By the end of the high school years, girls often appear "together" again. The doubt and uncertainty, the willful self-protection and fears, are covered over and rationalized. Still intensely interested in relationships, many girls hold their own needs, desires, and knowledge at bay so that they can have "good" relationships and get along with others. Others put on a protective coat of bravado and find themselves emotionally isolated as they speak their minds. What they think, say, and do differs from what they *really* think and would like to say and do. They lose touch with their authenticity.

As Lyn Brown observes, "Doubting what they know, these fifteen- and sixteen-year-old girls look to external authorities to define what is of value and what is legitimate knowledge." Not trusting themselves, they look to the culture and the media to define them. They look and sound good because they now fit into the expectations of the culture around them. Yet at each new opening in their lives—as they enter college and the work world—the compromises they have made can be once again opened to questioning and confusion.

CYCLE OF BETRAYAL

With their mothers at their sides, girls move from power to betrayal, from the power born of mother daughter relationships to a cultural betrayal wrongly blamed on mothers. From the wholeness of early childhood to their encounters with the Perfect Girl and into resistance (first political and then psychological), girls sustain painful and unnecessary losses as they approach and collide with the wall of Western culture. Mothers grapple with the harrowing task of reconciling their overriding desire to keep their daughters safe with their desire to keep them strong and free in a world that insists on women's inferiority and subordination. Only at adolescence, when the capacity to bear children begins, do girls become of any real interest or value to patriarchal culture. A door opens—narrowly—then, and mothers usher girls inside.

"Young women express the greatest scorn for their mothers at this time," observe Judith Herman and Helen Lewis, "the greatest desire to be different from their mothers, and the greatest fear that nevertheless they will turn out to be just like their mothers." While the conventional explanation for this struggle is that girls are trying to separate from their mothers, an interpretation closer to what girls and women actually say and feel is that girls feel betrayed or let down by their mothers, and they are searching for ways to liberate themselves and their mothers.

"In late adolescence," explains psychologist Terri Apter, "the daughter tends to be highly interested in her mother's gender strategies—that is, in how the mother treats the father, how their domestic roles are divided, how this division is negotiated, and what compromises were made from these negotiations." While girls actively observe such things at a much earlier age, as a girl gets older, she will often openly criticize her mother's choices. "Much of the barrage of criticism leveled at the mother by the daughter is an inner dialogue assessing the model she believes her mother presents her." Girls want to know: Do I have to make these sacrifices? Do I have to do what you have done to survive or to keep your love? Tied to their mothers by a deep attachment, daughters see their mothers' sacrifices and feel betrayed. Generation after generation, daughters translate betrayal by the culture into a betrayal by their mothers. Ironically, and tragically, mothers are blamed for the very betrayal that they themselves suffered.

Mothers repeat the lessons they learned as girls to their daughters. They teach girls to be women like them, to survive in a world of male privilege and power by pleasing men. As psychologist Dana Jack observes, "The growing girl experiences how maternal authority is overruled and replaced by paternal authority, both literally and metaphorically. Female authority teaches her by feeling, word, and example how to relate to male authority." Girls search for ways to liberate their mothers from unhappiness, while mothers seek to help their daughters adapt and be safe. They admonish girls to be careful, careful of men, and as girls grow older, the fears that fuel mothers' concern grow, too. Teenage girls share their mothers' fears of physical and sexual violence, yet with a sense of invulnerability, they act as if they continually think, It couldn't happen to me.

While men create the dangers, it is mothers who most often are "forced to be their daughters' jailers." Girls usually discount their mothers' warnings and respond with anger and contempt to unwanted—and in their minds, unnecessary—limits on their freedom and independence. Mothers' fearful, but justified, efforts to protect their daughters, their implied and explicit injunctions to do as they do, and their daughters' angry realization that their mothers' powerlessness mirrors their own future all join to place an unbearable strain on a relationship between mother and daughter.

This relationship, a mutual and deep attachment, is vital to them both. After all, girls and women value relationship with a felt intensity that the culture does not allow men and boys. Young girls' connections and their capacity to engage with others—learned in mother daughter relationships—are their deepest sources of strength and resiliency. The collision with the wall and mothers' culturally ordained responses threaten adolescent girls with a dreadful violation of their trust in and their relationships with their mothers. As a result, girls question their mothers' integrity, "strict personal honesty and independence," and personal "completeness" and "unity." This breach of trust is a loss and disappointment that causes girls to wonder, "Why didn't she warn me?"

For girls of color, the losses and disappointments are different. Educator Beverly Jean Smith, an African-American woman, comments on the differences: "When I read the psychological research about mother-daughter relationships, mostly what strikes me is daughters' pain, anger, hate, rejection, fear and struggle to find self. . . . This way of speaking about the mother-daughter relationship runs counter to my experience." In fact, Smith tells us, it runs counter to the experience of most African-American women she knows, despite their dissimilar backgrounds.

What research there is certainly suggests stronger connections between African-American mothers and daughters: "A decisive 94.5% expressed respect for their mothers in terms of strength, honesty, ability to overcome difficulties, and ability to survive." Respecting their mothers' experience may lead some poor African-American girls to worry that having children will keep them from being able to have the future they want. Jill McLean Taylor and Amy Sullivan (two white researchers) write about African-American girls in a study of urban girls who are considered to be at risk: "Most notably, three-fourths of all the Black girls specifically stated at least once in their three interviews that they did *not* want any children. . . . There is some evidence that how these girls understand and relate to their mothers and their mothers' experiences influence their assessment of their own futures."

Racism, the extended families and stronger community ties of African-American communities, and the role women play in those families and communities all contribute to African-American girls' experience. Anecdotal evidence from Latinas suggests differences in their experience of mother daughter relationships. They, too, report a stronger connection with their mothers, although Latinas play a very different role in their families and communities than do African-American women.

But all girls suffer some loss and disappointment, which is covered over, first, with fear and, later, with anger and hostility. Dealing with anger in such a crucial relationship is certainly difficult, especially in a culture that demands that women and girls be nice, and that trivializes women's anger and disagreements as silly "cat fights." Many mothers respond to their daughters' anger with the unsettling remnants of their own girlhood anger, as old disappointments and fears are revived. Their discomfort with their daughters' anger is heightened by their own unacknowledged hostile feelings and memories. Some mothers express this anger, others convert it into depression, and others deny it. Few are able to teach their daughters how to stay with the anger, to use it, and to understand that "anger is loaded with information and energy."

Why? Because mothers are daughters, too. As girls, they came up against the wall, turned to their mothers questioningly, experienced a painful breach of trust, and felt disappointment and anger shake their relationship with their own mothers. Having passed through the wall, they no longer see it or remember what it felt like to live outside its confines. Their mothers didn't know how to deal with their own or their daughters' anger either, so an unspoken and unforgivable betrayal haunts many women's relationships with their mothers.

"Girls, astute observers of their mothers," writes psychologist Annie Rogers, "seem to know when women can and cannot face squarely into a struggle with them. Unfortunately, women's reluctance to experience another shattering loss becomes a powerful psychological defense. . . . The defense—the story of inevitable loss and betrayal designed to protect from repeated losses—repeats itself generation after generation, handed down unconsciously from women to girls, from mothers to daughters."

PATHS OF LEAST RESISTANCE

As girls approach adolescence, they encounter the two well-trodden paths that women take into patriarchy: conventional femininity and "girls will be boys," the culturally approved adoption by women of male models for how to be and act in the world. Both paths require that a girl betray herself and her connections with women—but in different ways. Both are paths of least resistance, paths through which girls' healthy and political resistance are internalized and become a self-destructive psychological resistance that allows them to fit into the culture. In fact, these paths are offered up as the roads to success, the paths their mothers chose—or wish they could have taken.

Within conventional femininity, the traditional role for women, women give up power and authority in the world in exchange for being taken care of and protected. This is the familiar romance story: a woman trades her power so she can attract a man for security in the home. At home, women are allowed a certain kind of power—to nurture, to manage a household—but the purse strings and the real authority rest with husbands or fathers. Some women, in certain eras, were led to believe that they were indeed powerful within this private sphere, which, as they were told and sometimes believed, was simply different and not less important than the public sphere that men inhabited. With industrialization and technological advances, traditional women's work (making clothing, preparing food from the harvest, healing, making crafts) has moved into the public sphere or disappeared, and homemakers' contributions have increasingly been devalued.

Women's lack of real power and their economic vulnerability are evident in the increasing number of households headed by single women and in the increasing poverty of women and their children in the United States. While on a day-to-day basis, a homemaker may feel powerful because of her influence in her family and community, too often the serious illness, death, or departure of her spouse forces the realization of how powerless she really is. Yet the hope and promise of care is still held out to women as a justifiable reward for subordination and a loss of power in public arenas. White women, Latinas, African-Americans, Asians, and Native Americans are all encouraged to marry, but some, like African-American women, are also warned not to rely on or trust men, to guard their independence. Some groups acknowledge more than others that conventional femininity asks women to betray their public voices and power, and places them at risk.

The other path increasingly sanctioned for girls is a "girls will be boys" strategy of striving for success and achievement in terms defined by patriarchal culture. In the 1970s, attempts at gender-free parenting often resulted in girls being pushed to do what boys do—just as more women were doing what "boys" do. For middle-class women, this usually takes the form of pursuing professional careers and power within contexts designed for men who have wives at home. Tacitly, their success depends on women accepting the norms and values of male privilege without question, while maintaining a thin veneer of femininity.

Psychologist Jean Baker Miller notes the drawbacks of this strategy: "Usually they are not wholly accepted, and even then only if they are willing to forsake their own identification with [other women]." Women are asked to betray other women, particularly women who are raising children, to deny nurturing aspects of themselves and, thus, to give up deep emotional connections with others.

Women who want to "have it all," in the terms now offered by the culture, find themselves in the role of Superwoman, balancing conventional femininity at home and male standards in business. The inherent conflicts in these ways of being "work to undermine a woman's sense of adequacy both within and outside of her intimate relationships." As Dana Jack notes, these conflicting standards are both "male definitions of the female self" either as the perfect helpmate and supporter or as an imitation of male-defined independence and achievement. In interviews with women, Dana Jack further observed that the cultural standards of the Superwoman created new and impossible ideals for women's appearance and behavior.

The impossibility of these Superwoman standards can lead girls into serious psychological problems. Psychologist Catherine Steiner-Adair has discovered that girls who adopt the image of the Superwoman as their own personal ideal appear to be more vulnerable to eating disorders than girls who are critical of Superwoman perfection. Steiner-Adair asked high school girls about society's ideals for women and about their own personal ideals. As one girl said, her personal ideal is "the way you see models and everything. . . . The gorgeous lady that had perfect grades in school and went to all the right schools and knew all the right people and just had the best job and did everything right. And I think that is a real honest picture." All of the girls in Steiner-Adair's study who sounded like this young Superwoman scored high on a test for eating disorders. Girls who were able to criticize the Superwoman ideal did not seem to be in danger of disordered eating. Steiner-Adair called these adolescent girls "Wise Women."

The paths of conventional femininity and "girls will be boys" Superwomen are very familiar to women, to the mothers of older girls and adolescents. There is a new path of modern girls' devising that women must now figure out. Researchers Michelle Fine and Pat McPherson, both white, talked with four teenage girls in 1991 about being women in the 1990s. Their discussions with the girls, two African-Americans, one Korean, and one white, gave these two women a glimpse of a different strategy that sounds familiar. These girls wanted to be "one of the guys. . . . Their version of feminism was about equal access to being men." Many women who work with girls have noticed this new strategy among girls with some alarm.

Although this sounds like "girls will be boys," it is actually very different. Girls devised this strategy from the margins of the culture. As "one of the guys," girls take a swaggering stance in the face of sexism, a stance that adopts sexism's complete devaluation of femininity and women themselves. The "girls will be boys" strategy involves an understood element of expediency, some internal conflict, an absence of certainty about the complete superiority of all things male, and a lingering appreciation of things feminine. With the "one of the guys" strategy girls want to *be* boys.

One of the most extreme versions of the "one of the guys" strategy springs up in certain urban communities: girls form gangs. Increasingly, they dress and act with the familiar toughness and bravado of boys. By "fronting," that is, putting up this tough front, girls are set up to betray themselves and to hurt each other in a war for survival. Girls who are "one of the guys" reject other girls—and themselves. Dismissed as untrustworthy, weak, ridiculously prissy, and nice, other girls are regarded with an alienating distaste. The flip side of the pursuit of the Perfect Girl, it is a strategy that feeds on self-loathing. Faced with the losses at adolescence, girls idealize maleness and want it for themselves. In self-chosen and self-denying identification with the oppressor, girls equate male behaviors with honesty, integrity, courage, and strength. Frighteningly, girls buy the whole package, even when it includes violence. Many of these guy-girls find that the violence they accept and find cool is turned on them sexually. While they may feel like one of the guys, the guys know that they are still girls.

The paths of least resistance—traditional femininity, "girls will be boys," and "one of the guys"—are short-term survival strategies with enormous costs. All of them require that girls surrender parts of themselves —their agency or their compassion. All of these strategies compromise girls' self-love and integrity. Within the context of our culture, these are the options that mothers have to pass on to their daughters. Mothers lose their daughters' trust and, horribly, are rewarded with contempt. These limiting individual strategies perpetuate fear, isolation, and divisiveness. With a politicized awareness of the forces of disconnection, women can find ways to resist the pressures of oppression and to join against loss.

THE RESISTANCE MOVEMENT

Tracing the path from power to betrayal, from girlhood to young womanhood, shifts blame from mothers to a culture that insists on the subjugation of women. That shift of blame does not, however, mean that mothers have no responsibility. Mothers have a profound responsibility to resist and to support their daughters' resistance. While individual resistance may be difficult and, perhaps, even doomed to failure, a group of women, a politically aware movement or organization, can compete against the pressure and power of the culture to prevent the losses girls typically suffer as they become women. History confirms the effectiveness of collective action. Our growing national awareness of domestic violence is the result of a movement that arose from the feminist movement of the

1970s. Without the support and resources of this movement, people might have continued to avoid acknowledging just how prevalent and damaging violence is in our homes.

Pointing to sexism and away from mothers, however, sounds easier than it is. Girls understand that the world they are entering is one in which women's knowledge is devalued and their power is illusory. But this *is* the culture. For now, there is no place else to go. What is a mother to do? Sociologist Pat Hill Collins relies on historian Elsa Barkley Brown to describe the "delicate balance between conformity and resistance . . . as the 'need to socialize me one way and at the same time to give me all the tools I needed to be something else.' " Girls have to know how to fit well enough while resisting. But they cannot fight alone without the risk of being overwhelmed. They need a network of women and girls to support their resistance against loss.

What is ultimately at stake in adolescence is a loss of the power of love. What girls once knew as love, the love that was the foundation of their selves, changes in the shadow of the wall. Living in a culture where "true love" is supposedly the romantic love between adult men and women, girls' fierce love for their mothers and for each other is easily ignored—after all, they are just little girls. But girls' loving, particularly of their mothers, may be the most intense loving women do in their lives.

As girls struggle and lose what they have known as love, they are offered another version of love in its place, the "true love" of romance. If the power of the culture were just oppressive, women would surely organize and march at every opportunity. But with subtle seduction, power creates desire. Perfect desire, perfect love, and perfect happiness are held out as women's reward for giving up the power of psychological integrity, passionate child love, the child world of girls and women, and the potential for being a force in the world. The story women are told is quite a story.

3

The Stories We Live By

And it is a hard thing to make up stories to live by. We can only retell
and live by the stories we have read or heard. . . . They may be read,
or chanted, or experienced electronically, or come to us, like the
murmurings of our mothers, telling us what conventions demand.
Whatever their form or medium, these stories have formed us all; they
are what we must use to make new fictions, new narratives.

Carolyn Heilbrun
WRITING A WOMAN'S LIFE

Once upon a time (that's how this story begins) there was a girl who
didn't quite realize that she'd become a lovely young woman. (The
story most often starts here, at the edge of womanhood. When these
stories start at birth, it's usually just so that a curse can be put on the baby
by other women.) She's pretty and quiet and good, and sometimes she
seems sad, mainly because her mother had died when she was just a baby
(a typical twist in the story). She is often being raised by other women
who are mean to her and make her work every day from dawn until dusk
(which is the fate of all but the wealthy in the kingdom, but the implica-

tion is that she should be spared). Sometimes she is sent away to the woods. But she doesn't say much about any of this. No, she never complains: she endures it all cheerfully. In fact, she seems quite perfect.

At some point, despite the evildoings of all the older, ugly women, she meets a rich, handsome man. He happens to be pretty perfect himself: he is very important and does exciting, adventurous things, but his father insists that he find a wife so there will be grandchildren. Prince Handsome isn't thrilled with this until he meets this girl. Of course, he is immediately taken by her beauty. Sometimes he is also impressed by all of her hard work, and a few times he likes how level-headed and wise she is. (After all of her years working from dawn until dusk, she doesn't tolerate much nonsense.) The handsome guy turns out to be a prince, and the young woman is revealed to be a long-lost princess (a common turn of events). Eventually (not right away, because he has some adventures in which he rescues her and others in which he defeats the evil schemes of various women), they get married in the biggest wedding anyone has ever seen. She wears the greatest dress. And, as we all know, they live happily ever after.

What happens during "happily ever after"? Oddly enough, the importance of the princess's life seems to end here. Few stories are written about what happens to the princess after the wedding. Reading between the lines of other stories, we can sketch out her "happily ever after": The princess gets pregnant and hopes for sons. As long as she is faithful and bears sons, she is considered to be a good wife. We don't hear whether or not she's a good mother, unless something goes wrong with her children. She's safe and cared for in the castle. Occasionally, something might be written about the good deeds she performed, acts of charity and the like. But, by and large, she's not heard from again. That is because this romance story is merely a subplot, almost a diversion from the *real* story: his. All of history has been written about the subsequent adventures in the chapters of his life. The prince goes back to his life of pursuing adventures and ruling the kingdom.

In many ways, this cultural story-to-live-by is the illusory American Dream of middle-class success, which has become a story of adventure and romance for people all over the world: once the wedding is over, the home has a thirty-year mortgage, and the kids start coming, everyone is happy, and everything is great and easy, right? The prince in the story is a man of the world who controls his own destiny and fortune. He is very powerful, strong, and, in most outward ways, invulnerable. He briefly takes time out of his public life for courtship, but he is rarely at home long enough to be warmed at the hearth. Wealth and influence signify his success, the measure of his manhood. The princess's life begins near the hearth and ends there. Her path to success and security is through the man she marries. Marriage is supposed to lessen her burden, take care of her, and allow her to jump up the economic ladder. Her husband's money and status are the signs of her success. Perhaps this, too, sounds familiar and a bit closer to home. Yet, if the basic plot and expectations for our life stories are determined by these cultural stories, then, like birds flying toward a picture window, we are in for an unhappy surprise. The story-to-live-by is an alibi that covers the losses hidden beneath its candy coating of perfection.

This story is so familiar that it seems almost ridiculous to examine it as an important source of knowledge about expectations for women's lives. And who believes in these fairy tales anymore? Aren't they pretty relics from a time gone by? Not exactly. We begin here because these stories—ones that most anyone would admit are foolish fantasies—exert a surprising power over our choices and expectations. "Myth and its little sister, fairy tale, make stories out of what we don't know we know," writes novelist Lore Segal. Fairy tale and myth are the forerunners of psychology: they explain, and give structure and meaning to, the lived experience of human life.

The depth of this relationship between story and culture is amazing. Anthropologist Peggy Sanday reviewed the creation myths of cultures worldwide. Western culture, with its solitary omnipotent creator, represents an extreme end of a global continuum that stretches from myths that describe the earth's creation by a matriarch to creation by a couple to creation by a patriarch. Creation stories that involve a Great Mother goddess, or an original divine couple, describe an attachment to the earth's body as part of their description of how life came to be. These cultures tend to be more egalitarian in their sexual politics. When only a male deity is recognized and the early experiences of the culture involve hunting animals, dislocation and migration, and warfare for survival, as in our culture, male dominance tends to be more severe. Sanday's analysis also suggests that the ubiquity of male dominance has to do with our culture's violent conquest of other, more egalitarian and less warring cultures.

The actual stories of our lives often follow the plots of those larger-than-life stories for several powerful psychological reasons. The hallmarks of loss, to paraphrase Carol Gilligan, are idealization and devaluation. These seemingly opposite responses cover rage, and under the rage lies sadness, which in turn covers the terror of our powerlessness. After experiencing the unnecessary and traumatic losses that are the price of admission to Western culture, our psyches "forget" the pain and fear (just like with childbirth). We then idealize and devalue crucial aspects of what was lost —a response that, oddly enough, protects us from our pain.

For men, the cultural story-to-live-by is the *hero legend*. For women, it is the *romance story*. These stories have immense and subtle power because they spring from the deep longing and pain brought about by these sacrifices. On entering adult society, men must sacrifice intimacy, emotional vulnerability, and community. Women must sacrifice their public life, voice, and power, as well as their trust in other women. As children, we take in these stories as important prescriptions for our lives. Eager to learn how to live in the world, children grab hold of these stories as guides and as a balm that soothes the pain of the sacrifices made to fit into Western culture. These idealized stories define true love and morality, but their glossy veneer obscures the lived truth of the violence and suffering that darken the root of our culture.

These cultural stories-to-live-by provide the unseen, and often unspoken, context that shapes mother daughter relationships. We need to understand how these stories have the power to shape our desires. Consider this an invitation to a favorite play—but this time, from backstage, where the mechanisms of the magic are revealed.

THE HERO LEGEND: MYTH BECOMES SCIENCE

"In all times and under every circumstance, the myths of *man* have flourished," says Joseph Campbell, equating *man* with *human* and, in this one sentence, unerringly and unwittingly, proclaiming men's story to be the basic story of human life. He has called the protagonist of these myths "the hero with 1,000 faces" because his story has been told so many times in so many civilizations. The reason the hero shows his face in so many places is that men dominate almost everywhere. This hero story codifies and glorifies the pain and sacrifices asked of men as they create and perpetuate their systems of superiority. In our technological age, the hero myth has moved from popular story to science to truth.

Who are heroes? The classical heroes—Odysseus, Aeneas, Hercules. The Greek gods like Apollo, who rides his chariot across the sky to bring humankind light; Zeus, who can destroy worlds with his thunderbolt; and Ares, who presides over wars. The Vikings Thor and Odin, Arthur and the knights of the Round Table, the Hindu Rama, and, even, in some ways, Christ or Buddha. Hero legends are not confined to ancient history, however. Hitler used hero images of the pure, powerful Aryan as part of his emotional siege of the German people. The Lone Ranger is a classic hero, as are Superman, Robin Hood, James Bond, the Terminator, and the whole host of caped crusaders, superheroes, and adventurers. Stories of the American cowboy (out West or in his modern urban incarnation), personified by John Wayne and Clint Eastwood, follow the hero plot.

The hero story is about a young man who separates himself from mother and home to search for greatness and supernatural powers. After engaging in a lengthy search and adventure in which he is put to grueling tests, he wins the powers that protect him in his conquest of the Queen Goddess of the World. After marrying her, he returns, powerful conqueror, to his home, where he then rules triumphantly. The hero has to leave his home and family and become invulnerable in order to rule over others.

Perhaps, at one time, these separations and the illusion of invulnerability were actually a necessity for men—"adaptive," as evolutionary biologists might say. When women were confined to the home by work and child rearing, men were alone in exploring, guarding, and expanding the resources that the family and community needed to survive. If men's lives have to be sacrificed through war and, these days, through a commitment to corporate wars against competitors, then the sacrifice of their feelings may make sense. At least this way, they will feel no emotional pain, and their physical pain will be sanctioned and justified.

Boys in early childhood (ages three to five) enter the hero legend at the same time they learn what *male* and *female* mean. For most boys, the person who has been physically and emotionally most present and nurturing has been mother. Once they realize that mother is different—a girl— they struggle to disconnect from mother in order to be not-mother, to become little men. They distance themselves from all of what mother has meant to them—including the nurturing intimacy of infancy. They lose the relationship with their mothers for the sake of relationships with others. In other words, many boys face a true dilemma: to be male, as they see and understand it, means not to behave like mother—not to be close physically and emotionally. Thus, they give up on that closeness and change the relationship with the person who has loved them most directly and who has kept them alive. While boys don't stop loving their mothers, they separate the experience of close intimacy from their construction of themselves as male. Intimacy becomes a threat to the self they are creating.

Sigmund Freud, through analyzing himself, called this struggle the Oedipus complex, after the Greek tragic hero Oedipus. Freud observed that small boys, within traditional nuclear families, connected the pleasure in their bodies at their mother's touch and the desire to have a possessive relationship with her to the realization that their father was a rival for the mother they love. From Freud's perspective, too, boys have to give up relationship with their mothers and identify with their fathers. All in all, this change in boys' lives is very powerful, confusing, and painful. The emotional "adjustment" that boys make often creates anger and hostility; they resist this disconnection with their mothers for the sake of their burgeoning "male" identity.

Young boys, therefore, throw themselves into the story of the hero because it resolves a profound psychological need. By idealizing themselves as invulnerable, by re-creating themselves as superheroes, boys "forget" the pain of emotional separation. The hero story enables them to make sense of their own experience. Yet it covers the lived truth of their pain and vulnerability.

Freud believed that boys' resolution of the Oedipus complex and entrance into the hero legend were necessary for Western civilization. He institutionalized the myth of separation by declaring that the myth held the key to individual human development. Separation—from mother, from emotional connection—became the cornerstone of Western civilization. Freud's stance and status lent his "discovery" of the Oedipus complex the stamp of science; after the turn of the nineteenth century, the myth became science. Other psychologists—such as Erik Erikson—would build on Freud's theories, and over the years we have come to call these interpretations objective truth.

The hero legend provides a justification for the sacrifices that men are asked to make for the sake of the culture. The legend promises the reward of immortal recognition—the next best thing, perhaps, to actual invulnerability—for giving up, first, one's closest emotional connection in childhood, and, then, one's life in adulthood. Because the hero is invincible and, therefore, unafraid, this damaging story-to-live-by leaves no room for pain and complaint.

At bottom, so much of the hero-legend psychology is a lie, a cover-up for the disconnection and pain that boys are asked to bear in their lives. What they get in return is the run of the place: entitlement to live and act in the public world. Power in the world—power to dominate and to ensure that they do not suffer inequality—is the compensation men are promised for giving up the power of emotional connection. Equally troubling, perhaps, is the fundamental illusion of going it alone, of separation, of an independence that too often borders on emotional isolation. With this illusion operating, men who have attained the status of heroes can never deeply join others, be joined by them, or acknowledge joint efforts. Power is understood only in terms of this independence and disconnection.

As psychologist Jean Baker Miller observes about the "separateness" of the hero self: "Few men ever attain such self-sufficiency, as every woman knows. They are usually supported by wives, mistresses, mothers, daughters, secretaries, nurses, and other women (as well as other men who are lower than they in the socioeconomic hierarchy)." Miller questions whether, from the perspective of a "separate self," it is even possible "to conceive of the possibility that freedom and maximum use of our resources —our initiative, our intellect, our powers—can occur within a context that requires the simultaneous responsibility for the care and growth of others and of the natural world." Power and freedom are imagined as possible only at the expense of responsibility for others and for the planet —a frightening scenario that's hardly heroic.

This story-to-live-by frames human life in Western culture and contains the stories of extraordinary men who have sacrificed greatly in pursuit of their goals. The hero story, an idealization that has arisen out of that loss, is the bribe for men to persist. Yet, hidden in inarticulate feelings, in rage, in violence, and in shame is the lived truth of the pain that this hero-self story attempts to conceal. The lived truth of men's vulnerability and suffering, particularly in early childhood and at adolescence, is a secret in this culture that the hero legend protects. All of us in this culture pay dearly for this sacrifice. For women, it means they fit into only one chapter of the hero story: the romance story.

ENTERING THE ROMANCE STORY

Girls' seduction into the romance story begins early, with fairy tales. Walt Disney, the Hans Christian Andersen of the latter half of the twentieth century, created extraordinary animated versions of these romantic classics. He reaped a fortune and found that a spoonful of sugar helped the medicine go down (to borrow a line from Disney's *Mary Poppins*). Set to catchy music, these pretty cartoon romances teach girls simple lessons about being a woman.

Disney's *Aladdin* shows girls that by lying and trading sexual favors, they can get what they want. *Beauty and the Beast* gives girls the dubious message that "true love" can transform a beast into a prince (which is a recipe for a relationship with a batterer). *The Little Mermaid,* which was a blockbuster both in revenues and in related merchandise sales, shows how a girl gets the man she has fallen in love with by giving up her voice and transforming her entire nature.

The classics *Sleeping Beauty, Snow White,* and *Cinderella* are no better. *Sleeping Beauty* presents adolescence as a time of total passivity—sleep —from which one can be awakened only by a man. In *Snow White,* the stepmother is so engrossed in the cult of beauty that she is willing to kill her stepdaughter for it. Snow White's innocence and transcendent beauty are her "protection" from this evil woman and the lure for the handsome prince. *Cinderella* presents another terrific (literally—as in "terror") model of female relationships. Cinderella can only escape from the drudgery that other women assign to her through captivating a prince. The bubbly, winsome presentation of these romances all end with the promise of true love and happily-ever-after.

This promise is the balm for the wounding losses inflicted by girls' collision with the wall. The loss of connection with women, of what they have known as love, leaves girls searching for true love, a perfect love that will never disappoint. Relationships with women become less important, devalued. The idealization of romantic relationships with males and the subtle devaluation of female relationships are the hallmarks of the loss of relationship that girls suffer as they move into adolescence. The dangers of sexuality are safely scripted in the romance story, giving girls ways to speak of their passion. By seeking a man to fall in love with and follow, a girl's agency, that sense of self that gives her confidence to act in the world, channels into providing some man a home base for his quest for financial and worldly success. Within the few pages of the hero legend devoted to romance, a woman's powerlessness is transformed. By succumbing to love for her, the hero—briefly—loses his head and heart and, thus, his power. While the romance story fits perfectly into the chasm created by girls' losses, it masks power relations as love.

"The hero," explain the 1981 guidelines for potential authors of Silhouette Romances, one of the larger serial romance paperback publishers, "is 8 to 12 years older than the heroine. He is self-assured, masterful, hot-tempered, capable of violence, passion and tenderness. He is often mysteriously moody." The guidelines require that the hero always be older, as well as "rich and successful in the vocation of his choice. Or he can be independently wealthy with some interest to which he devotes his time. He is always tall, muscular (but not muscle-bound). He is not necessarily handsome, but is, above all, virile." He is, after all, the prince in shining armor.

In contrast, the heroine "is young (19–29)." Furthermore, "she is not beautiful in a high fashion sense, is basically an ingenue, and wears modest make-up and clothes. Frequently, she does not consider herself to be a beauty, and this attitude is used to play off against the other woman (women)." While she has a good figure, she is also slight and petite. "Naturally, when she dresses up she is stunning. Her outfits are described in detail, as is her physical appearance. In spite of her fragile appearance, she is independent, high-spirited and not too subservient. She should not be mousey or weepy." Often, she is in transition, "leaving college, unhappy with her present job." Just starting a career, she is sometimes "too caught up in her work." The heroine is basically alone in the world: "She is usually without parents or a 'protective' relationship. Sometimes she has lived with an elderly female relative but breaks away to lead a life of her own."

This is the setup for an extraordinary story about power. All of the culturally sanctioned modes of power—physical strength, economic might, social class, education, worldly experience, sexual prowess—are on the hero's side. The heroine could very easily be victimized in this situation. In some senses, that is her struggle: to turn her relative powerlessness into power by holding the hero prisoner of his own emotions until he simply must marry her (and, thus, share his economic power and privilege) or lose his mind. Her tools are her innocence (which often means that she is sensible and sincere, is not wise in the ways of the world, and is sexually "pure") and her beauty. She is *not* like the other woman (as the romance tip-sheets emphasize) who is "usually mean, over-sophisticated, well-groomed" or, as another description says, is a self-conscious narcissist. Often, as the descriptions indicate, the romantic heroine's beauty is enhanced by her naiveté.

Girls know how to tell this story and make their experience fit its plot. Sharon Thompson is a researcher who studies adolescent sexuality. In one study, she asked boys and girls to tell them about their puberty experiences. Boys wouldn't speak to her, so she ended up interviewing twenty-five-year-old men who told "pubertal anecdotes revolving mainly around early heterosexual play or disconnected homosexual episodes like circle jerks. Upon being questioned about puberty, girls of fifteen and sixteen, on the other hand, rushed into full-blown narratives about sexual and romantic life." She was amazed by girls' breathy accounts of love and passion that sounded as though they came right out of a paperback romance story. The romance plot line shapes girls' understanding of their own experience. Good girls have sex when it is "true love." As many girls and women come to find out, this is one of the biggest manipulations that boys and men figure out—tell her that you love her and you can do anything.

When Victoria is a seventh-grader, she and her mother read romances. Her mother explains to Victoria that "her life just hasn't turned out the way she has wanted it to." Victoria understands that the trouble with her mother's life is that she didn't marry the real prince—another man who was courting her. Her mother, Victoria explains, had it tough: "Her father died when she was 14 and I think she expected to marry the guy of her dreams and everything and have a happy life. And my Dad bought her chocolates and everything." But, as her mother (and Victoria) found out, "he is not like that at all," meaning that her father is not really a prince. For Victoria and her mother, the solution to their problems resides not within themselves nor in the arrangements of the world but in choosing, as Victoria says, "the perfect prince." Her dream is to marry this perfect prince who "is going to be at least six foot and have a beard and mustache and he's going to be really nice and gentle. . . . He is going to be rich, too." As she says, this would feel like "happiness, a lot of happiness" to her.

Girls learn that they are to put all of their desire for life and their longing for perfect relationship into romance. One man is invested with the power to make all of their desires come true. "Abruptly now," writes sociologist Frigga Haug, "all the stirrings of a childhood yearning which resided in colours, in the forms of the hills, the shimmering of rivers, the breath of wind on the skin, the first glimpse of mountains, sunlight on the fields, are bundled together, their energy directed towards one person. Bewitched as we are by that one love, we strip the rest of nature of a magic we can only revivify—though never in its previous glory—through the beloved." Girls are told from every direction and in every possible way that their every desire is for sex with a man. The only way to have sex with a man, and still be "good," is to fall in love, to enter romance. As girls' bodies awaken to genital sexual feeling, the cultural messages that equate desire with sexuality collide and collude with the romance story: "Yes!" girls hear their bodies as saying, this *is* what I wanted after all.

Girls and women are guided to look outside themselves—to men— for their deepest satisfaction. "When we live outside ourselves, and by that I mean on external directives only rather than from our internal knowledge and needs," writes Audre Lorde, ". . . then our lives are limited by external and alien forms, and we conform to the needs of a [social] structure that is not based on human need, let alone an individual's." Having lost their deepest connection to their own desire and knowledge, women latch on to men's drive and power. They devalue themselves and their potential as they idealize the possibility of true love. Little is as important.

To enter the romance market, girls and women shape their desires around the enticements of the consumer market. Advertising and the media promise girls and women desirability—for a price. Women are told that they need an ever-lengthening list of products and fashions to perfect their desirability. Adolescent girls are a particularly lucrative and malleable market. As Susan Faludi notes in *Backlash,* throughout the 1980s, predominantly male fashion designers tried to sell women romance. The makers of Guess jeans made a fortune selling jeans through advertisements that never showed their products. Instead, they offered romance laced with danger— "the threat of discipline"—that caught adolescent girls' attention because the jeans offered them the illusion of a starring role in a romance thriller. "Jeans," notes Faludi, "are mostly bought by teenage girls, who are more vulnerable to fashion dictates."

Few women realize that the desperate scramble for romantic involvement with a man through the extraordinary expense of time, energy, and money is a cover-up for the loss of true desire within themselves. This is not to say that relationships with men aren't important or wonderful. But the sense of being nothing without a man plagues many women—and has made some psychologist-authors wealthy. Too many women feel that without a man they are nothing at all. While women strive increasingly for economic independence, this feeling persists and continues to compromise women's ability to be truly autonomous—that is, able to care for themselves within their relationships.

The classic romance plot links the idea of economic and social advancement with a woman's attracting and marrying a man of higher socioeconomic status. Although this notion may be less real than ever before, romance still lures many adolescent girls with the promise of a better life. In studies of working-class girls in England, the girls' reliance on romance increased as their hopes for a viable or satisfying career were lost. The realities of a weak job market, coupled with the virtual inevitability that they would not earn enough to support themselves, helped these girls willingly embrace the culture of romance. In sociologists Dorothy Holland and Margaret Eisenhart's study of young women's career aspirations at two colleges in the South, they found that "as the women became discouraged with schoolwork, they increasingly turned their interests and identity to the world of romance."

In a study of American adolescent girls and romance reading by researcher Linda Christian-Smith, the girls are clear that their lives will probably not be like those of the heroines they read about. But faced with a poor economy and the knowledge of how difficult their mothers' and other women's lives are (juggling paid and unpaid work), these girls use romance as a wish for a more promising financial future. "It would be nice to think that Tommy and me would end up like Janine and Craig [the couple from the popular *Blossom Valley* series]," says Patty, a fifteen-year-old white girl whose working-class roots place her and Tommy far from the fictional Janine and Craig, "you know, married with kids and having a nice home, car and money." Many of the girls to whom romance is marketed most aggressively are struggling and failing at school. Romance provides a way out of the dead end that their school failure signifies. For these girls, many of whom are poor and working class, these romances offer false hope.

But romance's alluring promise of a rosy economic future doesn't affect only working-class or poor girls. A survey of 13- to 17-year-old girls reported that 81 percent of these girls do not expect to work outside the home when they have children. In a 1992 study by Girls Count of middle-school girls in Denver, most of the girls said that they did not expect to have to work full time as adult women; they were going to be married and raise children. In fact, many of these girls are living in the aftermath of divorce. Their mothers, struggling to work and support children, are actively encouraging the girls not to make the mistakes they did. As a member of the Girls Count project reported, rather than encouraging the girls to find work that they love and that pays well, most of these girls' mothers are telling their daughters to put on a little mascara and make sure that they find a man. If the daughters do this, the cycle of false hope followed by disappointment will be repeated.

Within the African-American community, however, many mothers don't buy into romantic illusions of security. Educator Beverly Jean Smith was taught by the aunts who raised her to take care of herself and to make sure that she had her own money. "No Prince Charmings would be coming on white horses. In America, the concept of a 'powerful black male' is an oxymoron." She asks, "How can black men rescue black women when they cannot save themselves?" The African-American girls in a study of urban high school girls did foresee "relationships getting in the way of their futures," observe white researchers Jill McLean Taylor and Amy Sullivan. "In this case, however, their emphasis tends to be more directly on children with less discussion of how the expectations of a spouse or partner might interfere with their plans." The popularity of romances among African-American girls and women seems to hold a very different wish— the wish to be truly known and intimate. African-American girls are so deeply "dissed" (disrespected, discounted, dismissed) by white culture that their longing for recognition is profound.

As girls find themselves adrift in betrayals, they grab for the romance story and its promise of perfect happiness and true love. Now *this,* they seem to say, is what life should be all about. The ideals of true love and perfect happiness are not only unattainable goals but lies against which we measure the truth of our living and find it wanting. Set up by losses, girls search for a romantic happiness by ignoring reality. But when they take parts of themselves and their knowledge underground, they develop a false innocence that leaves them open to violation.

The romance story also puts a pretty face on the violence and fear in many women's relationships. Women learn to confuse fear with the thrill of passion. Particularly in "bodice rippers" and best-selling romances, women are chased, trapped, and molested or raped in the name of love. The heroine's fear—the panicked uncertainty, the butterflies in her stomach, the chills—are reinterpreted first as sexual attraction and then as love. Being open and vulnerable to another person—fearing exposure and rejection—are a part of developing intimacy, but the feelings ascribed to women in these romances are about real danger. Women who use the story of romance as their benchmark for understanding love learn to reinterpret warning signs within their own bodies as "true love." In the moment of a heartbeat, women reinterpret as love and longing what they, as girls, would have recognized as fear in their bodies. Psychological resistance to embodied feeling allows for such dangerous reinterpretations.

When girls' psyches are searching for a way out of the frightening problem of loss and powerlessness, the romance story provides the solution. The changes of adolescence leave behind an amnesia, bordered by fear. Girls suppress and "forget" their fears of betrayal, their oppression, and their previous knowledge of relationship. As their psyches respond to the loss, they desire romance and its requirements as the model for a perfect relationship. Only this perfect relationship seems capable of soothing the deep pain of the loss.

THE IDEALS OF PERFECTION

The romance story perfectly solves the problem girls face, but it leaves them with another dilemma: How can a girl make sure that she becomes the heroine of her own romance story? She has to be really nice, good, cheerful, generous, self-sacrificing, dependent, loving, pure, and, above all, beautiful. She can't be angry, sad, sexual, ambitious, autonomous, assertive, sarcastic, or intensely intelligent. If she has the misfortune to be unattractive, then her only hope is to be voted "Miss Congeniality." In a word, girls must be perfect. Girls' developing intellectual capacity enables them to monitor themselves and compare themselves to the ideal romantic heroine. Their potent young minds imprison them in perfection.

Trying to attract men is a dangerous gamble for girls in this culture. To secure a relationship, girls supposedly must make themselves physically and emotionally attractive to men. But if they overshoot and are "too" attractive, they may become objects of lust and rape. Walking this fine line, girls skirt danger by employing different tactics. Some try to embody the images of perfect women; others make themselves ugly to deflect the male gaze. Still others come up with their own unique approaches. Cynthia, age fifteen, finally tells her therapist why she constantly wears a large, eye-catching hat everywhere she goes, even in therapy: "It was just weird being checked out all the time. If I wear the hat, at least I know what they're looking at." Critical and unrelenting, the male gaze violates and triggers girls' self-awareness.

In an attempt to avoid danger, girls self-protectively internalize rigid standards of beauty and perfection. They become self-critical as they become self-conscious. Victoria, at fourteen, speaks of being "bad" for wanting to eat a pastry and worries about her leg muscles, which she calls "flab." The power of these internalized standards gives them moral authority in girls' minds. Looking good becomes confused with being good. Liza, in the eleventh grade, struggles with anorexia. Internal demands to become thinner and blonder threaten to erase her self and to tear apart her relationships with others. She resents her psychologist's telling her that she is perfectionistic, because, as she angrily insists, "I'm not perfect." What she doesn't understand is that her compulsive desire to be perfect, in looks and grades and sweetness, is the problem. Victoria and Liza measure themselves against an internal yardstick of perfection. Aspiring to perfection can result in a progressive loss of self-esteem as a girl inevitably "fails" over and over again.

On the other hand, challenging the standards of perfection by adopting their opposites doesn't work to free girls from their tyranny. Girls who appear to resist by acting and living in direct opposition to these standards simultaneously reinforce their power. As Frigga Haug observes, "A simple reversal—'It's fun to be fat,' or whatever—merely reinforces the validity of the negative evaluation of fatness in the very act of affirming it." Either embracing or reacting against internalized demands for perfection brings girls into an inner dialogue with those demands. Authorized by the culture and by girls' personal experience, these demands hold the key to romance and its illusory rewards—safety, relationship, and true love. This morally persuasive voice demands that girls meet the ideal and punishes them for any shortfall.

At the point that girls are caught in this inner dialogue, they have fully entered the culture because the culture has entered their psyches through the voice of self-blame. By adopting the model of perfection, a girl tries to protect her vulnerable, authentic self. But, as in a horror movie, this invited guest turns out to be a Fury: it punishes and disciplines in its deranged blaming. As clinical psychologist Dana Jack has observed, the Fury "speaks with a moralistic, 'objective,' judgmental tone that relentlessly condemns the authentic self. . . . It says 'one should, you can't, you ought, I should.'" Negating girls' personal authority, it assumes the high ground of objective, moral authority, thus giving it an indelible quality. It cannot be challenged in the same way as an erroneous fact because it mouths "truths beyond question." A girl's authenticity struggles with the Fury within her. This ongoing battle saps her strength and diverts her energy.

The Fury's voice echoes in the halls of a woman's psyche every time she confronts impossible societal ideals of perfection. At each confrontation, the Fury asks that a woman give up some of her authenticity to get the security she thinks she wants. In writer Dalma Heyn's controversial book *The Erotic Silence of the American Wife,* Heyn describes another such confrontation—that of the "Perfect Wife." As she notes, " 'Good' as it applies to the Perfect Wife inevitably modifies and diminishes the word 'self'—as in self-sacrifice, self-abnegate, self-restraint, self-denial—the prefix always restraining or containing in an effort to make that woman's self a little less *something.* Her virtue exists in direct proportion to how much of her self is whittled away, and how much of what is left she is willing to not keep to herself." To create "happily ever after," the Fury's demands of perfection declare women's true selves too threatening, so women sacrifice themselves.

"Because the tie between *mother* and goodness is even stronger than it is between *wife* and goodness," writes Dalma Heyn, "we must be alert to our assumptions of how this link affects children." A mother's "goodness," her self-sacrifice and self-denial, is assumed to be good for her children. A mother's genuine desire to "do right" by her children leaves her vulnerable to the Fury's harshness. The loss of power that many women feel as new mothers, the sense of incompetency and of being in charge of a vulnerable newborn, pulls women once again into the tyranny of perfection. Wanting so much for our children, we mothers rationalize self-sacrifice as a small price for our children's happiness. Through the eyes of the Fury, a woman's imperfections seem to be the problem, a sign of inadequacy, rather than simply the human condition.

For women to join their daughters in a resistance that leads to mutual liberation, they must transform this perfectionist Fury into an ally. The Fury's basic motivation is protection. When a woman or girl is presented with the limited options for women in the existing patriarchal culture, the Fury tries to keep her safely in her place. But a woman can claim the Fury's desire for her safety and protection and turn it to her advantage. Recognizing and freeing their authenticity enables mothers to join their daughters as they come of age. A young daughter's knowledge and love help a mother to remember and find the wellspring of her own resistance, which is essential for courageous change. When we women and girls join collectively to "practice self-love as a revolutionary intervention that undermines practices of domination," we begin the "undefined work of freedom."

TWO

Lessons in Resistance

ELIZABETH:

It took me a long time to learn to listen to girls. I remember my first interviews. Young girls' directness startled me and made me want to look away from their intense gaze. They told me stories of a love that seemed so much richer and simpler than the love I knew or remembered. "How do you know that your mother loves you?" I'd ask. "Because she does. She hugs me and kisses me. She listens to me. And she tells me she loves me." At first, I listened to this as a naive adult: how cute, how innocent. Then they spoke of anger as a powerful and dangerous feeling that was a sign of connection with another person. While their stories of unfairness and not being listened to seemed so simple, my colleagues and I began to realize that these girls knew a lot about love and friendship and conflict and they felt emotions more deeply and more easily than we did. Their feelings were accessible to them in ways that mine were not. In order to really listen to these young girls, *I* had to change; I had to learn from them how to listen.

My experience listening to adolescent girls taught me to hear in a different way. With them I found myself in a maze of truths: one "truth" would give away to another and then another. Beneath defiant or "good girl" responses were doubts and feelings and keen observations. I began to listen for the moment in the interview where everything would shift as a girl would move from telling what she thought she should say to telling what she *really* had on her mind. I learned to ask questions of these older girls that would draw out knowledge shared so readily by younger girls. The process of listening to these girls has changed me.

The voices of these girls brought to the surface feelings that I had buried long ago. I had a dream one night as I was about to begin a new stage in my work with girls and women. I was in a huge marble building that looked like Harvard's main library. There were men in uniform carrying guns stationed three deep around the perimeter. I was trying to escape. I had two children with me—a young boy and girl. As I moved to sneak past the guards, the boy ran to safety. Where was the girl? I panicked. I heard her running back into the building. She was heading for a dark, watery canal in the basement. "Stop! Don't go!" I called to her. She turned and looked at me. While she refused to speak, I knew that she wanted to swim underwater to safety. "No," I said, "it's too far, you can't stay under water that long." Suddenly, I had paper—the wide-ruled kind used in grade school—and crayons. "Here. Write," I said. "Write and you can get out of here. That's what the boy did, he wrote." She took the crayons from me warily. She wrote and handed me the paper. "My name is Beth," it said. "Beth" was what I was called as a girl. She looked at me, intensely, with a challenge in her eyes. Was it really going to be safe? she seemed to ask me. I woke up.

I have learned that I am writing to get girls to safety. I often wish that I could say to this dream girl and to the real girls that I have known: "Yes, it's safe for you to say what you think, to feel what you feel. Just say it." But that's not true—yet. I am working to be an ally for girls, someone who will really listen so that they don't have to take themselves and their knowledge underwater. This is the first step.

4

Reclaiming

But we can practice being gentle with each other by being gentle with that piece of ourselves that is hardest to hold, by giving more to the brave bruised girlchild within each of us. . . . We can love her in the light as well as in the darkness, quiet her frenzy toward perfection and encourage her attentions toward fulfillment. Maybe then we will come to appreciate more how much she has taught us, and how much she is doing to keep this world revolving toward some livable future.

Audre Lorde
"EYE TO EYE"

Grace, in her mid-forties, is the mother of two vibrant young women, both now in their twenties. Thinking back to her daughters' coming of age and memories of her own experience, Grace tells of how "I was caught up quite short one day when my oldest daughter talked about cheerleading tryouts. I asked—with some eagerness, having been a champion cheerleader—if she were trying out. She answered with an emphatic, 'No! I don't want to cheer, I want to play.' I was stunned. It still hadn't dawned on me to 'want to play.' And here was my daughter that I, inadvertently, subvertingly, was leading by my question into a repetition of my own adolescence."

Grace's adolescence was a prison of perfectionism. "I had determined that I would be perfect in body, mind, and spirit. Religion became my vehicle for perfection. I would be sinless. I began to say constantly that I was sorry. My mother was crazed at how often I was sorry. And I was— sorry that I lived because I just couldn't be perfect enough. I was sweet and perfect enough to be the Queen and leader of the school. God knows I didn't make anybody angry! Over the years in high school, my ceaseless driving for perfection and its predictable failure took its toll. I began to come home and run butcher knives across my wrists; I couldn't live up to the model I had laid out. No one, not even my parents, guessed how I tortured myself, or how often I thought of killing myself."

Yet, Grace's acute suffering and deep religious beliefs made her a champion for others. "I had a keen sense of justice, and I both spoke up and acted when I saw injustice in any form. Of course, I didn't notice the injustice of being born female and the price I was daily paying for that basic sin." While struggling with perfection and on behalf of others, Grace was engaged in another battle, one for which she had no words and no support. "All the way, something inside me continued to fight. I even canceled my wedding at first, bringing shame on my entire family, but eventually I succumbed to the external injunctions that were by now deeply inside me and got married."

Within a culture where women are supposed to make themselves perfect so they can be chosen and live within the narrative of the romance plot, women, like Grace, have often found themselves inwardly resisting conventions at the same time as they are working hard to be "good" or "perfect" women. Mothers can find themselves unwitting accomplices; they re-create in their daughters' lives the choices they made in their own lives. Women may find themselves subtly encouraging their daughters to accept the same limitations on dreams and power that they had accepted because women know of no other ways to survive in a hostile culture.

Conversely, women may find themselves urging the opposite choices for daughters, ones that mirror the hero. But the independence of a female hero leads to isolation in this culture where the rules as men play them define success. When a daughter chooses the hero role, she faces betraying her mother by living so differently. She also abandons her own healthy desire for connection and community.

The choices presented to women within patriarchal culture, ones born out of the trauma of loss, leave mothers in a double bind. If mothers decide to join with daughters who are coming of age as women, mothers must first reclaim what they themselves have lost. Reclaiming is the first step in women joining girls' resistance to their own dis-integration. Reclaiming is simply the process of discovering, describing, and reappropriating the memories and feelings of our preadolescent selves before we became, as activist and writer Gloria Steinem has said, "female impersonators."

The goal is not to become a preadolescent girl. That wouldn't be desirable even if it were possible (which it isn't—the trauma of girls' collision with the wall changes the psyche). But women can reclaim and, thus, re-integrate the vital parts of themselves that they discarded or drove underground. By realizing exactly what they gave up in order to fit into society, women gain an authority that comes from the conscious awareness of their own life experience. From this authority, mothers can develop the confidence to be ever more courageous in relationships and in life.

The process of reclaiming leads up back to the wall where, psychologically, women entered patriarchy and where patriarchy entered women. To seek evidence of this collision and to begin the process of reclaiming, we need to understand how the psyche translates our experience.

READING THE PSYCHE

Understanding how our minds—conscious and unconscious—work is a tricky business. But Carol Gilligan offers "five psychological truths" or basic grammar rules for the language of the psyche. The psyche is a dynamic process (not a thing, like the brain) that is in constant dialogue with parts of itself and with others. Using these rules, we can begin to understand how we have internalized the losses in our lives and how those losses continue to instruct our actions as women and mothers.

Rule Number One:
The psyche's logic is a logic of association as well as a formal logic of classification and control.

Our "logic" is the way that we recognize patterns. While we find logic in mathematical principles and in ordered sequences, we also find logic by making associations between different things that bear some analogous relationship, for example, between the color "red" and the feeling "anger." Our capacity to draw analogies between very different things is the basis of our capacity to use symbols and the core of creative human intelligence.

Gloria Steinem provides a good example of the psyche's associative logic at the beginning of *Revolution from Within.* When Gloria was a child, her mother "suffered spells of depression, delusions, and long periods as an invalid both before and after [Gloria] was born." Her father left Gloria and her mother when Gloria was ten: "Basics like regular school attendance, clean clothes, a bedtime, enough money to pay bills, and," she adds, "after I was ten, any kind of consistent parenting at all, had gone the way of my father's wandering lifestyle." While Gloria felt that she had built a "wall between me and my childhood," she began to wonder "if it hadn't seeped into the present in spite of all my bricks and mortar."

Then Gloria "began to follow the clues backward. Why was the sound of a radio so depressing, though television and records were not? *Because the radio had been the only sound in the house where I lived with my mother.*" For Gloria, a radio playing in a room was an association to the frightening loneliness of her childhood. So she avoided the radio. Her adult "apartment [filled] with cardboard boxes, stacks of papers, and long absences" was created out of her deep associations with what she knew and recognized as home. As she wrote, "Old patterns, no matter how negative and painful they may be, have an incredible magnetic power—because they do *feel* like home."

The associations made by the psyche are often surprising. They cover up painful, sad, or frightening experiences. We end up going out of our way to avoid the associations and, thus, the memories and feelings from the earlier experience. Patterns form from this avoidance, and until we recognize and explore these associations, the patterns too often rule our behavior. People don't do things, even seemingly harmful or destructive things, for no reason. Our odd obsessions, irrational fears, and pet peeves all make sense if we follow the trail of associations to the root.

Rule Number Two:
What is unvoiced or unspoken, because it is "out of relationship," tends to get out of perspective and to dominate psychic life.

We consciously and unconsciously censor ourselves as we try to fit into our families and society. We want to figure out what will bring us love and security. But as we grow, we discover, directly and indirectly, that aspects of ourselves (our anger, our messiness, our playfulness) jeopardize our relationships with those we depend on and love most. Yet what we take "out of relationship" with ourselves and with others—what we censor and push underground—ultimately gets blown out of proportion and colors our feelings and thoughts.

Judy, a thirteen-year-old at the Laurel School, found out how her entire family "got out of proportion" when she and her sister visited her father, his wife, and their preschool children. She and her sister were extra nice to her stepmother, who was also acting extra nice to them. "It was really tense like the whole summer," she said, "because everyone was trying to be extra special nice to people, like the whole time . . . because we all feel awkward." Unaccustomed to living with older children, Judy's father and stepmother imposed house rules that felt babyish to Judy and her sister. They were roped into babysitting all the time without even a thank-you. One night near the end of their vacation, Judy's little sister refused to eat her vegetables. Everything blew up. "The whole thing was not about carrots," observes Judy perceptively, "it was just about everything else." The pressure of the unsaid, what had been pushed out of relationship, was just too intense: "We were so tired of being nice, that everything blew up and we got in like huge fights."

> **Rule Number Three:**
> **What is dissociated or repressed—known and then not known—tends to return, and return, and return.**

When we push our true feelings underground, we get out of touch with and lose parts of ourselves; we "dissociate." Dissociation and its less dramatic cousin repression are protective mechanisms. When we experience fear, we shake and cry. But often in situations in which we feel powerless to stop what is happening (and what is happening is really bad), then the psyche detaches: we "numb out" while our bodies and minds go into a hypervigilant state, ready to take action. After the situation has safely passed, then our feelings of fear finally rush through us. Dissociation can give us the time to act or to distance ourselves when we are threatened, rather than be debilitated by fear.

When we find ourselves repeatedly in frightening or powerless situations, particularly at the critical points of early childhood and adolescence, dissociation becomes a habit that reshapes the psyche. In mild cases, we feel out of touch with feelings—spacey, not vivacious or fully alive. In the most extreme cases, the psyche splits into different selves, "multiple personalities," to hold different experiences, thoughts, and feelings. When dissociation happens, a part of the psyche freezes over and becomes stuck, holding the thoughts and feelings of the frightening event. We lose our wholeness and integrity: we dis-integrate. Whenever a situation that is similar to the original traumatic event occurs, the frozen part of the psyche resonates.

Judith Herman, in *Trauma and Recovery,* vividly describes how dissociated or repressed experiences can return. As she writes, "Traumatized people find themselves reenacting some aspect of the trauma scene in disguised form, without realizing what they are doing. The incest survivor Sharon Simone recounts how she became aware of a link between her dangerous risk-taking behavior and her childhood history of abuse:

> For a couple of months, I had been playing chicken on the highway with men, and finally I was involved in an auto accident. A male truck driver was trying to cut me off, and I said to myself in the crudest of language, there's no f——ing way you're going to push your penis into my lane. Like right out of the blue! Boom! Like that! That was really strange.
>
> I had not been dealing with any of the incest issues. I knew vaguely there was something there and I knew I had to deal with it and I didn't want to. I just had a lot of anger at men. So I let this man smash into me and it was a humongous scene. I was really out of control when I got out of the car, just raging at this man. I didn't tell my therapist about it for about six weeks—I just filed it away. When I told I got confronted—it's very dangerous—so I made a contract that I would deal with my issues with men."

Sharon's recklessness was also a courageous attempt to rework what had been done to her—to be able to stop a man from bearing down on her, to rage at him, to have the power to end it. Her repetition of her early incest happens more on a symbolic level this time. As is typical, Sharon's psyche holds several, often conflicting, voices within it. One, the most hidden, holds the unexpressed feelings and thoughts from the original event—the fear and rage. Another voice propels her into risk-taking behavior so that she can try to triumph over her early powerlessness: "there's no f——ing way you're going to push your penis into my lane." Yet, another part of her psyche speaks to prevent her knowledge and experience of the original events from fully coming into conscious awareness: "I knew vaguely that there was something there . . . and I didn't want to" deal with it. That part of her self defends Sharon from her knowledge, as though doing so will prevent her from reliving the experience.

We defend ourselves psychologically from knowledge when we have found ourselves to be defenseless. And there is usually a last voice, what we have called the Fury, that warns of things we must avoid to prevent such terrors from happening again. The Fury acts as an internal monitor containing the messages that we felt would have saved us. The Fury voice demands to protect us from further harm: "don't ever talk back," "if you can know what others think, then you'll be safe," "when you feel good, then bad things happen." Overall, the psyche tries to figure out *why me?* It will develop answers, which often become serious rules to live by and very frightening, dangerous rules to break, because the original experience was so horrible.

The power of our psyches to repeat in order to re-integrate these terrifying experiences is extraordinary. According to one recent study, girls who experience family violence or sexual victimization before adolescence are far more likely than other girls to experience rape or attempted rape as adolescents. In turn, those who experience rape or attempted rape as adolescents are far more likely than other girls to face similar experiences during their first year of college. Repressed knowledge and experience return in dreams (although they are often nightmares); in psychophysical symptoms where our bodies repeat, often symbolically, what was experienced; in compulsive play or routines; in spreading of feelings we originally couldn't have felt onto others or onto entire classes of people; in strange feelings of shame and guilt that seem out of touch with present reality; and in sudden, seemingly unwarranted bursts of rage or sadness. As we move further from the original events in which we repressed or dissociated, the pattern of the return becomes more symbolic and less immediately recognizable. All of these experiences and voices within the psyche need to be reclaimed in order to regain balance and free-flowing feeling.

> **Rule Number Four:**
> **The hallmarks of loss are idealization and devaluation, which cover rage, and under the rage, feelings of sadness, which hide feelings of utter helplessness and vulnerability.**

As noted in previous chapters, threats of loss—loss of one's sense of basic power or ability to be effective, loss of relationship, loss of one's physical wholeness, and near loss of life—lead to dissociation and repression. In the face of real or threatened loss, we split our feelings and thoughts into polar opposites. On the one side, we *idealize,* and then desperately long for, part of what was lost. When we idealize something, in our minds we need it to be perfect, larger than life, the best, the most, the only thing we need for perfect happiness. On the other hand, often simultaneously, we *devalue* and say that we could care less about having what we once lost: we're fine without it, no problem, and who cares anyway? These dismissals and putdowns indicate that something we really desired was, in fact, lost and that we feel a need to minimize its importance so that we don't have to feel our feelings.

Frequently, when what has been idealized is found to be imperfect or simply human, we feel enraged, cheated, and betrayed. Sometimes, we both blame ourselves and try to prevent further harm. We tell ourselves: The reason I lost my mother is that I was (and still am) deeply bad, so I will busily and exhaustively create perfection in my home and be perfectly loving. In this way, I will ward off the possibility of such a loss again. Like a fire wall, feelings of anger and rage just below the surface keep the good and bad intact. Beneath the rage is a sadness that hides our immense vulnerability and powerlessness—the overwhelming feelings that set up such a protective pattern of polarization in the first place. Our fear of dipping into the well of rage not only locks idealization and devaluation in place, but it also protects us from feeling vulnerable and helpless in the face of loss. But we must experience this grief at our frightening yet noble mortality to be released from the psychic hold of the loss.

Rule Number Five:
One learns the answers to one's own questions, which change over time.

This final rule is deceptively simple. Our psyches try to rewrite and master what has hurt us. Gloria Steinem wrote a first draft of her book on self-esteem, *Revolution from Within*, without including herself or her experience. A friend suggested that she, too, might actually have a self-esteem problem because, as the friend said, "You forgot to put yourself in." At that moment, Gloria learned that she was trying to answer her own questions about self-esteem.

Psychiatrist Lenore Terr, who studied childhood trauma in her book *Too Scared to Cry*, explains that her lifelong interest in childhood trauma began when she was a fourth-grader attending a Saturday movie matinee. She saw a newsreel about the American soldiers entering Hiroshima after the atomic bomb was dropped. "What got to me was a shadow." The newscaster, in appropriately neutral and detached tones, described a "foot bridge at ground zero or near to it—and the bridge had been bleached of all color. But a man's shadow lay obliquely across the bridge. He must have been walking there, the movie announcer said, when the bomb vaporized him. (Vaporized!)" Terr continues, "From the moment I saw that newsreel, if a light was turned on in the middle of the night or if a sudden noise awoke me from sleep, my heart would start pounding at once even before I awoke. I would breathe in gasps, sweat, and say to myself, 'This is it. The bomb.'" She identifies her interest in figuring out what effect trauma and extreme fear have on children as an attempt, in some way, to discover the different self she became after seeing the news-reel of Hiroshima.

The nature of the questions we ask changes over time, reflecting changes in our capacities to think and to know. As a nine-year-old, Lenore Terr reenacted her traumatic fright in her dreams, but as an adult she made a profession of studying the effects of trauma on children. The most difficult task for our minds is identifying our own patterns of feeling and behavior. Most of us are well into adulthood before we begin to see how our childhood patterns persist in our adult choices. As mothers, we have to become conscious of the questions that our own patterns ask in order not to visit those patterns on our daughters.

RECLAIMING OUR RESISTANCE

In chapters 2 and 3 we discussed the losses we suffer when colliding with the wall of the culture. But at each decision point, at each moment of sacrifice of our integrity, moments of resistance occurred. We didn't go down without a fight. Using the five rules of the psyche, we can begin to decode and revisit the moments where we compromised ourselves. By recalling those moments of conflict, of resistance, we come to see those rebellions as the markers of our authenticity.

Traveling back to the scene of the collision, the first trail to follow is the line of our resistance. The word *resistance* may seem a curious one to bring into mothering. But the "resistance" we are speaking of here refers to the ways that we opposed or withstood the pressures to conform to narrow expectations for women. The ways that we struggled against the pressures to disconnect from parts of ourselves, from our knowledge and authority, and from other women and girls. How did we resist the pressure, usually evident by age twelve, either to become a Perfect Girl or to be branded as selfish? Either to put up a tough front or to be ridiculed as weak?

Although each woman has faced a struggle unique to her, we can begin our exploration through the understanding of the dissociations and disconnections that the dominant culture, in general, demands of women. From this grounding, we hope that individual women can begin to trace their own unique paths through their associations, their patterns of repetitions, and the splits of idealization and devaluation to find the line of resistance—the ways they refused to accept their own disempowerment. By reading the language of the psyche, women can find where they were most torn by pressures to conform.

For most women, resistances reclaimed from childhood will seem small because children have few options other than to make harmful compromises to protect themselves. What may appear to be a small act of defiance by a little girl was, most likely, an act of great risk for her. For some of us, too, resistance may be difficult to find. Our psyches, accustomed to being cut off from the knowledge of these years, have organized our "selves" without this knowledge. Reclaiming takes time, gentleness, and permission to know what terrified us as young adolescents. As grown women, we have more strength to face what was overwhelming at ten, eleven, twelve, and thirteen. By giving ourselves permission, by being curious to know what we once knew, our psyches will begin to open up. Memories and feelings will arise, and we can begin to see how and why we sent them underground, thus separating from our selves and our loves.

Begin at the age of eight or nine and try to remember any and everything from that time through early adolescence—room, friends, teachers, clothing, games, books, family dinners, favorite and least liked things. Perhaps there are stories, told by the family or shown in photographs or remembered, of incidents that happened through that time. Tell the story of coming of age, or stories of critical incidents, over and over again, each time adding as much detail as possible. At first what is remembered may not seem even interesting. Allow yourself to free associate, to let your mind wander from these first, uninteresting details and incidents to whatever connections come forth. Gradually, the psyche will begin to reveal what it has held for you to reclaim.

Our first step is to reclaim double vision, the "outsider's eye," as Adrienne Rich calls it. In an old folktale about the fairy people, a little girl finds an ointment that her ugly, grouchy caretaker puts on the eyes of her grandchild. Curious, she rubs a little of the ointment on one eye, and the splendor of the fairy world is revealed to her in all its beauty and romance. Forever after, the girl has double vision. Girls possess double vision: they can see and play the games of the adult world and at the same time stay grounded in the reality of their experience. After passing through the wall, girls and women are often left with a dizzying after-image from life before. Seeing, and naming, that double reality can give us the clarity for action.

As an eleven-year-old said to her friend within earshot of psychologist Annie Rogers, "Lying? I know all about lying. My house is wallpapered with lies." What this girl knew as "lying" is the ordinary half-truths that cover over the cruelty and dishonesty of the adult relational world. A group of young African-American girls said that they were angry at their mothers for always lying to them. What did they mean by lying? How their mothers covered over their own feelings and thoughts. As girls move into adolescence and begin to feel pressure to give up their experience for the "reality" of the adult world, they view the adult world as a pack of lies rather than a kind of game they used to play.

Barbara remembers being raised to have children, yet she resisted the ways that she was raised. "I was certain from the time I was four years old that I was going to have children. That was how I was socialized and I wanted them. But I knew that the way I was treated—like a piece of property that my parents could order around—wasn't how I wanted to do it." While her parents kept telling her that they were raising her to be "good," it didn't feel good to Barbara. Out of one eye, she could see the sense that her parents made out of things, but out of the other, she knew that their code of good behavior robbed her of her freedom and strength. Struggling to hold on to what she knew and felt was right, Barbara was lucky enough (within her affluent household) to have access to books. "Winston Churchill and Virginia Woolf" were her reading diet, she says, laughing. At thirteen, Barbara read and reread Woolf's "Three Guineas," a powerful essay on war, the education of women, and the creation of a female "Society of Outsiders." "Then I knew that I had been right—girls didn't have to be treated the way I was treated." Barbara had Virginia Woolf to validate her double vision, to help her maintain the outsider's eye.

Jill's religion gave her double vision. The daughter of a minister, she saw her father beat her mother while proclaiming love from the pulpit. While she loved what her Bible said, she saw the hypocrisy of those around her—particularly her father—who sanctimoniously called themselves "Christian." Marianne remembers that during church her mother was more pious than the pope. But one Sunday, while zooming out of the church parking lot, her mother was almost cut off by another driver. "You son of a bitch!" her mother screamed—five minutes after wearing her holier-than-thou face.

Along with the knowledge of the outsider, we need to reclaim our voices. "Voice" is not to be confused with loudness or mere speech, although girls are often incredibly loud and talkative. We are talking about the voice of courage to speak one's mind, not the courage we have come to know after scores of war and wild West movies. As Annie Rogers explains, "When courage is linked to one of its oldest meanings in the English language, 'to speak one's mind by telling all one's heart,' the embodied or ordinary courage of eight to twelve year old girls becomes readily visible and audible."

Our cultural notions of courage currently imply an ability to override one's vulnerability and to outrun fear in order to risk one's life. Rogers observes that "the courage of girls has been rendered all but non-existent over the centuries as the word came to signify the bravery and heroic valor of men, so that neither men nor women were likely to discern the courage of girls. This cultural loss is doubled by a developmental loss of ordinary courage that occurs in girls' lives in early adolescence." In a sense, courage has come to mean a form of dissociation.

Melissa wondered where her courageous girl's voice was. Try as she might, she couldn't recall any memories of telling her truths. Then she remembered that when she was nine, her mother used to tell her that she must be going through adolescence early because she had such a "big mouth." While Melissa can't remember what she said as a girl, she remembers that her mother noticed her courage—and discouraged her from speaking. "The recovery of ordinary courage in women's lives," Annie Rogers notes, "is nothing short of extraordinary, because it depends on finding a voice to speak what has been unspeakable. Often this process begins in a safe, playful and challenging relational context among women or women and girls together."

Internal disconnections don't happen only in the realms of thinking and speaking. Certain feelings are often outlawed within the straitjacket of "nice and kind" behavior. These "outlaw emotions," to use a phrase from philosopher Alison M. Jaggar, will vary within each cultural group. For many middle-class women, anger is an outlaw emotion that is repressed and denied. However, for working-class women and certain women of color, anger—often expressed as hostility and defiance—is an almost omnipresent defense that tells the world to watch out. Yet almost all women have lost the righteousness of anger, the power of anger to demand change. Whether stifled completely or rehearsed over and over again, anger that is not about conviction leading to action is about powerlessness. Anger warns us of violation so that we can act to change things. Because acting usually requires conflict, which can risk safety and relationship, our anger has been rendered ineffectual. Ironically, expressing anger directly and entering into the conflict often encourage real intimacy and connection.

While young girls often express anger during small skirmishes, these confrontations are very important in the scale of their worlds. Cecilia remembers an incident of outrage from when she was nine. "My best friend, Susan, was really a chicken. The kids in the neighborhood could say almost anything to her. One time this boy, Jimmy, from down the street said some really nasty things to her, right in front of me. And she just stood there. I insisted that he had to take it back. But he wouldn't and it made me furious. He told me just to shut up but I wouldn't, I wouldn't stop. He started threatening me with his fists, you know, and I still wouldn't stop. And then he hit me. We fought and I know he won the fight, but it didn't matter because I stood up to him." From this story, Cecilia remembers the power of her anger to move her to act courageously.

Anger is not the only outlaw emotion. Many girls give up hope for themselves and their futures when they learn about racism, classism, and sexism. Two African-American girls responded to questions about their future plans with a series of joke responses (custodian, bag lady, or pigeon). Finally, one of them whispered softly that she wanted to be a lawyer. Diana, a working-class mother who "never made anything" of her life and "was just a housewife," always wanted to be "an archaeologist, and go on digs." As girls, we learn that life isn't fair and that we have to "settle" for far less than our dreams, and as women, we often continue to accept this self-limiting view.

Other women have given up their joy and playfulness. "I used to do stand-up comedy routines for my family and friends," recalls Aida. "I would impersonate everyone in the family, and I did a killer Milton Berle. What amazes me is that I was so un-self-conscious. I just did it. I loved the thrill of performing." Remembering running in fields, playing hopscotch and jump rope, or swimming like a fish can help women reclaim the sheer joy of being alive that was so present for them as young girls.

Some women find that they have had to give up their vulnerability. As life became tough and frightening, the experience of being vulnerable to hurt or fear had to go. "Oh, God," says Marlene, "I remember saying 'I don't care, see if I care' over and over again. As a teenager, it was my mantra. But before that I cared a lot, about everything. I used to come home and cry on my mother's shoulder—really soak her dress—about the slights and fights at school." As children, many of us crawled into bed with our mothers or asked for comfort—to be held—when we needed it. Too many of us, now supposedly "all together," have altogether lost our capacity to seek comfort directly and straightforwardly, which affects our capacity to experience intimacy and closeness.

The process of re-membering, of reclaiming our resistance to limits on our knowing, speaking, and feeling, brings us in touch with what we have lost. One woman at a workshop run by Carol Gilligan recalled noticing as an eleven-year-old that the women around her seemed unhappy. She and her best friend talked about how women had lost the secret of life. As girls, they made a pact to remember: they wrote each other letters and kept journals about secrets and joys of life. But in adolescence, this woman took her books filled with these secrets and burned them without rereading a word. While she doesn't remember why she did this, she now wonders if her girlhood truths were too overwhelming to her in adolescence.

The experience of loss, as the grammar explains, holds many layered feelings: grief, rage, terror. As we remember more and more the ways that we spoke courageously, knew what was true for ourselves, and felt the entire range of human feelings, we can't help but wonder: What happened? Where did these parts of me go? No one cried for us when, gradually, more and more, our spirits left us or were confused by messages that we were bad. We will have to mourn for ourselves but also celebrate that, fortunately, the psyche holds everything for us. The girl who experienced joy and anger, who had a "big mouth," who could tell the lies from the truth, and who collected the secrets of life is still with us. By remembering our resistance, we begin to re-member our selves and reclaim the authority of our experience.

RECOGNIZING OUR SURVIVAL STRATEGIES

As we reclaim our resistance, inevitably we will become more conscious of the ways we were unable to resist for reasons of physical or social survival. Many women, particularly middle-class women, caved in to what Jo-Ann Krestan and Claudia Bepko, family therapists and authors of *Too Good for Her Own Good,* call the "Code of Goodness." In sum, the code pledges us to perfection by requiring that we be competent at everything while remaining responsible for the happiness of family members, children, relatives, co-workers, and friends, without ever acting tired or exposing anger. For many women, "goodness" wears a face of helplessness, while for others it has a tougher face, a tough-it-out face. Regardless, the code makes women responsible for everyone around them while setting standards of perfection for themselves.

We recognize the necessity of validating the clever and often deadening ways we survived as young women in a world where sexism made excruciating demands and where personal loss was the key to entry. For some of us, our survival strategies provided "success": we were athletic or charming or beautiful or smart in school. For some of us, our survival strategies led to pregnancy, alcohol abuse, and a future that looked like a dead end. Whatever the cost of success in each community, many women paid it in triple to ensure survival. Some of us found that our survival strategies did, in fact, provide the skills—the education or smarts—to find our way out of the restrictions we had placed on ourselves in order to survive.

"When I was newly twelve," recalls Carly, "I changed my voice. I know it must have been about then because it was the time when the boys on the swim team seemed to assume a certain command, an authority I thought I remembered being mine once, an authority that I believed came from their voices, newly even and deep. I remember noticing that I was not being heard anymore, and thinking no one would ever listen to me or take me seriously if I did not remove the 'hysterical' rise and fall in my speech, the music in my voice."

Flattening her voice into a limited range of a few low notes, Carly tried to impersonate the voices that held authority around her. Some girls, like Carly, take on "girls will be boys" strategies for success. Recognizing that what boys do or what authorities value is the way to safety, many women hold to male standards, temporarily.

Psychologists Tracy Robinson and Janie Ward write of a destructive pseudo-resistance that is actually a survival strategy. African-American women, they argue, "have become expert appropriators of resistant attitudes and behaviors [that are] forms of resistance . . . not always in our best interest." Even though this defiant resistance is often destructive, they call this "resistance for survival" because, in the short term, it helps a girl survive in her community. Some women recall their experiments with risk taking that gave them connections with friends through the wrenching betrayals of early adolescence. "We had sort of a club," recalls Donna. "We would carve each other's names and the names of our boyfriends on our arms. We smoked together, cut classes together, went on joy rides with boys. When I look back, I'm amazed that I'm alive."

Many women will recall moving into "goodness" in order to survive. By "calling back the fears, hopes, feelings and derailing train of thought" that were hers, Anna tries to recapture her younger self, at the age of ten, the child of immigrant Greek parents in the South. Anna remembers a decision she made: "This year I will not be the loud, outspoken Anna of Mrs. Raspberry's class. . . . I will be liked by everyone this year. I will be quiet and even a little shy. Parents always like that and so do boys and so do the nice girls." She also recalls, "I felt numbed as I walked, like I was in a bubble that protected me from the outside. I could see the outside but did not truly interact with it. I walked straight as a stick." Reflecting on her recollections, Anna says, "I definitely see this ten-year-old in me *now*, concerned about being 'too loud,' 'silly, spastic.' I am sensitive to my concerns that led me to the point where, as a ten-year-old, I didn't talk too much, I didn't want to drive them away. I remember numbing myself out, thinking that not feeling would protect me from the pain. I did not realize that it also protected me from feeling entirely (or if I did, I considered the tradeoff worth it)."

In beginning to recognize survival strategies and to validate the sheer ingenuity it took to survive, we remember the ways we have been betrayed and the pain of our betrayals. Anna remembers her mother urging her to go to charm school. "Boys don't like girls who are too smart," Rita heard her mother say over and over again. The countless warnings from those who loved us (If you don't have anything nice to say, then don't say anything at all. . . . You have to suffer to be beautiful. . . . Boys don't make passes at girls who wear glasses. . . . Don't be a show-off. . . .) restricted our voices, our desires, and our actions and, despite the adults' good intentions, betrayed our hearts, minds, bodies, and spirits. In re- claiming, we bear witness to the ways that we were betrayed by our moth- ers, fathers, teachers, and counselors as they sanctioned our loss of voice and unwittingly urged us into a struggle for perfection.

RESOUNDING WITH OUR DAUGHTERS

Through reclaiming resistance, recognizing survival strategies, and bearing witness to betrayals, women can begin a process of re-integration. This process is an odd one, filled with stops and leaps, grief and joy. For those of us who have begun to cross these divides, one of the most power- ful guides along this journey has been the voices of preadolescent and adolescent girls. Voices of girls call to the girl *we* once were. Listening, *really* listening, to girls, taking their voices into our psyches, is critical to our own process. For the Harvard Project researchers, listening to and being with girls directly called forth the past. Girlhood memories seeped into our waking moments; girls walked in our dreams. Reading novels about girls, stories written by girls, and the words of girls sends a call deep into our psyches. Mothers of preadolescent and adolescent girls are lucky: they have a girl guide in the house to point the way to reclaiming. By listening to those feisty nine- to twelve-year-olds who prefer playing to cheering on the sidelines, women can get the cues they need.

Our daughters are extraordinary sources for the process of reclaiming because our deep emotional resonances with them provide a psychic sounding board. As Belle said, "When I see Sandra go farther than I would —particularly with her father—and hold her ground, I think about how I must have had this strength in me when I was nine. It makes me wonder about where it went. And if she can do this at nine, why not do more of it now, at forty-seven?" Watching young girls' courage and spirit, women can begin to reclaim their own. While mothers learn a lot from their daughters, this is often considered to be somehow not directly a part of mothering. Claire said that, while her first daughter seemed so much like her and was easy for her, her second daughter "was sent to teach me about myself."

"At eleven," says Iris, "my oldest daughter came and asked me to rock her. She spread her lengthening legs across the arms of the chair, pushed her body close, and told me how she felt she was supposed to be doing something—moving away—and it didn't feel right. She was scared." Iris's daughter heard the injunctions in the culture and began to realize that she was going to have to disconnect from a woman's world to move into patriarchy. "I was moved. This daughter was a dancer in life, a risk-taking twirler in space. She stuck to her guns, fiercely stood up for her friends and for herself. She had a keen sense of justice and injustice." At the moment, though, Iris thought that she might have failed to help her grow up enough, that "for all her bravery, she was not ready, which was a sign that I had 'overmothered.' " Reflecting on this time for herself, Iris recalled that there was a popular song on the radio, "Slow Boat to China," when she was eleven. "Each time I heard it on the radio, I shook and cried with premonitions of danger and loss as Frank Sinatra—I think that's who it was—crooned: 'I'm gonna get you on a slow boat to China, all to myself alone. Get you and keep you in my arms forever more. Leave all your lovers waiting on the faraway shore.' " Remembering her terror, Iris remembers that "unlike my daughter, I didn't have the courage to tell my mother how much that song scared me and how much comfort and assurance I needed about not being turned over to some world where some man would have me all to himself alone."

Because motherhood is such a consuming responsibility, women can find themselves so overwhelmed by caring for daughters that they lose sight of them as young people in their own right. In fact, it can seem that learning from daughters and exercising authority in mother daughter relationships are somehow at odds. Mothers are supposed to have all the answers to keep our daughters safe and happy. To open deeply to learning from our daughters, to hearing their unique voices, brings women into relationship with girls and with themselves in a new way.

Ingrid was concerned about her fourteen-year-old daughter's lousy grades. Cara did well in subjects that she liked when she liked the teacher, but she was flunking Spanish and doing poorly in two other subjects. Ingrid talked to Cara: they went around and around about how important it was to get good grades so that Cara could get into a good college. Cara seemed to agree with her but came home with a report card the next quarter that was even worse than before. "I lost it—I mean I really lost it. I started to cry and scream at her about how she was ruining her whole future. I heard her talking to a friend on the phone and she said, 'Your mom might be upset but my mom's really upset—she was sobbing and everything.'"

Ingrid was a little taken aback by her own response. Asked what would have happened to her if she had brought home such a report card, Ingrid was shocked: "But I couldn't! My parents would have killed me—" She started to laugh and shake. Ingrid realized that her fears for her daughter, while based in a real concern for Cara's future, were blown out of proportion by her own experience. Later, Ingrid talked to her daughter about what, in her own past, had caused her to react so strongly. A few days after that, she confronted Cara when she found her smoking in her bedroom. Cara began to sob and told her mother about how pressured and inadequate she felt. From there, Ingrid and Cara have joined together to tackle Cara's problems with school and her teachers.

We often forget that our daughters know us perhaps better than we know ourselves. While their knowledge is often inarticulate, they know where we have stopped short, where we feel bad about ourselves, and where we have disconnected from ourselves, our voices, our desires and dreams. In many ways, Ingrid's daughter couldn't have picked a more sore spot than academic achievement to make Ingrid panic. For many mothers, their sorest spot is around sexuality. Melinda, at fifteen, made her mother, Lonni, crazy with her open exploration of her sexuality. "If you had a boyfriend or weren't so uptight about sex," Melinda said to her mother, "then maybe I wouldn't have to do this."

In often uncanny ways, daughters carry their mother's unresolved conflicts with them. At least a half dozen of the women we have spoken to have told us how, in their early twenties, they accidentally got pregnant, outside of marriage, and were consumed with pain and guilt. Later they found out that one of the biggest secrets of their mothers' lives had to do with a child either aborted or borne outside of marriage. Perhaps girls are so uncanny because they sense that in these places where their mothers have silenced themselves they will have the freedom to explore and to figure out something for themselves.

"The places where I haven't looked, where I am still unconscious," said Bonnie, "those are the places that I see that my daughters are stuck." We react most strongly to the things that our daughters do that transgress the boundaries that we ourselves learned to keep ourselves safe. The things that make women most crazy are girls' actions that evoke women's fears, anger, betrayals, or grief. These are usually the places where women have suffered loss and disconnection. Psychotherapist Leslie McGovern observes that the "issues that arise around teenage daughters often appear to be, and are culturally assumed to be, the daughter's problem. While in some cases this may be true, largely our adolescence was and is so painful and unaddressed that we misplace our unresolved feelings onto our daughters."

Taking in our daughters' voices forces women to confront what was pushed underground. As Natalie took girls' voices into her psyche, she began to feel "as though I was underwater." Others have felt dizzy or as if in a waking dream or chilled. This is fear—the fear that we experienced when we made these psychic disconnections. We need to experience the

121

chills running down our spines, the fearful tears and shaking that most of us were too overwhelmed to experience when we were adolescents. If we can recall, as Iris did, a "Slow Boat to China," or anything that made us frightened or made us cry as early adolescents (another woman used to sob at Stevie Wonder's song that goes "Mary wants to be a super-woman . . ."), then we can listen and let the feelings come now that we are safely here, well on the other side of adolescence.

Working through the fear that holds the dissociations and repressions intact is certainly serious business. But, oddly enough, the psyche will not reveal what it has repressed or dissociated by being afraid of fear. The fear is a psychic warning about a situation that no longer exists: while women still live in a violent, sexist, and racist society, women can make choices that were not available at ten or twelve. The fear that threatens to numb us during this process is a friend to be greeted with joy and real pleasure. Chills, trembling, numbness, and dizziness are messages that, yes, we are crossing the chasms in our psyches. Pleasure at the evidence of fear allows the release of feelings that have acted as the fire wall in our psyches. Working through these strong feelings, with our daughters' voices as a guide, brings women back in touch with the parts of themselves sent underground so long ago. This allows us to be fully present for our daughters as they journey to the crossroads of womanhood.

RECLAIMING OUR MOTHER'S COURAGE

"How are we to be the mothers we want our daughters to have," asks activist Letty Cottin Pogrebin, "if we are still sorting out who our own mothers are and what they mean to us?" For many women, one of the most profound losses upon entering patriarchy is losing the relationship with one's mother. For many women, what is lost is a sense of being able to be oneself in relation to one's mother. What is often lost at adolescence is the deep faith that our mothers are truly our allies. This loss, notes Adrienne Rich, leaves behind "a girl-child still longing for a woman's nurture, tenderness, and approval, a woman's power exerted in our defense."

As we realized, in adolescence, that women exert little power in the world, we lost our belief in our mothers' courage and strength. Out of this loss, some of us have extremely polarized feelings about our mothers: we love and trust them deeply while reviling them and distancing ourselves from them at the same time. As Anne St. Germain, coordinator of the Adolescent Health Program for Minneapolis Public Schools, a nurse administrator, observed, daughters reject mothers for those feminine characteristics that threaten to cost the daughter part of herself and her power.

In *Don't Blame Mother,* psychotherapist Paula Caplan advises her female clients and students to interview their mothers. In fact, her book contains an appendix with sample questions to get the interview under way. Caplan urges that women realize that the culture of mother blaming is the cause of much of the guilt, anger, and pain in mother daughter relationships. "I have found that nearly all women," she writes, "are filled with a mixture of anger, guilt, fear, and uncertainty about many aspects of their relationships with their mothers and/or daughters." The double binds in which mothers find themselves in patriarchal culture are as hurtful as the binds that cut into girls at early adolescence. By escaping those binds, adult daughters build new relationships with their own mothers.

"Until we give some room for who our mother is, there's not enough room for ourselves," says family therapist Lois Braverman. "It is in our interest to learn the context of our mother's life, when and where she grew up, what her relationships with her parents and siblings were like, what her struggles as a daughter were." Talking to a mother to learn about her life as opposed to exploring places where we are blocked in our relationship provides useful information. "Knowing the context of a mother's life can help women get distance from their mothers and allow space to see the differences and then the similarities, and appreciate who she really is. Otherwise we spend time endlessly organizing against our mothers, or living out unthought through parallels. Both are reactive positions, taking up the life energies of mother and daughter," continues Lois Braverman. By doing this, we can begin to understand that our mothers often taught us what they knew to help us survive. More than that, though, they were often conscious and courageous in the ways that they tried to make our lives better than their own.

Mae was shocked when she interviewed her mother. For years, she had deeply resented her mother's capitulation to her father. While Mae loved her father, her mother's apparent weakness infuriated Mae. While interviewing her mother, Mae was surprised at her mother's awareness of having "toned down her life" to appease Mae's father. She had chosen to do this in order to keep the relationship. Mae found out that her father had "made it clear that [Mae's] mother had to mute her voice as a condition of the relationship." Her mother felt, as good mothers in patriarchy do, that she was doing well by her children, her daughters, to keep the family together. Mae was shocked at how conscious her mother was. She felt a great deal more respect for her mother for having chosen to give the best that she could—even when it required that she sacrifice herself for her daughters.

Claire was raised by a mother who, for almost all of Claire's life, seemed rather distant and untouchable. When asked to tell a story of her mother's courage, Claire told the story of how, when she was three, the stove in their kitchen exploded and set the house ablaze. Her mother was burned over most of her body while trying to rescue Claire's sister from behind a wall of flames. "I never put together my experience of my mother with this story. I had never thought of it that way—as courage," she said, with some surprise. "It's a miracle that she survived. I think it was just her will to live. In several weeks, she was sent home to us—three children under the age of five. I don't remember it well but she must have been bandaged from head to foot. There was no one to help her take care of us. She must have been in excruciating pain."

Claire was very young when all of this happened, but the overriding memory that she carried with her was of a mother who was distant and somehow unloving. "It may seem crazy but all these years, I never put it together as a story of courage. Everything around me just told me to think about what my mother didn't give me—and she didn't give me a lot of physical affection. How could she? She was so courageous to have fought to be with us." Within a culture of mother blaming, Claire could not hear her own mother's story as powerful and courageous. Claire says that the "biggest bonus" from talking about her revolutionary mothering has been that it has "given me my mother back." Claire has a powerful story to tell her daughters of courage that flows through the women in the family.

Many of us have lives circumscribed by stories from our mothers that have been passed down in limited interpretations: stories of immigrant women, of uneducated women, of official or unofficial slaves. These stories of struggle have often been hidden because of shame or told to make later generations appreciate how easy they have it. Reclaiming these stories as tales of power that flow through a mother's line puts a new spin on the suffering of previous generations of women. Every mother's heritage is filled with the adventure stories of courage, stories that have never been told or, if they have been told, never focused on the woman's strength and glory.

Enlightened by the story of how mothers fare in patriarchy, women can relieve themselves of the need to hold mothers responsible for doing their prescribed roles as well as they could. We can begin to move beyond the anger and the associated guilt that many of us feel toward our mothers. Perhaps we can genuinely begin to forgive what they couldn't help and to feel gratitude for our mothers.

"Many of us," writes Adrienne Rich, "were mothered in ways we cannot yet even perceive; we only know that our mothers were in some incalculable way on our side." She continues by exploring the variety of ways that mothers have been betrayed by patriarchy's institution of motherhood and have, thus, betrayed their daughters:

But if a mother had deserted us, by dying, or putting us up for adoption, or because life had driven her into alcohol or drugs, chronic depression or madness, if she had been forced to leave us with indifferent, uncaring strangers in order to earn our food money, because institutional motherhood makes no provision for the wage-earning mother; if she had tried to be a "good mother" according to the demands of the institution and had thereby turned into an anxious, worrying, puritanical keeper of our virginity; or if she simply left us because she needed to live without a child—whatever our rational forgiveness, whatever the individual mother's love and strength, the child in us, the small female who grew up in a male-controlled world, still feels, at moments, wildly unmothered.

By understanding the cultural context that warped the foundation of our first relationship, the rage, desire, and mistrust begin to make sense in a new way. But then, further work needs to be done to heal the relationship.

Women can reclaim the desire for mothering and care that is split off and twisted into a desire for romance and a man's protection in patriarchy. These feelings of being "wildly unmothered" are a legacy of patriarchy and the psychological hook that pulls girls and women into the culture of romance. Putting the blame where it belongs, we can begin to forgive what has felt unforgivable. By facing "to the utmost in ourselves the groping passion of that little girl lost," writes Rich, we can transform that passion to alchemize "the blind anger and bitterness that have repetitiously erupted among women trying to build a movement together." By reclaiming our passion for our mothers and feeling the loss that we suffered, we strengthen our heritage for our daughters and our daughters' daughters. Out of the oppression of our pasts, we can create a story of courage passed from mother to daughter.

RECLAIMING CONNECTIONS WITH WOMEN

Several years ago, Carol Gilligan was asked to consult at a number of clinical psychology training institutes to assess trainees' case presentations. As these things usually go, each trainee presents the story of a person he or she has seen in therapy, and then the invited consultant discusses the case. Whether intentionally or not, the consultant's greater experience and knowledge typically leaves the trainee feeling naive and obtuse. Carol didn't want to play that game. She had been invited by women who were placing themselves in a vulnerable situation with her. Carol wondered whether she could model something different for these women and their colleagues who would be present. Before she began her schedule of appearances, she made a commitment to herself: first, to speak to each woman presenter, knowing that inside the woman was a girl who wanted real relationship and connection; second, never to compete with the woman who was presenting the case; and, third, not to stand by in silence and allow women to be "trashed" or put down at any point in the discussion.

Carol Gilligan's three precepts are a great starting place to reclaim connection among the community of women. The collision with the wall leaves girls mistrustful of their mothers and other girls. Particularly in the adult domains of love and work, competition among women and the prioritizing of relationships with men over relationships with women have been principle survival strategies. Reclaiming a community of women begins with a commitment to resist the temptation to compete against and put down other women. Remembering that all women were once girls who had to compromise themselves provides women with a different way of understanding the pain and hostility that often make working and living closely with other women so difficult. While this recognition does not make relationships among women easier automatically, it may take some of the sting out of the initial disappointments.

Each time women enter into friendships or into working or living arrangements with other women, there is usually the hope that—at last—the deep connection and community that they have been longing for since childhood will return in ideal form. Many women idealize these relationships with other women, hoping that if only "nice and kind" thoughts are expressed among women, then they will rediscover what they once lost. But they didn't lose perfection—the desire for perfection is a defense against the pain of the loss. What these women have lost is the ordinary way that girls related to each other, where horrible thoughts and feelings are expressed along with affection and playfulness, before images of the perfect girl disrupted their ability to be truthful.

Reclaiming connection with women, a woman reclaims her complicated and typically troubled history of relationships with girls. First, recall your own playmates and best friends for as far back as you can remember. What happened to those relationships? Did they change? If so, how? Call forth all of the details and activities that your girl friends enjoyed from childhood through adolescence. Beginning with the rather uncomplicated relationships of childhood and moving through the times of backstabbing and complicity, you, like other women, will need to try to put the pieces back together.

Girls lacked the knowledge, skills, and permission to work through their difficulties. But women can begin where girls never had any real chance by taking the risk to build support and community among women. "If women truly want to make a difference in their daughters' lives," Annie Rogers has said, "then the most important thing that they can do is create a community of women for daughters to grow into." Her comment is echoed by Adrienne Rich's words: "Until a strong line of love, confirmation, and example stretches from mother to daughter, from woman to woman across generations, women will still be wandering in the wilderness."

We have spoken to a number of women who have created supportive communities of women for themselves. Mae lived and worked in San Antonio, where she had raised her five children, built a thriving counseling practice, gotten tenure at a university, and enjoyed deep relationships with her peers. For several years, she talked to her friends about wanting to move to New York. Her friends were unanimously discouraging. At age forty-six, Mae decided that she would move to New York. Mae had made up her mind. She gathered friends around her and told them what she needed. First, she said, her decision was final. Next, she said she needed their help. From this time on, none of them were to talk to her about the difficulties of leaving San Antonio; they were *only* to offer direction or assistance that would move her toward her goal. With this new commitment and assistance from her friends, things began to change. Within two years, she had moved to New York and had begun to rebuild a life for herself and for her family.

Mae's story bears witness to the strength of will it takes to make big changes, the necessity of asking for what one needs, and the powerful and necessary role a supportive group of people can play. For mothers, the need for a supportive community is doubled. With other women, mothers can do the difficult work of reclaiming the painful and proud stories about their own lives that their daughters evoke. It is helpful to have a safe place to cry about loss while focusing on "getting out of San Antonio"; a place to share fears about what happens if girls keep saying what they see, being who they are, and looking like they desire life. Women need other women to talk to about fears that their daughters will become outsiders in the world by standing outside the romance narrative for their lives. Within a group, women can name their experience in the world and practice saying to each other what they see, words that are outrageous because they evoke conflict with "good girl" injunctions. Women need a place to talk about what daughters teach them, to construct new narratives for women's lives, to connect across the divisions of race and class, and as Carolyn Heilbrun says, to "speak profoundly to one another."

The work of reclaiming resistance as individual women and as a community of women takes women into new territory. The survival strategies of disconnection and mistrust that have enabled women to maneuver in patriarchal culture were learned for good reasons, and they are frightening to give up. Women cannot do this work comfortably in isolation.

Pat Flanders Hall, former Dean of the Laurel School, speaks for herself and the sixteen other women who formed a community of support for themselves at the school, when she writes that they realized that

> unless we, as grown women, were willing to give up all the "good little girl" things we continued to do and give up our expectation that the girls in our charge would be as good as we were, we could not successfully empower young women to act on their own knowledge and feelings. Unless we stopped hiding in expectations of goodness and control, our behavior would silence any words to girls about speaking in their own voice. Finally, we dared to believe that one could be intelligently disruptive without destroying anything except the myths about the high level of female cooperativeness.

But, as important, this knowledge itself changed the way they were able to take risks with each other and with the school administration, which inevitably led them into conflict over the vision of the school they cared about. This work was too frightening to be done alone by a single woman and was possible only in the supportive bonds of a community. The researchers of the Harvard Project have also found that working together by, for example, jointly authoring papers and giving presentations, enables women to speak more easily about the effects of patriarchy on girls —traumatic knowledge that author and audience alike resist.

Within the larger community of women, our respective collisions with the wall have created divisions among groups of women. The alliances that white women and middle-class women have made along race and class lines to ensure their safety and "success" in patriarchy have created deep pain and divisions within the greater community of women. Different women hold different information about the wall because of varied experiences in the culture. The anger, fear, and guilt that different privileges cause block women from realizing their wholeness and integrity. What we fear in each other holds the key to what we fear in ourselves. Reclaiming our connections with women means that we have to work through the boundaries that the culture has created between us.

While chapter 9 contains suggestions to mothers about how to form groups, reclaiming connection with women begins with the promise that Carol Gilligan made: to speak, knowing that each woman carries a girl inside her, and not to compete with or devalue other women. For that promise to be fulfilled deeply, however, women must bring their healthy, resistant selves into community among other women. In community and in solidarity with each other, women can speak of the ways in which they silence themselves, avoid conflict in relationships, and struggle with perfection. Within the safety and power of a group, women can find a healing response to the trauma of growing up female in our culture through what Judith Herman's research has found to be essential for victims of war, domestic violence, and rape—recognition and restitution.

By creating community, we women provide a way for girls to maintain their connection to women as they grow. Through shared social action, we can find that our personal experience of trauma has deep meaning that transcends the personal. By giving daughters this shared, communal approach to the dilemma of coming of age in this culture, we ensure change and eventual success. By refusing to be isolated and silenced, women can create a new set of societal rules. While we may not be able to secure restitution in the immediate future, we can demand it and acknowledge that it is due. In so doing, women use the experiences of the past for a promising future. We call forth our reality and, supported, we truly join our daughters in decreasing the likelihood of the replication of our self-sacrificing experience.

5

Voice Lessons

What would it mean for a girl—against the stories read, chanted, or murmured to her—to choose to tell the truth of her life aloud to another person at the very point when she is invited into the larger cultural story of womanhood—that is, at early adolescence? . . . To whom would a girl speak and in what context? Who would listen to the story she dares to author? What does she risk in the telling?

Lyn Mikel Brown
"TELLING A GIRL'S LIFE"

Describing her early adolescence, writer Maxine Hong Kingston tells of having a pain in her throat from "a list of over two hundred things that I had to tell my mother so that she would know the true things about me." She decides that she has to tell her mother these things. "If only I could let my mother know the list, she—and the world—would become more like me, and I would never be alone again." Squatting down beside her mother, who is starching shirts in the family laundry, Maxine begins to describe, one by one, the items on her list—stories of cruelty and longing. For several nights, she whispers her secrets to her mother, the secrets that separated them by silence. But soon her mother says, "I can't stand this whispering. I wish you would stop."

"So I had to stop," writes Kingston, "relieved in some ways. I shut my mouth, but I felt something alive tearing at my throat, bite by bite, from the inside. Soon there would be three hundred things, and too late to get them out before my mother grew old and died." But the pain in her throat continued into adulthood. "The throat pain always returns, though, unless I tell what I really think, whether or not I lose my job, or spit out gaucheries all over a party." Maxine Hong Kingston has learned that the tightness and pain in her throat guide her to her truths, the truths that first became important to tell to her mother as she entered adolescence. This daughter's struggle for voice and for connection with her mother are deeply interrelated: she goes first to her mother to speak so as not to be alone in the world.

But Maxine's mother, in her exhaustion from overwork and her need for some quiet time herself, never heard or understood that the crazy whisperings about killed spiders or longed-for white horses were an opportunity for her daughter to express her true self. They were her daughter's voice lessons. Not being heard, Maxine Hong Kingston began to write. Perhaps this mother's unwillingness to listen led her daughter to have such a powerful literary voice. The psyche finds ways to speak the truth of its experience. Perhaps, then, the silent misunderstanding that caused this mother and daughter pain and suffering was, in the long run, worth it.

But most mothers and daughters (probably including these two) would prefer not to be separated by misunderstanding and unspoken truth. Maxine Hong Kingston struggled, as many adolescent girls do, to be known by the woman closest to her. We have heard girls complain most loudly about three things in their relationships with their mothers: not being dealt with fairly, not being truly loved for themselves, and not being trusted with the truth. All three complaints are directly linked to entering the world at adolescence and colliding with the wall.

At adolescence, a girl first becomes aware of an inner, authentic voice that struggles to articulate who she is in relation to others in her world, particularly in relation to her mother. While eight-year-old girls might find thinking about their "selves" to be silly, adolescent girls tend to be preoccupied with their "selves." Adolescent girls become aware that they are thought about and judged, because they can now think about and judge themselves—and others—as not measuring up to often-conflicting standards at home and among peers. Girls begin to see that life is complicated and that they can safely reveal only certain layers of what they know. This leads them to wonder who they are and who really knows them. "Their courage seems suddenly treacherous, transgressive, dangerous," notes Annie Rogers. "But the 'true I' lives on in an underground world, waiting and hoping for a sign that she may emerge, whole, and open herself again."

Of all the acts mothers can engage in with their daughters, one of the most radical seems at first blush the most basic: listening to and validating the way daughters experience the world. Listening and responding are the basis of all relationship and are so much a part of what every mother does. A revolution within mother daughter relationships does not require that mothers take on more work in listening and responding, but rather that mothers bring themselves to these tasks in a different, gentler way.

The enormous responsibilities and overwhelming expectations placed on mothers often create internal noise that drowns out the simple act of listening and responding. The tension to mother the "right" way can leave a peculiar silence within mother daughter relationships—the silence of a mother's own truth and experience. Within this silence, a daughter's authentic voice can also fall silent. This is the silence of perfection. This silence of perfection prevents mothers from listening and learning with and from their daughters.

THE SILENCE OF PERFECTION

Claire vividly remembers "the hurt and disappointed faces of my children when they would try to get my attention or ask for something and I couldn't hear them. I was too busy trying to be the model mother and getting them to do what I needed them to do to be model children to really listen to what they wanted and needed." Of course, Claire wasn't simply ignoring her children, but her responses and reactions showed them that what was most important was keeping to her schedule, her standards of behavior: no questions, please, just go ahead and do it. Of all of the mothers we have listened to, Claire most fully described how she broke the silence of perfection.

"My mother- and father-in-law both died, my younger daughter was in and out of the hospital with some disease that no one knew how to cure, my husband lost his job, and the girl who was in our foster care was in deep trouble," Claire remembers with a sigh. "It was the most horrible time of my life. I was about to lose it. I didn't know where to go—but I remembered that I liked the woman minister at a local parish. She was no longer there, but I decided to go anyway and speak to someone— anyone."

Claire went, her two young daughters and little son in tow, and spoke to a minister. "He said, 'Oh my God! I think this is one of the worst stories I've ever heard. You're handling more stress than almost anyone that I've ever talked to. You need some time to yourself.'" The minister turned down the lights in his office to a warm glow, took Claire's three children, and instructed Claire "to just sit and breathe for fifteen minutes." Afterward she was surprised that she felt just enough different to get a little perspective on the craziness of her situation. "He gave me the validation that I needed. It may seem odd, but he gave me permission to say, 'Yes, this is too much for me to handle.'" Claire learned what theologian Valerie Saiving says that many mothers learn: ". . . that a woman can give too much of herself, so that nothing remains of her own uniqueness; she can become merely an emptiness, almost a zero, without value to herself, to her fellow men [sic], or, perhaps, even to God."

Simultaneously, Claire was getting signals to break the silence of perfection from another source: her daughter, Jessica. "Twice Jessie came into my room in the middle of the night, having nightmares about me. Once she dreamed that my head fell off, rolled around on the street, and my brains spilled out. At that point, I just 'shushed' her and told her it was just some nonsense, a silly dream. But, in the middle of all the craziness that we were going through, I was kind of haunted by her dreams. I thought, Now what is this crazy kid of mine trying to tell me?" Listening to the language of her daughter's psyche, Claire began to translate the message. "I realized that she was right—I had pretty much lost myself and was in danger of losing it completely. I had to stop living the way I had been living." Claire's response to her daughter's acute perceptiveness was to open more to her children, to let them guide her more. "It happened almost overnight. I threw it all away. I realized that I couldn't do everything. I decided that the most important thing for me to do was to listen, *really listen,* to my children—to really get to know them and allow them to be themselves as fully as possible."

Claire had been exhausted, humorless, and angry at anything that got in her way. Yet, caught in the isolating silence of perfection, she was trapped by her expectations that everything had to be a certain way or her life would go completely crazy. Paradoxically, it was trying to keep everything together, being responsible for everyone's happiness and laundry and schoolwork, that was making her crazy. When she let down the ideal, Claire realized that she got more done than she had before.

The pressure to be perfect—and thus blameless and worthy of love— is one of the ways that patriarchy psychologically silences many women's authenticity and saps their strength. For many women, being the Perfect Mother means being utterly selfless and nurturant. But just as Liza was confused when she was told that her anorexia displayed her perfectionism ("But I'm not perfect!"), the very idea of being perfect seems to make no sense. We all know how perfectly imperfect we truly are. But, to a great extent, that's the point. Mothers don't experience the trap of perfection in actual perfection (which is impossible anyway) but in a constant awareness that they are falling short. Sometimes mothers experience a fearful vigilance that suggests that if they let their guard down and stop running at a frantic pace and go out without looking totally together, then everything would come crashing down. While women cannot live outside of the culture, by identifying and contradicting its conceptual traps, women can, psychologically, begin to live free of its dictates.

The constant striving for perfection creates rage, isolation, and exhaustion. Claire's exhaustion and loss of any sense of humor were signs of her isolation in perfection. While the demands on women's lives are intense, the feeling of tiredness that comes from living hard is completely different from the exhaustion of perfection. Marjory heard that the adolescent daughter of a friend had made a serious attempt at suicide. Sitting by the girl's bedside, Marjory said, "At last, you're getting some rest, right?" The girl was shocked that Marjory understood what was happening. Marjory said, "Yes, I understand very well. I tried the same thing when I was about your age. I was just so tired from living up to everyone's expectations." Exhaustion from goodness begins in adolescence. One in four adolescent girls attempt suicide. None of these attempts could be classified simply as exhaustion, but many of them result from early induction into being perfect.

Words of comfort and love are hard to hear and accept while women are inside the noise of perfection. Such words seem false: How could anyone really feel that way when I don't measure up? Thus, trapped in the ways perfection silences a woman's authentic feelings and thoughts, women cannot connect fully or be nurtured. Out of touch with themselves and with others, women push ever harder to be perfect. On this treadmill, the urge for perfection causes women to run and run without being able to stop. Whatever gets in the way triggers acute frustration and rage.

The constant running and out-of-proportion rage act like a barbed-

wire fence keeping women from what lies underneath: fear and powerlessness. Women often struggle to find ways to seek their own fulfillment
other than through their children. But they find few ways to experience
their own desires and needs within the narrow breathing space of the
patriarchal institution of motherhood.

Mothers in patriarchy, as we said earlier, are also held responsible for
the "outcome" of their children and yet are often denied the power to
provide for their children. The profound depth of a mother's responsibility, coupled with these dichotomized pressures, makes it difficult for
women to maintain a sense of themselves as competent and capable human beings. The weight of mother blaming robs women of their power to
mother as they would like to. While mothers crave support and guidance,
particularly during the first years of a child's life, mothers are too often
isolated in their homes with the sword of blame hovering over their heads.
Isolation, layered with loss of authority and control, leads women into the
self-critical frenzy of perfection as a way of compensating both for these
losses and for the fear of mothering poorly, which carries the greatest risk
of all—the loss of one's children.

The often-overwhelming responsibility of motherhood gives the self-
critical Fury inside each woman a new opportunity to act as a moral
watchdog. The voice of a woman's Fury—the internalized patriarchal
critic—barks "shoulds" to ensure that a mother doesn't transgress and risk
this ultimate loss of her children. The Fury created at adolescence is roused
again in motherhood and draws its "shoulds" from each woman's unique
girlhood experience. The Fury voices the "shoulds" of femininity: You
should be all-loving, you should please everyone, you should be nice. . . .
The "shoulds" that it presents are what a woman should do to be considered a "good" girl or woman within the culture.

These shoulds keep women in line and silence their thoughts and
feelings because these directives have the unquestionable ring of moral
truth. Who could doubt the moral propriety of loving others more than

oneself? Or of giving one's life for one's child? The Fury's words often resonate deeply with the commandments and moral codes that are so solemnly intoned in Western culture. Yet these codes, too, were written for men, to circumscribe their tendency for self-involvement. While almost every mother would, if called on, sacrifice her life for her child's, the daily routine of sacrifice on the altar of perfection corrupts women's ability to love and to act freely as moral agents. To break out of perfection, a mother needs to call on her Fury as a resistant, not a negating, force to protect her authenticity.

RISKING IMPERFECTION

When the Ms. Foundation for Women was developing a slogan for its public education campaign on their National Girls Initiative, one slogan that was tossed around was "A girl is watching . . . what is she learning about being a woman?" The idea was to have a multimedia blitz through television, radio, magazine ads, and billboards that would startle everyone into awareness that girls observe women and the surrounding culture to learn how to be women. By shifting the gaze of women's Fury to align with the gaze of girls, women perform a radical act of psychological disengagement from patriarchy.

This double vision—seeing through the eyes of male power and privilege as well as the eyes of a truth-telling girl who is as yet unaware of the dangers of being female in male culture—is a powerful way to break the silence of patriarchal perfection. By simply asking our daughters what they see about women's lives in families, in workplaces, and in the larger world, we regain an authority as exemplars rather than as subordinates. For Claire, and for other mothers who have made allies out of their Fury, the shift was extremely freeing.

Breaking away from perfection sometimes comes when a woman taps into an underground stream of resistance that marks the presence of her own truth. Many women aren't even aware of such a stream (let alone aware of its power) until they are swept away by its currents. "My husband and I had been living estranged but pretending that we had a marriage for many, many years," says JoHanna. "He had begun to order me around, telling me what I could and couldn't do. I told him, 'Hey, you know, we just have an arrangement here—an arrangement for the kids. If you don't like it, then we should talk.' He thought he was calling my bluff and said, 'Yeah, I think we should talk—about getting a divorce.' 'Huh!' I said. I hadn't really thought about it. But then everything became crystal clear; I felt strong in a way that I never had before. 'Okay,' I said, 'enough's enough. Let's get a divorce.'" Some women break out of perfection by leaving their marriages because they cannot find a way to live as full people with their marriage partners.

Some women have broken away by having an affair. June describes her thoughts and feelings as she found herself at this brink: "I went to my room the night I met him and thought, 'I want that guy. I'm going to have an affair with him.' As if I were a practiced . . . adulteress. I was clear as I'd ever been. I shocked myself, and double-checked my thinking, kind of like, 'Come on now, June, that's not your style, that's the *opposite* of your style.' 'Are you sure?' I kept asking myself. And 'You bet!' was my answer."

Other women have broken perfection's prison by listening to their true inner voices that led them back to school or work. Many women do it by going on vacation for themselves, starting to meditate, or developing interests that are solely for themselves. Sometimes women have broken with the Fury by doing what is absolutely unthinkable in patriarchy— falling in love with a woman. For each woman, the particular confines of perfection will be different, depending on the taboos from girlhood. For many women, breaking the taboos of the Perfect Mother will mean find- ing pleasure and humor, the power of their minds, or time away from caretaking to allow for growth.

"I think that my kids would say that now I'm more fun," says Claire.

Each of her three children (Cristina, Jessica, and Nathan) can remember the exact week five years ago when their mom changed. "She became totally different, like a different person," says Cristina, her oldest child. They like the "new mom" better. "We have a gas together," says Claire. "Our house is a real loony bin." Humor is one of the best antidotes to the fear that silences a woman's authenticity.

"The art of playing with girls sustains both women's and girls' courage," explains Annie Rogers. "The art of playing—creating truthful illusions by shifting a single element; becoming characters through which we might play ourselves at one remove, touching the edge of what is most unspeakable in our own lives; creating those rituals and games in which danger suddenly shifts into wildness and helpless laughter—makes it possible to say what is unspeakable." Being able to laugh at ourselves, at our foibles and weaknesses, contradicts the Fury's warnings that women must be either perfect or unloved. Breaking through the fear of not being perfect catapults mothers back into real relationship with themselves and their daughters. Paradoxically, often by risking what we most fear, we are granted our selves back.

Claire believes that education has allowed her to begin an internal dialogue very different from the one fueled by self-hating perfectionism. "I'm a very intuitive and spiritual person," she says. "After I took refuge in the minister's office, he and I started a reading group, to read and think about spirituality." This has led Claire back to school for a master's degree. "I'm reading a lot of feminist thinkers, and a lot of theology; I'm putting things together my way." The discipline involved in Claire's schoolwork provides a space where she can hear her own thoughts. Within it, she has found a little solitude.

Solitude, too, contradicts the edicts because it affirms a woman's importance to herself. "One of my earliest memories," writes Pearl Cleage, "is coming home from school to find my mother seated at the piano playing 'Solitude,' the Duke Ellington classic that Billie Holiday made her own. Now, my mother often played the piano and sang, but not like this.

On these occasions she became somebody else entirely. She would close her eyes, throw back her head and sing with a fierce intensity and longing that I was still too young to understand."

After her ten-year marriage ended, Pearl, alone as a woman and as the mother of a daughter, found that she had a great deal of time to herself: "I was spending a lot of time alone, but my thoughts and spirit were more scattered than ever, and spending time by myself terrified me. Alone with my thoughts? Forget it!" Happening on Billie Holiday on the radio, she remembered her mother singing "'. . . *someplace quiet to collect my thoughts. That's the solitude I was talking about . . .'*" Pearl Cleage recalls, "Suddenly it made sense to me." She decided to give herself "at least one uninterrupted hour" in a week.

> When the appointed day and hour arrived, I dropped my daughter off with her father, unplugged my telephone, ran a hot bath, slid in up to my chin and waited. I have to admit I felt kind of silly, hunched down in the water with the moon shining in my window, waiting for immediate and magical revelations to occur. But I made myself be still. I closed my eyes and let my thoughts roam freely. And roam they did—to everything from my work, to my daughter, to my gentleman friends, to my health, to my friends and back again. I didn't try to determine the right or wrong of anything that popped into my mind, I simply tried to be the same open, non-judgmental ear for myself I try to be for those who are closest to me. And at the end of an hour, I was refreshed and energized in a way I hadn't been before. I was amazed, but still skeptical.

Slowly and fitfully, Pearl developed a practice of solitude. "And the quiet became the stillness and the stillness became the peace and the peace became a path to a new way of life. I know my mother would understand."

A woman's nurturing of herself—even if it is just ten minutes a day or an hour a week—breaks the silence imposed by the Fury's "shoulds" on the self's desires and vitality. Taking time for ourselves and our own pleasure and growth, relishing a sense of humor, looking through our daughters' eyes—all these things contradict the fear that locks mothers into selflessness, strangled by the silence of perfection. Yet these are not new warnings, new "shoulds" to add to the Fury's list. They are an opportunity to relax, to breathe, and simply to look around.

Breaking this silencing of the self even once or twice or from time to time enables a mother to connect more honestly with her daughter. Laura found that she started to be able to feel herself go into perfection "overdrive"—that breathless "ohmygodIonlyhaveanhourandthekidsneedandthestorecloses andthebankisn'topenand . . ." feeling—and began to laugh at herself whenever she started to feel her anxiety "shift into warp speed." The model of a mother's resistance to a "good woman's" sacrifice can help daughters move through adolescence without being trapped by self-silencing. Immersed in perfection, mothers can't possibly hear what daughters are saying very clearly. As Claire said, she did not really listen to her children because she was too busy trying to get them to be who she needed them to be.

LEARNING TO LISTEN, LISTENING TO LEARN

When Carol Gilligan, Lyn Mikel Brown, and other Harvard Project researchers began exploring girls' development at the Laurel School, they were trying to be "perfect" researchers in response to criticisms of their previous work. These women, professionally trained to ask questions and interpret answers, found that their perfectionistic agenda kept them from developing the relationships in which girls might feel both comfortable enough and respected enough to speak honestly about their thoughts and feelings. Lyn and Carol recall:

Within hours of beginning our research with girls on the experience of being listened to, we had simply become a new version of something to guard against, someone to protect themselves from, to be suspicious of, to be warned against. Perhaps most insidiously we became another reason for girls to feel bad or to feel judged. . . . We felt this, and then we overrode our own feelings. As women we found this easy to do.

Over time, however, these researchers decided to break with the traditions of their field (to risk breaking the model of the perfect researcher). They created a way of listening to the girls in which both the girls and the women researchers had greater voice: "Out of what could be seen as a collapse in form—a letting go of our planned research design for the messiness and unpredictability and vulnerability of ongoing relationship— a way of working emerged which felt more genuine and mutual, precarious at first, disruptive, unsettling to those of us used to our authority and control in professional situations." In rejecting conventions of "good" research, the Harvard Project researchers became more radical—going to the roots of the research relationship. They began to listen to learn and, in so doing, learned to listen to girls.

While a mother is an ongoing and necessary authority in her daughter's life (and a researcher clearly is not), a mother, too, can impose an agenda with her daughter that can obscure the daughter's voice. What mother wouldn't say that she wants what's "best" for her daughter? that she wants a good relationship with her? But what a mother feels is best is shaped by her own particular combination of desires and fears. A mother's "agenda" is to protect her daughter from danger while allowing her opportunity. Yet a mother's sense of danger is shaped by her life, her experience, and her response to it.

Girls enter into experiences and situations that women would often prefer to forget or ignore. As mothers listen to their daughters, they will inevitably face experiences that sexism has taught women to condone (such as being put down or not being given resources) or to dismiss (such as serious fights with friends, the power of a child's love, or their struggle to understand injustice). Why, as one girl asked, would a vice-presidential candidate force a girl to have a child if she were raped?

As things are now, "good" mothers must prepare their daughters for their role within a world defined by men. Judith Herman and Helen Lewis explain that a mother's role is to "protect her daughter from the worst excesses of male exploitation, teaching her to avoid molestation, rape, incest, prostitution, and physical assault. Although men create these dangers, it is the lot of women to explain them to their outraged and uncomprehending girl children." As noted earlier, this "training" that restricts girls' freedom to be wholly in the world accounts for much of the hostility between mothers and daughters. A mothers' fear for her daughter simultaneously binds the daughter to the mother and prevents both from living as whole people. Mothers find themselves needing to be jailers and teachers of servitude. They train their daughters to muffle and disguise their voices to keep them from sounding out of tune with the culture. But mothers can be inspired teachers of voice who en-courage the full expression of girls' true natures.

The best voice teachers have good ears. They appreciate the full range of the human voice from whispers of fear to shouts of joy, from bass bellows of anger to piercing shrieks of laughter. In the sounding rooms of mother daughter relationships, inspired voice teachers demonstrate, cajole, mimic, and play with voice. While a mother need not herself be a great performer, she at least has to sing—and to have the ear to appreciate a fine performance. But the true essential of voice lessons is practice, practice, practice. When learning a new song to sing, only the rare few can belt it out without a wrong note. Mother daughter relationships are the practice space for voice lessons.

The paradox of mothers teaching voice to their daughters is that a mother's best teacher will be her daughter. This is the critical and ongoing component of a mother's own reclaiming, resounding with her daughter.

In speaking about learning to listen, we will refer mostly to *what* is said, not *how* it is said. But the free, full-bodied voices of young girls, especially, offer an incredible lesson in voice. Mouths open, lungs full of air, young girls can belt out what they feel. The classic breathiness of women's voices and their high pitch apparently are not justified by the structural differences between men and women. The narrow range of the traditional feminine voice is a constant, everyday message that says, Please don't take me seriously; can't you see that I am too meek and frightened to be any sort of threat? As attentive voice teachers, mothers listen and encourage daughters to be powerful, open channels of expression.

What does it mean to listen? By *listening* we don't mean the basic function of hearing, although that is usually involved. Mothers who are deaf can be extraordinary listeners. Listening means an awareness, an openness to learning something new about another person. In ordinary conversation, people often speak in a shorthand with each other, assuming an understanding to make the conversation flow. Interrupting, even for clarification, can seem to be rude or a breach of some unwritten code of sympathy. But listening with the intent to learn is both an approach to conversation and a different type of conversation.

"She really listens," says Amy, eleven, about her mother, "and she understands and she'll give me advice if I need advice, but sometimes I'll say things like: 'Just don't tell me what to do. Just listen.' " Listening to learn isn't about giving advice—at least not until asked—but about trying to understand exactly what someone means, how it is that someone looks at and feels about her particular situation. Listening to learn is a conspiracy—which literally means "a breathing together"—in which one person breathes in the words and feelings of another.

In conspiring together, women do not collude in silencing girls by ignoring or avoiding the potential places in which a mother's experience might differ from her daughter's. Instead, they ask for clarification, ask to know more about the other's thoughts and feelings. A mother can give a daughter "permission" to say the unexpected by going even further than asking her what she thinks—by asking what she *really* thinks. Our daughters know to protect us from what we find uncomfortable. Sometimes what a mother hears could literally take her breath away because it is painful for her daughter (and, so, for her) or frightening, particularly in relation to the mother's own experience. Breathing in a daughter's thoughts and feelings, allowing them to stir up the mother's own experience, grounds a mother in her own thoughts and feelings before she responds. This conspiracy has a tremendous power to communicate to a daughter, Yes, I respect you enough to take in your words and to be with you in your thoughts and feelings.

"When either one of my daughters, the fourteen-year-old or the nine-year-old, is acting funky or mopey, I know that something's up," says Lisa. "Sometimes I might not notice right away, but after a couple days with a long face, I'll pay attention." Lisa will approach the troubled daughter. "I'll say, 'You've been looking kind of down lately. Is something the matter?' My nine-year-old daughter sometimes isn't sure, and so we'll talk about what's been happening at school, with her friends, in the family until we get to it. When we finally do hit it, this incredible stream will come out of her mouth that makes sense out of everything." But the fourteen-year-old daughter acts differently. "Often she'll shrug and turn away from me, mumbling that there really isn't anything wrong. So sometimes I'll just mimic her and slouch down beside her and say, real mopey, 'Nooo, Mom, I'm just great,' and she'll laugh kind of sheepishly. Sometimes I'll just sit next to her and ask her to look at me. Almost the second we make eye contact, the tears start flowing." Lisa persists gently: "But it takes so little, really. I just touch her shoulder, squeeze it a little, and— whoosh!—all of what's been bottled up comes rushing out."

Lisa is learning to listen differently. As soon as she notices that there is something happening with one of her daughters, Lisa brings full attention to her. Heart and mind open, she watches her daughter's eyes, breathing, and body language. Lisa knows that painful feelings hide behind downcast eyes, short breath, and slouchy posture. And those feelings are a wall to free connection between her daughters and others, including herself. The strength of her warm attention, eye contact, and gentle urging gives her daughters the faith that their mother wants to know and will listen to learn.

Lisa's story also begins to show that there are differences between listening to young girls and listening to adolescents. The younger the child, the more direct the relationship between her trouble and her actions. Adolescence calls on different listening skills. At this time of crisis and extraordinary change, daughters fight to be recognized both as the young women they are rapidly becoming and as the unique selves that they are.

"My mother and I used to have these conversations. They were sort of fights, struggles," says Rachel, at twenty-one. "I would say something about myself and my life, and my mother would agree and then say something that showed me how off she was. I would say, over and over, 'No, Mother, that's not it at all' and then try to explain. At points I wondered why I bothered. She didn't seem to know me at all. But that was the point—I wanted her to know *me,* not some version of me that she had made up to suit herself." Rachel feels unknown and unloved (two deeply related things) because, in her mother's eagerness to connect and instruct, Rachel doesn't feel heard or understood.

"Girls tend to be touchy and sharp-witted with a mother who assumes that they think alike, or that they think as one," explains Terri Apter. She heard complaints from many adolescent girls that their mothers didn't really love them for themselves but only loved them because the girls were their daughters. "The complaints about how well she [the adolescent girl] was loved," she writes, "were linked to how well she was seen.

"It was accuracy of perception, far more than strictness, which preoccupied adolescent girls. They complained about a mother's personality, about her 'hang ups,' her limitations, her prejudices—but most of all about her vision." Girls' most consistent complaints were about their mothers' shortcomings in not seeing the daughters, their new selves, accurately, apart from the children they once were (even though sometimes they want to be childish). "I've finally started to confront my mother about how she only says she loves me like—'Goodnight, honey, I love you,'" says Tricia, at sixteen, "and she says, 'Of course I love you!' but it reminds me of Tevye in *Fiddler on the Roof* when his wife sings, 'Do you love me?' and he basically says, 'Hey, I'm here, aren't I?' I don't want that 'if I didn't love you, I wouldn't be here' kind of love, not even from my mother. I want to know how and why she loves me for me." Listening to learn from a daughter in adolescence, conspiring with her thoughts and feelings, keeps a mother in touch with a daughter's growing and changing self.

As adolescents, Rachel and Tricia teach voice by using their increased self-awareness and a greater ability to compare and note differences between what is said and what is happening. They challenge their mothers more directly. As they are able to think about themselves in new ways, they become aware that others cannot know what they think and feel, who they are. Do their mothers, then, *really* know them? Would their mothers love them just the same if they did? To listen to a daughter with the intent to learn allows a mother to come to know the daughter's inner voice, her new self, and, as Maxine Hong Kingston said, make her mother and the world more like her so that she would never be alone again.

But "voice" is not so simple as what a daughter says verbally: a mother needs to honor the ways in which her daughter speaks through the language of the psyche. In Margaret Atwood's novel *Cat's Eye,* young Elaine "voices" her distress at the cruel treatment at the hands of her so-called friends by chewing her hair, lips, and fingers, and by avoiding direct eye contact with her mother. Elaine also peeled the skin off her feet every night. The psyche speaks indirectly through symptoms and behavior. Elaine was being peeled alive under the gaze of her "friends." In Jamaica Kincaid's autobiographical novel, *Annie John,* the heroine goes into a severe depression as she enters adolescence and finds that growing up means losing the close connection she had with her mother. Her maternal grandmother's cure is to hold and love her like a baby so as to reestablish the warmth of human connection. Watching for signs of distress, as Lisa does, in a girl's moods or liveliness or body language, and asking her what is happening, can help keep a daughter from finding herself alone with underground feelings that are too painful or shameful to let out. Listening without an agenda to a daughter at that unspoken place helps to keep her powerfully connected to her mother and a world of women.

"My daughters will sometimes tell me, 'Mother, you have just crossed the line,' " says Barbara. "They let me know when I've gone too far and then I back off." Listening to learn to an adolescent daughter, as Barbara has learned, means giving her space when she asks for it and respecting the "line" that she draws. Because a mother has had such a powerful influence on a girl's life, a daughter will sometimes want privacy—she wants not to be listened to but to listen just to herself for a while. "Sometimes when I'm trying to figure out something," says fifteen-year-old Angie, "I hear her voice inside my head. I wonder if I'll ever have my own thoughts." Angie and many other girls will carry on internal conversations with their mothers—anticipating what their mothers will say (often inaccurately) and then checking to see if they are right. Paradoxically, respecting a daughter's space, acknowledging her desire for privacy but letting her know that her mother is available, allows a daughter to create the inner space to seek out her mother's ear.

Voice lessons are also about practice. Even with the best of intentions, mothers can find it hard to listen amidst the cacophony of family life. But perhaps the place to start is in those serious *conversations* that happen between mothers and daughters. All mothers have conversations with their daughters—those times when either something has happened that has to be discussed or something just comes up that involves a serious subject. At those times, a mother doesn't have to instruct or come up with the "right" answer, she can simply take a deep breath and just listen. In time, listening to learn becomes a habit not reserved just for those tough times. Listening to learn to a daughter's triumphs is also a powerful voice lesson.

A great thing about a lifelong relationship is that there is time: to apologize, to ask questions, to remember together. Voice lessons begin by listening, by asking questions, by being curious and open to hearing about a daughter's thoughts, feelings, and dreams without categorizing or explaining them, unless asked. In conspiring with daughters, a mother may discover experiences from her own life that will accelerate her own reclaiming. In listening to learn, mothers may find themselves open to ways in which daughters are different from themselves and different from their own conceptions about their daughters. Listening to, and thus acknowledging, these differences gives daughters space to make their own choices in the world.

VALIDATING VOICE AND REALITY

Girls don't want mothers just to be all ears; they want, as Terri Apter has put it, "mothers with their mouths open." Girls will push their mothers into dialogue, to find out how they differ, by cajoling, baiting, pestering, or shutting them out. "I found girls highly ingenious in the way they would coax their mother into acknowledging them in various ways," she observed. Validating a daughter's voice and reality asks that a mother listen to and take seriously her daughter's self-presentations with the intent of acknowledging her daughter's experience. "Validation of a person," writes Terri Apter, "involves responding to those feelings and thoughts the person is trying to put forward, whether directly or indirectly. In a sense it is a way of responding which indicates 'I hear what you are saying, and what you are saying makes sense to me.'"

In their collision with the wall of the culture, girls learn that what they know is not considered to be valid knowledge. As Victoria was told when she complained about the fact that she was being paid less than the boys at the stable where she worked, "People will think you are stupid for saying things like that." To validate a girl's reality means to acknowledge that, in fact, she sees something in the world that is real and important. For girls, like Victoria, who are learning that what they know and think and feel is not important, a "reality check" is critical.

How many times a day do girls cry out, "It's not fair!" Contained in those words is a girl's courage and her developing sense of justice. Yet the constant barrage of "it's not fair" from a daughter can leave a mother utterly exhausted until "well, life's not fair" is her response. "I'll ask my daughter to help carry in the shopping," said one mother, "and she'll start explaining a hundred and one things to me about why it's really her sister's turn to do it, and I never ask anyone else, and if I let her go on, the ice cream will be melting in the car, so I just give up and do it myself." In interviews with girls from the Laurel School, the Harvard Project researchers noticed that girls often reported that their mothers said "life's not fair" to them, to stop the girls' complaining. Apparently, this particular response by mothers has a strong impact on girls. Struggling as they are with sociopolitical realities that are not at all fair, girls seem to play out their questions about justice within their families, particularly with their mothers. The mother with the shopping could acknowledge that her daughter might be right and that she herself is not perfect, ask again directly if her daughter would help her now and talk about the unfairness later, perhaps with her sister present.

Girls are extremely sensitive to unequal treatment—particularly when brothers are given more than they are. "My father gives more presents to my brother," says Amanda, at eight. "Do you say anything?" "Well, I tell my mother but I can't tell my dad or he'll get mad." If girls can find justice at home, then they might have the grounding to demand it in the world. A mother can admit that unfairness exists without blaming it on life as a whole. When "life is unfair," then the realities girls see that disempower them are fixed and immutable. There is no recourse.

Shawn Slovo's autobiographical film, *A World Apart*, ends with an "it's not fair" scene between thirteen-year-old Molly and her mother, the journalist Ruth Furst, who was imprisoned in South Africa for her work against apartheid. In this powerful scene, she created a fictitious confrontation between her young adolescent self and her mother. This is what Shawn wished had happened and what probably would have happened had she dared to speak. When her fictional character confronts her mother for being away from home so much and calls the absences unfair, her mother both reassures Slovo of her love and agrees with her. "Life isn't fair *yet,*" says this mother, who explains that in her work against apartheid she is trying to give her daughter a fair world. What the girl wanted was the promise from her mother of a love that went into the world to make change. Proving that it is never too late to validate a girl's reality, Shawn Slovo rewrote her life story to get a validation of her own voice from her mother.

In our experience, one of the deepest validations that a girl may seek is to know that she has an impact on her mother. Claire's daughter Jessica knows how to coax her mother into recognizing her existence. Claire looks at her daughter's often-exasperating behavior not as "badness" but as an expression of some unresolved question or issue that her daughter is struggling with: "Jessica, what is it? What's happened that you are acting like this?" As girls come to realize that women's voices are muted in the world, as they struggle with the extraordinary changes of adolescence, girls want to know that somewhere they are a force to be contended with. Girls want their mothers to respond to them for real—not to intellectualize ("you're just going through a stage" or "you're just doing this to bug me, and it won't work") and not to ignore ("that's nice" or "oh, really?") but to respond fully to what she is doing.

The trick to validating a daughter's voice in adolescence is to notice, to wonder at, and to applaud the growing edge of a daughter's self. "The mother validates the daughter not by responding objectively to what she is," writes Terri Apter, "but by perceiving her through her appreciation of what her daughter wants to be. The fantasies, hopes and irrational confidence of the adolescent must be shared in part by the parents." Building on listening to learn and learning to listen, applauding a daughter's new perceptions and capabilities as she shows them to her mother is a powerful validation of her voice and her reality.

Validating a daughter's voice is about practice, not perfection. No mother can validate—or should validate—everything her daughter says and does. A mother's best guide is herself: what does she wish her mother had said to her? "When I had troubles in junior high and high school, I remember my mother telling me not to worry, just be myself and everyone would like me," Claire recalls. "I hated that. It seemed so simplistic and dismissive. She was wrong, too. I promised myself that I wouldn't do that to my kids. While I may know that what they are hurt by will seem silly in the future—something else my mother said, 'You'll look back on this and laugh'—that's irrelevant. What they are living through now is their entire world."

Reclaiming and validating are often intertwined: a mother can often validate best what she has recalled and reclaimed about her own adolescent responses to her mother's advice giving. Validating daughters' voices is a matter of taking girls seriously. "Little girls are cute and small only to adults," writes Margaret Atwood. "To one another they are not cute. They are life-sized." And adolescents are often cute to no one but each other because they call to mind so much remembered pain. They, too, have life-sized problems.

AUTHORITY AND AUTHORIZATION

The words *authority* and *author* come from the same root, an old French word that means "to make to grow, originate, promote, or increase." What would it mean for girls to maintain their authority and author their own lives rather than making themselves fit into the stale roles offered by the romance story? What would it take to foster girls' self-authorization? Authorization is problematic for girls because women are denied the power of being the creators and authors of their own lives within the culture.

Authorizing in mother daughter relationships is a two-part harmony between the daughter's young soprano and the mother's more forceful alto. Authorizing goes further than validating. Not only does an authorizing mother validate her daughter's reality, but she adds her authority as a mother, as a woman who has experience in this culture, to amplify and harmonize with her daughter. Authorizing has two components: first, a mother authorizes her daughter by giving her permission to say what she sees and knows, and second, a mother authorizes her daughter by amplifying her daughter's voice with her own. Authorizing demonstrates to a daughter that her mother shares her view of reality enough to bring her weight to bear.

A mother cannot start too early, yet it is never too late to start authorizing a daughter's voice. Phoebe, at the age of three, climbed into bed with her mother and kissed her softly on the cheek. Patting her mother's face, Phoebe said, "I love you, Mommy." Emily, her mother, said, "I love you, too, Phoebe, and so does Daddy." "No," said Phoebe. "What do you mean?" asked Emily. "I know Daddy loves you very much." "I fears him, Mommy," she said with a solemn shake of her head. "He growls at me."

Emily knew that her husband was a growler, sometimes in play and sometimes when he was angry. She told her daughter that she thought they should tell her father. Taking her little daughter by the hand and leading her to her husband, Emily recalls, "I told him that his daughter had something to tell him and then I encouraged her to tell him what she had told me. I then said to him, in front of her, not to growl at her any more. Later, Frank and I talked about this—I told him again that he had to find some less harsh way to express his anger and frustration or he would hurt her and alienate her from him."

Emily authorizes her daughter to speak directly to her father, thus validating her daughter's sense that something is wrong with his treatment of her, and amplifying her daughter's voice by speaking to him herself. Emily has created space in which her daughter can be powerful and make change. Emily's authorization of Phoebe grounds her daughter in the reality of her experience. This mother authorizes her daughter by naming what she sees.

Overwhelmingly, the research on parenting shows that parents who are *authoritative,* rather than either *authoritarian* or *permissive,* raise children who can take care of themselves and confidently grow into responsible young adults. "I wanted my children to experience the consequences of their thinking from a young age," says Barbara. "So, for example, when they would see the sun shining and want to go outside without a jacket because they thought it was warm, I'd let them. They'd either come running back in or, at the worst, they'd get a cold. But they'd learn for themselves." By authorizing her daughters to learn from their experience and to develop their own base of experience in the world, she respects their authority. She also builds up their confidence in the rational basis of her authority. The respect for each other's authority and experience that they built together in childhood is standing Barbara in good stead now that her daughters are adolescents. As her daughters engage with things that their mother does not want them to experiment with themselves, they by and large trust that her warnings are about their welfare and not about her wish to control or thwart them. Barbara, as an authoritative mother, shows how power works through reason.

Within parts of the African-American community, mothers who might be considered authoritarian also produce responsible, assertive daughters. The community as a whole is embattled within a larger, racist context. Mothers explain this to their daughters from an early age. In addition, within segments of the African-American community, mothers are granted respect and authority that, by and large, non-African-American mothers are not. These mothers are recognized as fierce protectors of their children within a hostile, dangerous world around them.

When girls see their mothers as disempowered within a sexist culture where women compete against each other, they continually question their mothers' authority. Terri Apter observes, "Not only are mothers on the receiving end of far more criticism from their adolescent daughters, their authority is questioned in great detail, and under constant renegotiation." Just as a daughter questions her mother's "gender strategies" (the ways that she has negotiated being a woman—for example, Why did you ever marry him?) when exploring her own options and limits, a daughter questions her mother as a way of learning about negotiating with authority. The constant renegotiating that takes place between a daughter and her reasonable (and often exasperated) authoritative mother teaches a daughter that power doesn't have to come from position or status and that the exercise of authority benefits and empowers both people. Within a cultural context where women are subordinate, such a lesson gives girls tools to exercise power in nonarbitrary and nonauthoritarian ways.

Yet as many girls head into adolescence and begin to see how women lack authority and begin to hear how they, too, are supposed to behave, their ability to authorize themselves becomes imperiled. In Lyn Mikel Brown's original analysis of the interviews with the Laurel School girls, she saw that the second-grade girls gave their perceptions and feelings authority as well as looked to external authorities, such as mothers and teachers, for guidance. The tenth-grade girls found themselves confused about the appropriateness of their own feelings and granted others the power to judge them. The point at which girls' self-authorization begins to falter is seventh grade, age twelve. At this point, she observed,

> authorization takes a new turn for these twelve and thirteen year old girls as they ponder what aspect of themselves they will authorize, at least publicly, and what parts of themselves will they protect from judgment. The response to this question is in part expressed through their descriptions of themselves in relation to adult women, especially teachers and parents, as people who expect them to be always good and nice girls and who judge them according to this expectation. Thus it is safer and wiser to represent that part of themselves who never hurts others, who always helps, who observes closely and listens

intently for clues to people's feelings and needs, and to hide, and hence to protect, that part of themselves that has needs, fears, and wants—that part that they consider most valuable and at risk of being lost or endangered.

For mothers at this time, authorizing their daughters to use the full range of their voices is crucial to minimizing the loss of voice and self-esteem that occurs in early adolescence.

"Last year," begins Ruth, the mother of a seventh-grader,

Naomi struggled a lot with conflict over why she was being hurt by her peers' nastiness yet unable to be nasty back. This was Naomi the good girl—programmed into being the one everybody could count on to remain level-headed and nice. But she was suffering—and she did not have access to the voice that could tell other people to go f—— themselves when they deserved it. I saw incredible things—the whole vicious social game where girls don't think twice about stabbing their best friend in the back for a boy or anger directed and expelled at the easiest scapegoat as opposed to dealing with the real source of the anger and frustration. It was all unfolding like a dramatization but the players were sixth-grade children.

Ruth saw that her daughter was caught between her "good girl" upbringing, the expectations of everyone around her to continue to be good, and thoughts and feelings that Naomi couldn't even express.

I could see the pain this was causing her—she was getting headaches, she was demonstrating self-loathing, she was getting depressed. I knew what was happening. Carol Gilligan calls it "losing your voice." But I felt that Naomi never really had the voice she should have had. So I started to work on her. I gave her permission to get angry, to get pissed off at the appropriate objects—including myself. For the first time in Naomi's life, she was being allowed to and encouraged to let out strong negative emotions. We talked and talked and talked and have not stopped talking ever since.

Ruth connects Naomi's struggle with her own: "I'm afraid that much of my own emotional development was arrested at too early an age. I'm trying to catch up." By helping her daughter, she was able to help herself reclaim her own voice and power. Ruth's response to her daughter—giving her authority to name her anger, even at her mother—gives Naomi an even deeper lesson about the value of her voice.

Ruth and Naomi learned another lesson as Naomi began to break out of her "perfect girl" goodness. She was downgraded by a teacher not because her work had changed but because she was more outspoken and disagreed more in class. Ruth authorized Naomi by going to him and arguing on her behalf. "When I suspected that this kind of thing was operating in her teacher, Naomi and I talked about it, her teacher and I talked about it and all I can hope is that I sensitized him to the idea that people change, girls develop, their behavior changes, they process differently at thirteen than they did at eleven and a half, that Naomi should not be held to a higher standard than anybody else."

As Ruth says, she can "only hope" she was able to sensitize this teacher. In her statement lies the rub of authorizing one's daughter: authorizing can point out the *limits* of a woman's authority. What will it mean to Naomi if Ruth's authority as her mother is ignored or superseded by her teacher's authority? It will undoubtedly be a lesson to Naomi. But the depth of the lesson and its impact will depend in great part on Ruth. For her to maintain her authority, to use this incident as an example to Naomi that speaking with authority doesn't always work, can encourage Naomi's determination and her own authority. Naomi and other girls need to know that their perceptions and reality are not undermined by disagreement. The only way for her to learn this is to be able to speak in the face of differences and to fight for what she knows.

ACKNOWLEDGING DIFFERENCE

How a mother responds to a daughter's developing thoughts and feelings determines whether the daughter feels free to be her own unique self with her mother. Girls' growing ability to see themselves "from the outside" makes them more deeply aware of differences between themselves and others. They compare what they "should" be with who they are. Listening to learn gives daughters the space within their relationship with their mothers to present differences. By acknowledging difference, a mother teaches a way of loving voice that allows a daughter her autonomy, the ability to care for herself.

Mother daughter relationships traditionally have a double edge to the closeness. Daughters both trust and mistrust their mothers at the same time. Adolescent girls question whether a mother really knows them or not, yet they rely on mothers for advice and comfort, thus placing the relationship on emotional quicksand. Girls at adolescence often express concern about being "taken over" by their mothers and not being able to be "themselves" when with them. Because a girl usually has internalized her mother's voice from a very early age, the development of the girl's own unique inner voice at adolescence depends on the mother's ability to validate the daughter for who she is in her daughter's own terms. The "leave me alone" or "you don't understand me" of the adolescent girl signals that the mother is off target in her thinking about her daughter. Rather than being a sign of disengagement, such pronouncements warn that the mother is not hearing her daughter's perspective clearly enough for the daughter to feel listened to and understood. Girls hone their "selves" against their mothers. Each girl needs and wants to know that she is, and can be, different from her mother without losing her love.

Some mothers feel abandoned or rejected by their daughters at this point. For mothers who have not reclaimed their resistance, a relationship with a daughter brings back the closeness that they have longed for since their own adolescence. Frightened by their own experience with their mothers, they idealize their closeness with their adolescent daughters. Any threat to this "perfect" union is too dangerous because it once again isolates the mother from the kind of connection that she lost at her own adolescence and still longs for. Thus, some mothers go to great lengths to ignore or dismiss their daughters' difference. Often a daughter, sensing her mother's fragility, protects her mother from their differences, only to withdraw from her mother when gaining greater independence in adulthood.

What an adolescent girl sees within the family and explores for herself can be threatening to a mother's self-image as a mother and as a woman. At this point in a girl's development, a mother can be tempted to turn away: to let a daughter know that she cannot speak by setting up competitive dynamics within the family ("if you and your father think so much alike, then why don't you tell him all of this") or to ignore or put down what the daughter says.

While virtually every mother with whom we have spoken has wanted a different life for her daughter, a daughter's difference can feel like a pointed statement about a mother's choices. As girls see their mothers' choices and comment on them, they also proclaim that they are not going to make the same mistakes in their lives. "I'm not going to be so stupid as to fall for some guy who is a jerk just because he brings me flowers and chocolates," Victoria declared about her mother's "stupidity" in marrying her father. Her statement undoubtedly is difficult for her mother to hear.

Daughters' sharp eyes and tongues help them define themselves as different from their mothers. They aren't going to make the same stupid choices that their mothers made—whether the choice involved dependence on a man or the exhaustion of being a superwoman juggling career and family. Even when a mother most genuinely wants her daughter's life to be different, to be easier, than her own, it can be difficult for her not to gloat a little when a daughter's proclamations of difference get her into trouble.

"When I was in high school, I had a steady boyfriend for several years," says Deb. "My mother loved him. He was like the perfect guy. But I wouldn't get dressed up for him very much and I'd go out with my girlfriends, make them a priority. My mother seemed to appreciate my independence—I was determined not to become all dependent on a man the way she was." When this boy broke up with Deb in her senior year of high school, they "had a huge fight right before the prom," and Deb's mother was sympathetic. "I was crushed. He and I had been so close. My mother hugged me and told me that I'd be okay, that he was a jerk after all. But then she said something that made my insides recoil. 'And of course he'll find someone else right away who will want to dress up for him and be there for him.' I remember getting all cold inside."

Deb recognized that her mother was right—there are countless women who want nothing better than to make a man the center of their lives. "But it was her tone. She said that with a twist of glee in her voice. I'll never forget it. It was like she was saying, 'Yeah? You think you're so smart and are going to do things differently? Well, it ain't so easy, kid.'" Deb felt caught unawares and betrayed by her mother. Yet she and her mother had never had a straightforward conversation about her mother's choices, her strategies for survival.

Allowing for and being open to exploring differences in feelings and perspectives gives a girl safety to bring her explorations and questions into relationship with her mother. "Sometimes when we are talking about something, I will ask my daughters, 'What about this? You could look at this issue in this way'—something that they hadn't considered," says Claire. "I tell them that I want them to be able to think things through on their own, to be able to look at things in different ways so that they can really decide what they want and what they think. They know what and how I think about things. I want to know what they think and whether they consider different ways of looking at something as part of their thinking."

Claire makes different perspectives an explicit and important part of the discussions she and her daughters have about topics that are meaningful to them. In a recent conversation about abortion, she was concerned that her daughter had an opinion that was so close to her own that she pushed her to think the issue through from another perspective. She is less interested in having her daughters share her opinions than she is in having them be able to think things through.

We spoke in chapter 4 about mothers recognizing that many of their choices were survival strategies. Unfortunately, the world in which daughters are growing up is still not significantly different from their mothers': a mother's survival strategies are likely valid today. In fact, as it becomes more difficult to support a house and children on one income, pressure once again increases on women to align themselves with a male wage earner.

For a daughter, struggling against having her life defined by the romance legend is an important risk, one critical to her integrity. She desperately needs the support of other women, particularly her mother, to grow beyond conventional limits. While it is painful for a mother to have a daughter define herself by declaring her independence from her mother's survival strategies, it is critical to a girl's development that they enter into this conversation together, openly. A mother and daughter have the best chance to stay with each other through this period if a mother can share her ambivalence, her fears, and her experience with her daughter. This is why the process of reclaiming is so important for mothers. Reclaiming gives a mother the perspective and self-knowledge to be with a daughter more fully, to be her unambivalent ally in making her own different choices. As a mother's knowledge of the forces that shaped her own survival strategies become clearer, she can better acknowledge and accept the differences between herself and her daughter. This allows her daughter to have a separate and different outcome from her mother's life.

FIGHTING FOR CONNECTION

Anger, that signal of psychological trespass, changes dramatically as girls enter adolescence. Young girls know that fighting with friends is about connection, about bringing themselves—the whole range of their thoughts and feelings—fully into conversation (sometimes loud ones!) with each other. As Annie Rogers and Kate O'Neill write, preadolescent girls' "language of anger is very direct, and guttural exclamations are often used to express feelings. The girls make clear statements such as 'Sometimes I just go off stomping mad.' They also insist on speaking their anger: 'I have to say it out straight.' " As girls enter adolescence and discover their vulnerability in relation to boys' and men's greater physical power and greater propensity for violence, many girls send their anger and their ability to defend themselves underground.

These girls report that the women in their lives teach them that fighting is wrong and that good girls are always nice and kind, perfect girls. This standard of niceness, coupled with the potential danger of being angry in a male world, eviscerates women's anger. What girls need to know is how to fight, not *not to fight at all*. Some African-American and some working-class girls are encouraged to stand up for themselves and to fight when necessary. "You betta learn to open up your mouth and speak for yourself," Beverly Jean Smith reports having heard from the aunts who raised her. "Stand up for yourself. Don't go around here poutin'. Say somethin' to somebody. We can't help if we don't know. Don't let nobody mistreat you." Beverly was clear that her aunts included themselves there, too; Beverly and her sister were not to let their aunts or anyone else mistreat them. But for many middle-class mothers, teaching daughters about voice and fighting typically means that mothers have to begin by reclaiming their direct anger and learning how to fight.

Not only do we live in a culture that is shaped by male violence, but self-control and self-discipline have become cultural dictates. This means that emotional outbursts are not acceptable, are bad, or somehow show weakness. But as many young girls have noted and explained, when feelings are held in, they burst out all the louder at some later point, often indirectly. The only exception is male anger, which society condones because it is "manly" and the result of the "burdens" men carry. But in general, displaying emotion is a sign of sentimentality and foolishness, of "being a girl," which is supposed to be a nasty slur for men and women. "I can't fight," many women have said, "because I cry and then I look stupid and can't say anything." Fighting through the tears, letting out what has—too often—been held in too long, is fundamental to freeing voice.

Teaching girls that fighting and crying and yelling are part of strength, not shame, can be one of the most powerful voice lessons a woman could give a girl. As Terri Apter states, "But it isn't calm, unobtrusive relations between mother and daughter that give the daughter the strength she needs. It is a good fighting relationship, a relationship through which the daughter can define her differences."

Bonnie acknowledges, "I'm a strong personality. You have to be pretty strong to go up against me. But what my daughters have learned is that I will listen. I may have my own strong opinions and feelings, but I will listen to them and what they think and feel." Her daughters will go toe to toe with Bonnie when they disagree strongly with her. When girls are prevented by the code of goodness and perfection from learning how to work through conflicts within their relationships, they are prepared only for victimization.

Sometimes when the mother herself is in a threatening and powerless situation, typically through emotional or physical abuse at the hands of her partner, a daughter does not feel that it is safe enough to disagree with her mother. Their situation is too threatening to the mother to support a daughter's difference from her mother. The mother's need for support in the face of her own victimization creates a climate in which the daughter will often do anything that she can to "be there" for her mother. A reverse mothering takes place where the daughter tries to listen and counsel her mother.

Marta, at sixteen, feels deeply conflicted in her relationship with her mother, who is abused by her father; she describes her mother's screaming at her about the situation and feels her mother's feelings "gnawing at her." Marta tries not to be a problem for her mother and encourages her mother to leave her father. Encouraged by her daughter's concern and openness, and often with nowhere else to go, the mother takes the daughter into her life as her confidante. On the surface, this relationship may look extremely close. But closer scrutiny often reveals that the daughter's voice has been subverted into a backup chorus of her mother's voice. The daughter speaks to give advice to the mother and to present a perspective that supports the mother and the mother's existing ideas of the daughter. Oddly enough though, this close surface relationship often covers deep disconnection between mother and daughter. By naming this pattern and teaching a daughter to fight with her, a mother can give her daughter the lessons she needs to fend for herself in the world.

Fighting with daughters has certain unspoken rules, as should any fair verbal fight. Both mother and daughter should be held to these rules. The cardinal rule is not to humiliate or belittle the other. Comments about a daughter's looks, weight, or physical changes, for an adolescent girl in particular, are sources of deep humiliation. "My mother wouldn't get angry with me," says Sharon. "She would just make snide comments about my weight. When I'd complain, she'd act as though she was just trying to help me. It was really nasty."

The safest ground to stay on is to take responsibility by explaining the effect that another's behavior has on oneself:

When you do that I feel . . . because I know/think/feel . . .

When you keep asking for things instead of going to sleep, I get angry because even though I know that going to sleep is scary for you, I need some time at night for myself.

When you talk back to me like that, I feel hurt because I feel that you don't care about what I say.

When you lie to me about where you are going, I get worried sick because, even though you are capable and responsible, I figure that

*if you are lying to me then you are doing something dangerous or
you'd tell me.*

Going back and forth, allowing feelings to be brought out and expressed, and realizing the deep impact we have on each other are powerful
voice lessons. Such fighting gives a daughter information about the consequences of her actions within relationship. It also helps her to realize
the powerful effect she has on others and, thus, is enormously validating.

As we have said, voice lessons are just that: lessons. Anger and disagreement are learning opportunities for both mother and daughter. For a
mother who doesn't know how to express her anger and strong feelings
directly, or who finds it too painful to hear her daughter speak directly,
talking about that is the right beginning. "Any time I disagreed with my
mother, she would start to cry," says Michelle. "I could never say what I
felt because she would get so hurt and I'd feel like a monster." Michelle's
mother has created enough space in the relationship that her daughter can
speak about what she feels, but her mother's overwhelming feelings (probably related to her own fears of abandonment) stop their dialogue.

Many women feel hurt when their daughters fight with them, or they
don't know how to tell their daughters that they are angry with them.
Saying that, and describing angry feelings, not necessarily right as they
happen but afterwards, is good practice. Michelle's mother could have
gone to her daughter later and said, "When you disagree with me, I feel
bad but it's important that we keep trying." Or "I don't know how to
fight—I never learned. But I am really angry about . . ." The more
mothers and daughters try to discuss their differences and talk honestly,
the stronger their connection. One of the paradoxes of human relationships is that the very things that we are most frightened of saying because
we are afraid that they will lead to our abandonment (Oh, *that's* what you
think; well, then, I don't love you) are the things that keep us from deeper
and more intimate connection with each other and with the world.

Teaching daughters to fight will be a bumpy road. Sometimes the bigger bumps will make mothers "lose it." There are, however, voice lessons for daughters in "losing it." All of us can be expected to get pushed over the edge from time to time. "I remember crying and screaming that I didn't want to be here with them anymore, that it was driving me crazy," recalls Faith, a single mother to two little girls. "I felt terrible afterwards— the look on their faces was like a knife in my heart. But I talked to them, told them that I love them, and that when I have a lot of work to do I say things that I don't mean. I let them tell me how they felt, how scary it was. We cried together. I watched to see if they were tiptoeing around me for the next few days, and would talk to them, reassure them." While "I'm not perfect" shouldn't be a constant refrain or excuse for thoughtlessness, when women "lose it" (whatever "it" is), they show girls that they don't have to be perfect, that they can be vulnerable and angry and sad and human.

Susan, the mother of two girls in early adolescence, recalls with some embarrassment a particular incident. "Just last week, so it's fresh in my mind, I completely lost it—screaming, crying, raving, the works. I apologized and told them what had been going on for me. Afterwards my older daughter came to me and told me that she hated it when I lost it like that. She said, 'I think of you as someone who is so strong, that when you lose it, I get really scared—how can I keep it together if you can't?' " Afterward, Susan realized with concern that her daughter pushed herself to have it all together all of the time.

As Judith says, "I think it's important for my kids to see that I can lose it, but in an hour or a day or a few days, I'm back together again. I'll say, 'Mommy's losing it; I need some time alone and I'll be okay.' I think it allows them to see that you can feel those feelings and be okay—maybe even be better than before." Letting our daughters see that losing it— without violence—is all right teaches them that they can safely voice their rage and frustration and grief without disintegrating, being abandoned, or losing relationship.

TRUTH TELLING

What can women allow their daughters to know about their lives? The response to this question is both simple and complex; in a word, the truth. Teaching a daughter the truth by telling the truth about women's lives is a powerful voice lesson. Yet what is the "truth"?

"An honorable human relationship," writes Adrienne Rich, "that is, one in which two people have the right to use the word 'love'—is a process, delicate, violent, often terrifying to both persons involved, a process of redefining the truths they can tell each other." Truth and love are both processes, not static states. "It is important to do this," she continues, "because it breaks down human self-delusion and isolation. It is important to do this because in so doing we do justice to our own complexity. It is important to do this because we can count on so few people to go that hard way with us." For daughters to have mothers they "can count on . . . to go that hard way" with them, they have to enter together into truth telling.

One of the most dangerous lessons girls have traditionally learned from women is false-etto: how to pitch one's voice high to deny one's deeper, and perhaps darker, feelings. Carla, in eighth grade, says that she can tell that her teacher is playing favorites in math class because, when the teacher moves from a favored student to an unfavored student, "she changes her voice, like you can tell." As women move to protect their feelings and thoughts from their daughters—essentially move out of relationship with them—their facial and vocal expressions teach girls how to cover feelings with falseness. These dangerous lessons have been key to girls' learning how to dissociate and dissemble. Women hide anger and upset with raised eyebrows, wide eyes (Who me?), and a voice that quivers an octave above its normal range: I'm fine, really! Girls hear the false-etto and realize that women cannot be trusted.

At these points of denial, women shut girls out of their feelings and their worlds. They can try to keep pushing women into the truth or, if they have had enough experience to know that a particular woman does

169

not want to know, they will turn away. What girls see and feel anger about are the ways in which mothers conceal the truths of their lives and present a false, smiling face that warns girls to conform. A girl will feel betrayed by a mother who lies about her happiness and insists on the same route for her daughter. Girls basically want what women have wanted in relationship: honesty, directness, respect, response, and responsibility.

Girls in adolescence are walking lie detectors. They can spot phoniness and hypocrisy from a mile off. Lonni, the mother of twelve-year-old Melinda, was in the middle of divorcing her husband. One Sunday, at the end of the church service, Lonni nudged Melinda and said, "Let's leave quickly. I don't want to stay around because people, kind as they mean it, will put their hands on my arms and look into my eyes and ask soulfully, 'How *are* you?'" With quick recognition, Melinda agreed, "Yes, I hate that." Surprised, Lonni asked, "They're doing that to you, too?" "No," said her daughter, "but you do it all the time, and I know how it feels." Just as Lonni appreciated her friends' concern but didn't need their soulful looks of pity, Melinda also wanted concern, but not pity that robs her of respect, which then doesn't feel like real concern. Those very things that women complain about in relationships with others are what rub girls the wrong way in relationships with women. Their age often belies their sophistication about the dynamics of honest relationship.

Knowing that daughters are relationally sophisticated is important for lesbians who have to face telling daughters the truth about their own sexual orientation. Daughters who have known lesbian parenting throughout their lives begin to deal early and often with having two "mommies." Women who choose women later in life have a different reality. It takes courage to talk to girls honestly about an oppression that is so deep and painful, and that holds the possibility of losing a daughter through the courts or through a daughter's own choice and confusion. When Jeanette told her early adolescent daughter about her decision to live with a woman, her daughter's first response was concern: "Wouldn't it be easier for you to live with a man?" Jeanette acknowledged the difficulty of her choice in a heterosexist world both for herself and her daughter. But she also talked to her daughter about how respectful and loving relationships themselves are our challenge, no matter the gender of a partner. In this way, Jeanette created an opportunity to teach about both sexuality and love.

Mothers can tell the truth about their own struggles and admit to the strategies that they have used, even though these truths often feel painful or shameful. Mothers can claim their reality as their own and not as the destiny of their daughters. "I tell my daughters that I have struggled all my life with my dependence on men," says Barbara. "They see it. I'm not proud of it. They dress me down when my dependence affects my judgment about them. I've told them I was raised to be emotionally dependent, and I wish that weren't true, but it is. Just the fact that they have lived with my dependence, grown up with it, makes this also a tough place for them. But I am clear that they are living in different times and growing up differently than I did. They don't have to be dependent—certainly not the way I am."

For a mother to admit to her own struggles and to place it in the context of her own life within her generation of women can give girls the freedom to make different choices than she did. Telling her truths can also better enable a daughter to listen to learn from her mother because her mother respects the daughter's different situation.

Truth telling about struggles is different from confiding in daughters. Telling the truth doesn't mean telling everything that is or has gone on in a mother's life. By allowing a daughter to initiate conversations through her questioning of a mother's choices or her struggle to figure out her own life, a mother can keep her truth telling bounded and resist the temptation to confide in her curious and concerned daughter. When girls ask about aspects of a mother's life that feel too close (such as details of a mother's relationship with her partner), a mother can respond by saying, truthfully, that she isn't comfortable talking about this with her daughter. Even further, if a daughter is pointing out a place where the mother has capitulated or is unresolved, a mother can also admit that this place in her life is hard for her without confiding in her daughter about intimate details or engaging her to find a solution.

Providing a daughter with a mother's context gives a daughter permission to be a part of her generation and to resolve conflicts differently. "I think that one of the things that enabled me to consider my life in different terms than my mother," Paula notes, "is that I went away to a fancy college on scholarship and my mother's advice—coming from her working-class life—couldn't hold for me. Even though my mother insisted that her lot in life was the lot of woman, I was able to, well, kind of hold the question open because I was moving into a world far away from my mother's life." Rather than being given this space as a gift from her mother, Paula took it for herself.

Truth telling, too, takes practice. It starts with where a woman is right now: with her uncertainty or clarity, her love and anger, her frustration and pride. Truth telling is a way of speaking from experience—*this happened to me*—rather than from opinion. Truth telling fits nicely with listening to learn because it is a gift of one's self. When a mother responds, after breathing in and learning from her daughter's words, with the truth of her own experience (with the recognition that they are living in different times), a dialogue develops that allows for call and response, and expands the truths that mothers and daughters share.

SMART SPEAK/SMART MOUTHS

"What I'm concerned about," said Susan, "is what you do when your daughter is holding on to her voice, when she hasn't given it up, and she's getting herself into trouble because she won't *not* speak out." Susan told the story of her daughter, Alison, who has read newspaper articles about girls losing their voices at adolescence. Alison is determined not to get wiped out and has become very assertive. "She is in a battle with her history teacher, who is not a very bright guy," says Susan. "He told the class some misinformation about the Holocaust, and my daughter corrected him. She keeps challenging him in class. And I think now that he's out to get her."

While Susan will join her daughter and go to school to talk with this man, she has an ongoing concern with teaching her daughters the politics of voice. Girls who speak out are often considered troublemakers. "If Alison were a boy, I don't think he'd be half as upset," notes Susan. "He would consider a boy to be showing off how smart he is, and he'd show his grudging approval, but with a girl, I think it is too threatening—a girl isn't supposed to be this smart." Susan is trying to teach her daughter that voice is political and that silence can be a choice. Sharmaine, a fifteen-year-old, told a chilling story of having a gun pulled on her by a young male peer: "I started screaming at him and told him never to do that foolish shit to me. Stop waving that thing in my face." Sharmaine was lucky, although she, too, called the situation correctly—this time. Teaching girls to have voice does not mean letting them "voice" themselves into getting shot or flunked. Girls who speak out are often considered smart mouths; women can teach them to speak smart.

For mothers, members of another generation, it can be difficult to know exactly where the real risks are for a daughter. "My daughter has a *mouth*," says Ingrid. "I think it's great but it also scares me. We were in the car the other day, and some guy pulled up beside us and made some disgusting comment. Well, Cara just let him have it—she told him where to get off in the foulest terms. I thought, Oh my god! She's going to get herself killed for that mouth of hers." Yet Cara may have accurately assessed the risks in the situation. But Ingrid is uncomfortable because she doesn't know whether her daughter voices these things in situations where she might be more at risk. Furthermore, while Ingrid was raised to believe that cursing at men who make violating remarks is too dangerous to contemplate, her daughter goes to a school where she has to stand up for herself and tell boys where they can shove it.

By naming the political realities of being female in male worlds and discussing these different realities, mothers and daughters gain a chance to discuss strategies with each other. Within this process is further opportunity for mothers to reclaim voice and to rethink what can and cannot be said aloud within patriarchy. Girls can learn that they can use silence to their advantage when they are aware of why they are not speaking, why silence makes sense. Mothers may learn to speak out in public more often. The point is to make conscious choices, rather than being silenced or always "mouthing off." To teach daughters to feel the full power of mind, body, and spirit and yet to be conscious of where and how they speak allows girls the power to maintain voice within patriarchy.

VOICE LESSONS

As we women learn to listen and listen to learn, we discover how our own voices and lives have been shaped. Our daughters learn from us and we from them. This ongoing process of learning, of reclaiming self-knowledge and courage, is a deep act of love. As Adrienne Rich said, love is "a process of redefining the truths" we can tell each other. Love as defined and glorified by patriarchy rises out of the ashes of loss: the act of loving grasps for an idealized replacement of what was lost. This futile search for the perfect love who won't ever leave, abandon, or disappoint blinds us to the realities and truths of those whom we want so much to love and be loved by.

Mothers' collision with the wall of adolescence leaves them so frightened of losing their daughters that they idealize their closeness and deny difference with their daughters. The free flow of feeling from mother to daughter and daughter to mother becomes frozen and stuck within idealized notions of closeness and self-critical demands for perfection. And when the relationship inevitably proves imperfect, daughters, ironically, are left feeling unknown and unloved, and abandoned. Voice lessons, by providing a practice of knowing and being known, keep mother daughter relationships grounded in the truths of both mothers' and daughters' experience.

No matter how alike or close a mother and daughter may be, they are different people. Real love, as opposed to the so-called true love of romance, arises from knowing another individual fully in her own terms, not as we would have her be. Acknowledging difference and fighting for connection across difference are essential to a fluid love that allows both mother and daughter to know each other authentically.

Voice lessons lay the foundation for a true joining between mother and daughter that insulates a daughter from the hazards of disconnection at the wall of the culture. They give space for a daughter's voice and concerns in what is, for girls, a relationship of unequal power. Joining, grown out of a love based in knowledge and personal truth, brings love into social action by mothers on behalf of and in concert with daughters. Joining with daughters, the next strategy of resistance, continues the creation of an authentic relationship not based on self-negation and servitude. The goal is the mutual empowerment of mother and daughter.

6

Joining

And women in turn, taking in girls' embodiment, their outspokenness
and their courage, may encourage girls' desire for relationship and for
knowledge and teach girls that they can say what they know and not
be left all alone.

Carol Gilligan
"JOINING THE RESISTANCE"

In March 1992, mothers and daughters gathered at Wellesley College to
explore what mothers could do about the sexism that is rampant in
schools. A small group of mothers and daughters sat in a circle, sharing
stories, as part of a workshop about "The Hidden Curriculum"—violence
against girls in schools. One woman told of mobilizing mothers to join her
and her daughter in confronting sexual harassment by male teachers in her
daughter's high school. The daughter explained that she was touched inap-
propriately by a male teacher. The girls in school all knew about this man,

176

she says, but no one had ever complained. She decided that this time he was not going to get away with it, and so she told her mother.

Outraged by her daughter's story, the mother immediately called the mother of another girl who had also been harassed by this man. To the first mother's surprise, the other mother hemmed and hawed before finally explaining that her daughter was doing really well in this man's class and that, well, she just didn't want to upset things by confronting this man.

The daughter in this story has not disappeared into the silence of good girlhood: she's a resister. Trusting her own experience, she confronted the teacher—a man with the power to grade and to name her as crazy or foolish or wrong. Her mother joined her daughter and honored her daughter's voice. Her mother authorized her daughter to speak the truth of her experiences. She did not trivialize the experience or force her daughter to disconnect from her own sense of the event's importance. She didn't take the matter out of her daughter's hands or assume that her daughter should handle this situation by herself. She was her daughter's ally; she used her authority to take action and join with other women to organize for change.

While reclaiming is an ongoing process for mothers and voice lessons lay the foundation of a knowing, responsive love between mothers and daughters, joining connects mothers and daughters as they explore and confront the world around them. Joining with daughters protects them from the separations of the culture and creates a balanced relationship. Joining has as its goal the empowerment of both mother and daughter.

Conventional wisdom and traditional developmental theory both suggest that mothers can best support their adolescent daughters by separating from them. At a time when their daughters' experiences may be reviving painful memories of their own adolescence, distancing from the apparent source of the pain holds an understandable appeal for mothers, especially when they are told that this is the right thing to do. By resisting that impulse and contradicting the advice, mothers have an opportunity to mitigate the trauma of growing up female in a hostile environment. Connection, not separation, keeps girls strong and whole. With love, integrity, and dogged persistence, women can stay in relationship with girls through adolescence.

Joining with a daughter against patriarchy allows for the close, confiding relationship from which a girl's resilience grows. As we have said, the crisis of adolescence is a crisis of connection. Within this culture, many girls find that they must turn to men for protection and love in order to survive as women. Whether or not girls take the proffered path of romance, they are asked to give up some part of themselves as the price of becoming a woman. The trauma of this initiation into womanhood diminishes when girls have real company for their journey. By joining, a mother maintains her connection with her daughter and provides an antidote to separation. A daughter's powerful early identification with her mother can be a wellspring of self-esteem and strength to thwart the development of the punitive, perfectionistic Fury.

ENTERING PATRIARCHY TOGETHER

The messages of patriarchal culture to separate, to disrespect and blame mothers, and to enter the romance story swirl in and around every girl and woman. Billboards, magazines, television, and movies carry a subtext that the way to success is to separate from women and connect with men. Out of the mouths of a daughter's friends come the words of the culture: "Your mother just wants you to be her little girl—she won't let you have your freedom." Needing or accepting support is, too often, confused with dependence. American cultural icons of rugged individualism, like the Marlboro Man, celebrate solitary effort over collective action. This is truly a myth. No one does anything completely alone. In women's alliances with girls, women's role is not to rescue but to bear witness or exert power on girls' behalf, and to strive to live powerfully. As Alice said, "My mom's so cool. She'll say, 'What happened? What do you want? If that's what you really want, then tell everyone to look out—here we come! No one's going to stop my girls from getting what they want!' "

Bonnie remembers when her oldest daughter, Alethea, began to pay attention to these cultural messages—borne by Alethea's friends. "She was out with her friends and had told me that she would be at one friend's house when actually she was going elsewhere," recalls Bonnie. Remembering her own similar deceits as a girl, Bonnie recognized such lying as part of her own pulling away from her mother. " 'Stop!' is basically what I said to her," laughs Bonnie. " 'I am not your enemy—I want you to grow up and have your freedom.' I told her that I loved her and she didn't have to lie to me or shut me out to become a woman and to have more space." Bonnie told Alethea that she wouldn't restrict her unfairly, which was what Alethea's friends felt that their mothers were doing. While Bonnie doesn't think her daughter really understood what she was asking of her, Bonnie persisted. "When it happened again, I told her again," she says. "I told her that what upset me was being shut out—being cut off from her would kill me. It only happened twice and then she got it." Bonnie promised to listen fully to Alethea and to be fair with her. Alethea promised to be honest with her mother. By actively struggling to keep their promises, they have nurtured a vibrant connection with each other.

Girls also need an ally in their mothers as they enter a peer culture that, from grade school through high school, is often the arena for brutal power games. Girls' brutal social machinations are excruciatingly painful to mothers, as they can only witness what was undoubtedly painful for themselves while being powerless to do anything. A girl must have close friends (although one preadolescent girl reported that her mother told her that not being best friends with anyone would protect her from the abuses of cliques).

In the seventh grade, none of Gloria's close friends are assigned to her class, but the "popular" kids are. Shyly, Gloria begins to make friends with Kathy. Their budding friendship draws the attention of one of the leaders of the clique, Mary, who designs a plan to keep the established order in place. Mary has noticed that Scott, who inhabits the fringes of the clique, seems to like Gloria. Strategically, Mary pulls different members of the group into a plan to interest Kathy in Scott and to shift Scott's interest from Gloria to Kathy. Relying on Scott's desire to move from the fringe to the center of the clique, and on Kathy's induced jealousy, Mary succeeds in isolating Gloria. The coup de grace is a letter to Gloria written by Mary and signed by everyone in the class, including Scott and Kathy, detailing all the reasons why Gloria is disliked. Mary, backed up by a group of snickering cohorts, personally delivers the letter. Gloria is devastated. Haltingly she relates only small bits of her story to her mother. Her mother is shocked by the meanness of it all, but her first response is a question: "Did you do anything to these kids? Sometimes you're a little too smart for your own good." Stunned, Gloria answers, "No . . . I, mean, I don't think so. No!" "You can't let people treat you that way," her mother responds. Then, seeing her daughter's tears, she pulls Gloria to her in a comforting embrace. Gloria says nothing. She has not been asked to say anything.

In a well-meaning and probably frightened response to her daughter's obvious distress, this mother doesn't try to find out exactly what happened, what Gloria would like to have happen, what she, as her mother, can do. Instead, she subtly blames her daughter for her trouble by asking whether she has done anything to bring it on herself. Through naming and explaining the violence being visited on Gloria, and exploring with her what she wants to do, Gloria's mother would have begun to join her daughter in the face of her daughter's classmates' cruel, competitive exercise of power. By helping her devise a plan to deal with the aftermath of this painful incident and identify ways Gloria could defend herself from future onslaughts, Gloria might have reclaimed her own power and her own ability to fend for herself.

From a girl's first contact with the outside world—from television and child care through her contacts with peer culture and school—she needs an ally to join her as she enters patriarchy. "I couldn't bear for my daughter to have a Barbie doll," says Belle, "but she wanted one so much —and all of her friends had them. I told her relatives that I couldn't bring myself to buy her one but she seemed to need one. On her next birthday, she got five." Sandra, Belle's daughter, played with her Barbie dolls— "they look like Mommy"—to explore what women do. Joining a daughter in inventing explorations for Barbie, rather than leaving her to the mercy of Ken in the Barbie Dream House, gives a young girl new stories to explore.

"My daughters wanted to watch that television show 'Beverly Hills 90210,'" said Susan with a roll of her eyes.

My first reaction was to say, "NO! That's trash! I won't allow it." But they really wanted to. All of their friends saw it and, the day after the show each week, it was the topic of conversation all day long. I knew that they would be painfully excluded if they weren't part of it. So, I made it a family thing. The three of us watch it together every week. I comment and ask questions like—"Don't you think that she could do something more interesting than that? Does she just wait around for the boys all the time?" Gradually, they have started to make comments, too—"How could she just go along with him?" I see that they are looking critically at the show. They aren't just taking it in as though it was simply cool. And we have fun watching together. I think this was a really important lesson for them and for me, as a mother.

Susan enters into her daughters' world. Rather than condemning the culture that her girls are puzzling out (and making it even more alluring), Susan joins her daughters, explores what they think, and offers her own thoughts and feelings. Her stance is profoundly respectful.

"When my daughter Dottie decided that she was going to enter the Miss San Antonio beauty contest, I thought, well, I could lay across the driveway and block the car," laughs Mae, a feminist activist. "But I realized that wouldn't do any good. So I went and supported her, smiled and clapped. I have to admit, though, I was relieved that she didn't win." Mae, too, joins in with her daughter's interests. Mae discussed her views on beauty pageants with Dottie, but her daughter really wanted to compete in the talent contest and find out what being judged in front of a big audience would be like. Respecting Dottie's need to know, Mae joined her. Perhaps by jumping into such an arena of men's desires (in a bathing suit, no less), Mae's daughter was testing the roughest waters she could find. If she could survive and withstand such a display, then she knew she'd be all right. Mae says of her daughters, "They were good strong girls and I was a 'loose' mother in terms of trying to make them turn out a certain way, and they turned out good."

These women recognize the ways that the culture coerces emotional distance between mothers and daughters and among women themselves. They avoid unnecessary separations between themselves and their daughters that come from forcing a girl to choose between her mother and her peers, her own exploration of the world and her mother's politics, or her self-esteem and her mother's esteem for her. Aware of the needs and desires of their daughters to be with friends and to know about popular culture, these mothers can have fun and join in with their daughters' explorations. By exploring the expressions of patriarchy through a daughter's curiosity, a mother earns her daughter's trust—a trust that will stand them both in good stead when issues arise that involve greater risk. These women bring their own sensibility and concerns to their joining with their daughters, but they do not invalidate or devalue their daughters' interests. Real self-esteem in girls is not forged by "the passive passing down of the mother's self-image," writes Terri Apter, "but by the support she offers or fails to offer the daughter to build her own self-esteem."

A mother demonstrates faith in her daughter by willingly following her daughter's lead, even when the mother "knows better." Through this joining and entering the culture together, these mothers support their daughters and give them the opportunity to develop self-esteem and a respect for their own thinking.

REINTERPRETING

As women join with girls and as they enter the culture together, the women need to provide the girls with information and analysis to sharpen the girls' perspectives and hone the double vision that allows them to see the truth of women's experience in male culture. At the same time, women can help girls learn how to avoid unnecessary risks and undue danger.

The domination of white male privilege is never so complete that it doesn't allow for some measure of freedom, the freedom to see and name what we see, what feminist theorist and critic bell hooks calls "the oppositional gaze." Because of the "circumstances of domination," women of color, working-class women, and lesbians often have a defiantly illuminating oppositional gaze. Mothers can reinterpret the world for their daughters so that they learn about external and internal oppression. "Interpreting to a little girl or to an adolescent woman," argues Adrienne Rich, "the kind of treatment she encounters because she is female, is as necessary as explaining to a nonwhite child reactions based on the color of her skin."

Pearl Cleage, an author, performance artist, and single mother of a daughter, describes how her parents provided "a kind of sepia tone simulcast" to the nightly news. The "newsguy" comes on and says something critical about Patrice Lumumba, and the simulcast begins. Directing her remarks to the screen, Pearl's mother reminds the newscaster that the Belgians used to threaten to cut off the hands of captured Africans in order to terrorize them into being slaves. In the next story, he says something sketchy about the reasons for a violent crime wave in the black community. This time Pearl's stepfather fills in all the missing pieces, providing a full context of racism and its results, and ends by wondering aloud who put this fool on the air anyway.

Pearl's family educated her in the politics of racism, as most families of color do for their children. "By the time I was eight or nine," she explains, "I understood clearly that slavery and racism had created a complex set of circumstances that impacted daily on my life as an African American. Factors such as where I lived, how I lived, what job I could get, how clean the grocery stores were in my neighborhood, the probability that I'd get robbed and raped were all in some way circumscribed by the presence of white racism." Most of this teaching was taught in her home as an integral part of daily life and as a way to "filter the complex racial stimuli she received from books, teachers and the media. . . . These African American survival lessons were part of the fabric of family; expected, accepted and continuous." Pearl credits these survival lessons with her ability to be an authority in her life about being black, and by extension, about everything else. She says, "This self-confidence and clarity grew directly out of my racial self-awareness," providing "an oppressed person's most potent weapons: information, analysis and positive group identity."

Lena, an African-American mother in Iowa, describes her own simulcast activities with her eleven-year-old daughter. "I ask her questions all the time about what she's learning, what's happening with her friends. I'm always looking for what information she's getting and how it may need to be cast in the light of racism." This mother seeks information about the potentially racist context of her daughter's life so that she can analyze and provide her daughter with the knowledge that she needs to resist internalizing racist oppression.

For girls to maintain their double vision through adolescence, they need, as Pearl Cleage had, "information, analysis and positive group identity." Most women, however, even many feminists, lack knowledge about the extraordinary heritage of women. Stories of women fighting for their liberation and the liberation of working people and of the oppressed are only now being included in history and social studies texts. Women who were raised on idealized and sanitized biographies of pioneering nurse Florence Nightingale or Red Cross founder Clara Barton have not had access to works on such women as journalist Ida Wells, civil rights leader Fannie Lou Hamer, abolitionist and women's suffrage leader Susan B. Anthony, or abolitionist and women's rights activists Sarah and Angelina Grimké. These women may find themselves learning about women's heritage from their daughters' schoolbooks.

Even without the knowledge of the trials and triumphs of women, mothers can echo a daughter's cry "It's not fair!" in a more sophisticated way by pointing to the differences in expectations, opportunities, and roles for women as reflected in the world around them. "My daughter's only five," says Francie, "but whenever we read or watch television, I point out who is excluded from the picture. Already, she's coming to me, saying, 'Mom, look, there are no girls in this story,' or, 'How come there are no black people here?'"

"At some point," recalls Myra, "I realized that every time a commercial came on, all the children looked at me. I hadn't even been aware of it, but I was continually irreverent about commercials showing women dressed up doing housework and smiling, selling cars, modeling clothes posed in positions that would have broken a normal woman's back. I think they began to look forward as much to my version of commercials as any produced by the products. I never considered that I was instructing my children in sexism—but I was." Myra remembers that her daughter, in junior high, brought her a poem that her teacher had used to illustrate a kind of rhyme scheme, and she had complained about it: "Never give a woman money,/for it's sure to harm you./Even though she calls you honey,/never give a woman money." All of the other illustrations of rhyme involved validating stories of boys or men; this was the one that included a woman.

Myra's reinterpretation is humorous but pointed. While she doesn't provide her children with facts about sexism, she helps her children see the difference between the commercial version of motherhood and the reality. Finding ways to make fun of Superwoman expectations or model-thin perfection gives girls ways to become wise about the world. They then can learn that what they see and hear in the media is not to be taken as real. This, as the work of psychologist Catherine Steiner-Adair reminds us, may help girls to resist eating disorders. Humor like Myra's is an extraordinary tool because it robs the images of perfect womanhood of their power to make girls and women feel bad about themselves.

These mothers provide their children with the tools of reinterpretation, and the opportunities for reinterpreting sexist portrayals are, unfortunately, endless. As Gloria Steinem documented in *Revolution from Within*, "One study of books from fourteen U.S. publishers found that, in the process of learning to read, a little girl is exposed to more boy-centered stories than girl-centered stories by a ratio of five to two, to folk and fantasy tales with four times more male characters, and to biographies that are six times more likely to profile males than females. Even animal stories are twice as likely to feature male animals."

If "boys are twice as likely to be seen as model students and praised by teachers, five times more likely to receive a teacher's attention, and eight to twelve times more likely to speak up in class," as U.S. and British researchers found in one cross-cultural study, daughters need women to support a gender analysis and reinterpretation of this unfairness. Mothers who have been successful reinterpreters talk to their daughters about how women have been socialized to value men and how the priority that men and boys are given is not a comment on their abilities as girls, but a societal problem. It's not fair, *yet.* By reinterpreting the world through the daily lens of being different and helping girls not to personalize oppression, these families create space for the possibility of change in a world that could otherwise seem too vast and immutable to girls growing up in it.

If sexism is as dangerous a threat to girls as racism and homophobia, the question is: Can we women—as mothers and teachers—take sexism seriously enough to follow the model of Pearl Cleage's parents and begin our own "feminist simulcast" of the world for the sake of having daughters who trust their own authority, as Pearl Cleage does? Undoubtedly, her parents educated themselves about the history of slavery and oppression—

such information is not widely available in most schools. Neither is information about women's persistent and courageous struggle against sexism available in public schools.

Even women who have been educated in the most prestigious academies do not know about the history of sexism, about the length of time it took for women to get the right to vote and to be educated, or about the many other rights there are to fight for. Adrienne Rich, in addressing the 1979 commencement at Smith College, an elite college for women, stated quite plainly that "there is no women's college today which is providing young women with the education they need for survival as whole persons in a world which denies women wholeness." She suggests "that not anatomy, but forced ignorance, has been a crucial key to our powerlessness." Gloria Steinem addresses the importance of "un-learning" the implicit schooling about women's "place" that is swallowed whole through the words and discoveries of legions of men.

"Even short-term exposure to the past experience of women," observed the historian Gerda Lerner, "has the most profound psychological effect on women participants." Women's history changes women's lives by giving women the knowledge that undergirds a positive group identity. Time for mothers is always at a premium. How can mothers learn about women's history without adding to their list of "shoulds" and "to dos"? Some women have tried reading and discussing short selections—perhaps an essay by Adrienne Rich or by Alice Walker, or a short story—with friends at work during lunch breaks. National Women's History Month in March provides a flurry of free events and information. Claire decided to take time out for herself one night a week to go back to school. Bonnie also went back to school, but before she did, she found herself looking at her daughters' books and reading along with the girls. "My daughters learned more in school about women than I ever did—they taught me." Giving a daughter the power to teach a mother about their shared history allows both mother and daughter to contradict sexism, and the daughter to enhance her sense of competency.

Yet sexism differs from racism, classism, and homophobia in some critical ways that have made it difficult for women to be comfortable reinterpreting within their families. In race and class struggles, the intermediaries of oppression (those who wittingly or unwittingly teach and exemplify inequity) are typically outside the family. Children are encouraged to view their oppressor as other than themselves. Further, both parents have a stake in reinterpreting the world for their children. But with sexism, it is more complicated. Girls and women not only live with men but also love them. Very frequently, women and other girls act as intermediaries of sexist oppression more than the males in a girl's life. Women may find that they feel uncomfortable reinterpreting the sexism in the world for their daughters because it seems disloyal to their husbands, male partners, brothers, and sons. While some men struggle actively against sexist oppression, many more find feminist reinterpretations of the world puzzling, or they actually enforce gender stereotypes. In homes where women have less power, they are more constrained about how much reinterpreting and educating they can do.

We mention this here only to acknowledge reality. In chapter 9 we explore the positive and negative roles that men can and do play in their daughters' coming of age as young women. We have discovered, however, that one of the advantages of being a single mother is the greater freedom these women have to reinterpret the world for their daughters. This, too, we discuss more fully in chapter 9.

Reinterpreting joins women and girls by enabling them to form a deeper, shared way of seeing the world. This double vision enables girls to look to and see their mothers as authorities who possess critical information and analysis. From this perspective, girls can more freely negotiate the world around them. By reinterpreting, mothers can also present—or learn with their daughters—a positive group identity that comes from understanding the heritage of women's struggles for liberation. "Without such education," writes Adrienne Rich, "women have lived and continue to live in ignorance of our collective context, vulnerable to the projections of men's fantasies about us as they appear in art, in literature, in the sciences, in the media, in the so-called humanistic studies." Reinterpreting is an ongoing, conversational education that teaches us to see the difference between the accepted view of reality and the reality of women's experience. Through reinterpreting the world for daughters in the everyday ebb and flow of conversation and media, women join with girls and all share in the heritage of their foresisters. Girls discover that they are not alone.

BUILDING COMPETENCE

"I look around my neighborhood," says an eleven-year-old African-American girl, "and I see girls on drugs, girls getting pregnant, and I know I want something more for my life." The crowd at this reception atop the Dayton Hudson Building in downtown Minneapolis (far above this girl's neighborhood) is surprised that she has stepped forward to speak—she's so young and so confident. But that's the point. This girl and other girls from a multicultural low-income neighborhood in Minnesota have been paired with women photographers in an experiment called "Get the Picture." The women and girls have met weekly, and the women have been teaching the girls to take photographs. The women have learned much from the "in-your-face" way the girls use their cameras. But what have the girls learned? This confident girl continues, "Many people come to our community to change things, but no one ever teaches us to do anything. This project taught me how to make photographs. Maybe I'll be a photographer, maybe I'll be something else, but I know that I can take pictures." (Maybe, wonders the president of the Minnesota City Council, she'll be a powerful politician.)

What this young girl has recognized, and what specialists in adolescence are beginning to notice, is that there are few opportunities for girls to build competence in skills that can open the world to them. Anne St. Germain, a nurse administrator, worries that too many people believe that they "can give you self esteem by giving you 'other's esteem' " through praise and reward. Her point is that praise is great, but it can also encourage a dependence on others to feel good. Real self-confidence is based in competence, in knowing that one can do and make things happen that are meaningful.

The division between men as active and women as passive becomes set in the psyche when girls collide with the wall of Western culture at adolescence. In the American Association of University Women (AAUW) study of self-esteem in boys and girls, boys' positive feelings about themselves were linked to their assessment of their skills and talents. They saw themselves as competent, as capable of doing things that they thought were worthwhile to themselves and others. Girls, however, based their feelings about themselves on their appearance and had little faith in their accomplishments. When girls become aware of the value society places on their "looks," they lose their connection with the world of doing, which is the essence of personal power.

"I was surprised," said Inez, "when my daughter started to want to do things around the house, like cooking and sewing, at about age eight or nine." Other mothers also remember their daughters expressing an interest at this age in becoming competent at what women do by turning to cooking, sewing, knitting—the traditional arts of women. Erik Erikson, the psychologist, called this period in child development the "age of industry versus inferiority" because he saw children at this time before adolescence as striving to develop competencies. Erikson didn't ask what happens if a child tries to develop competence over things outside her control (as do fourth-grade girls who begin trying to diet their way through adolescence). Or what happens if the skills that a girl "masters" are skills that mark her as inferior or subordinate within the power relations of the culture?

Girls, as they approach and collide with the wall, need to develop competence that gives them voice and power to carry into a male-dominated world. Voice lessons within the context of mother daughter relationships are the strongest foundation. But encouraging daughters to sing in the school choir or to act in theater; to write in a diary or journal; to explore poetry, music, and storytelling; or to paint or draw or take photographs also provides powerful lessons about the importance of voice and of competence. While not all girls will become artists, engaging with the arts keeps channels open from the psychic underground to the world. Countless women have credited some aspect of the creative arts with saving their spirit and soul. Alice Miller, a renowned psychologist, found that her free expression through painting, described in her book *Pictures of a Childhood,* allowed her to find a way back into her childhood that even the most intensive psychoanalysis could not have provided.

"My mother is an artist," says Adele, "and on Saturdays when we were little she would paint with us. In our family, art was just a part of what you did as a person—and certainly as a woman. It wasn't a big deal. It was fun and important. No one judged anything. When we got older, my mother would ask us whether what we had done was what we wanted and would help us with technique to more clearly realize our ideas." Adele's mother saw her daughters' expression of their imaginings and ideas as the point of their making art together. What Adele's mother did is possible for mothers who are not artists. It isn't expertise that permits some mothers to join with their daughters, but a willingness to be open to experiences. By joining with daughters to explore voice or, at least, to give girls access to these experiences, mothers give their daughters access to layers of psychological experience and to ways of communicating that are valued in the broader culture.

"While it is strange for me to say that I have a daughter who rides horses—I grew up pretty poor in the hills of Tennessee," Belle begins with an almost embarrassed laugh, "I am amazed at how into horseback riding she is." Sandra started hanging out at a stable because one of her friends took riding lessons and she would tag along. The friend's mother asked Sandra if she would like to try, and Sandra has ridden enthusiastically ever since. "There was a little competition, a horse show, at the place where she rides. Every student performed and everyone got some kind of reward. She was so excited. When I was putting her to bed that night, she told me that it had been the biggest day of her life. I asked her why. She told me that she was learning something that her father and I couldn't do. She has her own area of competence, where she knows things that we don't know. I was really surprised!" Sandra has found an area of competence that is hers alone. At nine years old, she grooms and rides a large horse. On horseback, she is powerful and in charge.

Sandra's experience of power and competence gives her a touchstone from which to enter adolescence. There are so few arenas in this culture where women, or girls after puberty, are able to revel in their bodies, to feel fully alive and exult in being alive, without being subjected to harassment. Joann Stemmerman worked with Outward Bound to create a wilderness experience for girls in early adolescence called "Connecting with Courage." Her goal was to combine the best of Outward Bound with "inward bound" voice-enhancing activities—journal writing and talking —to tailor-make a program that would give girls a safe experience in pushing their limits beyond where girls are "supposed" to go. Liza, a girl from the Laurel School who struggled with anorexia, spent a summer in a wilderness exploration that she credits with giving her a different, more powerful sense of herself. Noncompetitive outdoor activities such as camping, biking, and rafting give girls the opportunity to test their limits and to explore the world around them.

Claire and her fourteen-year-old daughter Cristina were at a weekend camping retreat with their church. Someone had set up a ropes course: two parallel ropes strung high between two trees for participants to cross. Watching people trying to cross, Cristina turned to her mother and asked, "Are you going to do it?" Claire demurred and hedged with a few excuses. "Mom!" said Cristina, "you sound just like I used to sound." "Are *you* going to do it?" her mother retorted. "Sure," said Cristina, "just you watch." Claire did watch as her daughter, "without a moment's hesitation," crossed the high ropes. She was determined to do it, too. But, perhaps saving her just in time, the retreat leader called everyone in to dinner as her turn approached.

Claire was really struck by what happened. She isn't a person to push herself to take risks like the ropes course. But she saw in her daughter's remark—"you sound like I used to"—something that she didn't like in herself. Claire did not hear her daughter's comment as a competitive challenge but as shocked recognition. Her daughter had the courage to push herself beyond ways of being that were comfortable to her mother, and then, as often happens when mothers and daughters join, she turned around and asked her mother to join her. Claire's joining Cristina by supporting her through tough times has given Cristina the courage and strength to ask her mother now to join her in building her competence.

"I am not into sports," Katherine says with a laugh, "but I read the research that said that sports help girls get through adolescence more smoothly. The school that my daughter was attending had no sports program for girls, so I decided that I would start one." Katherine and a group of other parents created a mandate for a soccer program in her daughter's middle school. "I have always shunned sports," she says, "but this has really worked. My daughter is so happy—her entire class is much more cohesive now that they play soccer together."

Girls who play sports seem to have extra protection against the losses of adolescence. While some girls use sports to control their bodies and their weight compulsively, most girls who engage in sports for fun and for competition feel better about themselves. The Women's Sports Foundation conducted a nationwide study on minorities in sports and found that Latina girls playing varsity sports in high school, particularly in rural high schools, "were more likely than their nonathletic peers to score well on achievement tests, to report high popularity, to stay in high school, to attend college, to seek a Bachelor's degree, and to make progress toward that degree." The results were similar for white female athletes (but not for African-American female athletes). Perhaps within the Latina and white communities, being an athlete is connected with breaking stereotypes about women and so gives girls a taste of power and freedom that they carry into young womanhood.

"My mother didn't go to college," says Joy, "and she knew very little of the process that was involved. But she knew that I was smart enough in school to go on to college. She made me catnip tea to calm my nerves before I took the SATs the second time—I had blown them the first time around because I was terrified. She found out what I had to do and when, and stayed with me throughout the entire process." While Joy's mother didn't have the experience to know how someone applies to college, she found out so that she could join her daughter in attaining something that no woman in her family had attained: a college degree.

Linda, a high-school student, and Joan, her mother and a college math professor, spoke about joining for Linda's education. "When Linda was young," Joan says, "I constantly created math games out of whatever we were doing together, and I made time to play them with her." Joan is convinced that this is what led to Linda's competence in mathematics. But Linda disagrees. "That was good," she says, "but what was most important to me was when you went to my fifth-grade teacher and told him to put me in a higher math group." Joan had insisted that Linda's teacher give her a chance in the highest math group, even though Linda had not done well enough on the placement test. Linda herself is sure that it was her mother's support and confidence—not her math games—that gave her the confidence to become confident.

Education is the classic arena in which women build competencies to move into positions of authority. But the disciplines of the academy mold a woman's mind to align her vision with patriarchy. "Get all the knowledge and skill you can in whatever professions you enter," urges Adrienne Rich, "but remember that most of your education must be self-education, in learning the things women need to know and in calling up the voices we need to hear within ourselves." Academic competence, of course, is important for daughters to develop. Joining with a daughter to help her with schoolwork, to help her develop the skills that will enable her to earn both respect and her way in the world, is an important aspect of joining.

Yet success in the academy is not necessarily related to feeling confident or competent. Virginia Woolf, in "Three Guineas," her searing essay on women and war, wonders about giving a guinea coin as a charitable contribution to support women's entrance into the professions. Arguing that for women to ape men and their petty, destructive hierarchies of knowledge and power would be tantamount to "prostitution of the brain," she urges women who enter the professions to dismantle them as bastions of class and racial privilege. Woolf sees an extraordinary difficulty for women who enter so-called higher learning. By "mastering" the disciplines as they have been constructed out of male experience and desire, women risk losing their perspective as outsiders as they hope to gain the security of being accepted as insiders. Thus, says Gerda Lerner, "Now we also know that we have participated, although unwittingly, in the rape of our minds."

Mothers who join with their daughters to build competence are exploring ways for their daughters to fight the loss of voice and power. Tuning their ears to their daughters' voices, these mothers look for ways to connect their daughters with channels for self-expression and self-knowledge. Moreover, these mothers encourage their daughters to develop a physical competence that gives girls the experience of being fully and joyfully present in the world as active beings, not passive objects. If girls are to resist the loss of voice and power, the definition of *competence,* typically and narrowly thought of as school- or work-related, must be expanded. Other competencies encourage girls to keep their own perspective in the face of educational systems that favor boys and male ways of thinking about what is most important. For a girl, confidence in her own voice and competence matters more in the long run than her grades in eighth grade. Mothers who foster the development of a broader range of competencies in their daughters provide girls with the keys to trusting themselves as they enter increasingly and more subtly hostile arenas.

TAKING ACTION

Katie's mother talked a lot about sexism and women's rights. As a social worker specializing in domestic violence and as a single mother, she raised these topics often. But Katie, as she turned the road into adolescence, wouldn't have anything to do with such talk. She had a "that was then, this is now" attitude. And besides, as everyone said, Katie was gorgeous. Why should she have to pay attention to all of this negative talk about women and men? She was going to have fun.

Then Katie was sexually harassed in school, and she couldn't get the school administrators to consider the harassment anything but playfulness (boys will be boys, right?). Outside of school, friends of hers were raped. Not knowing what to do, she told her mother what was happening. Lucia, her mother, did know what to do: she took action. She went to the administrators and made sure that the boys were punished for harassment. Lucia taught Katie how to organize and to keep the pressure on the school. Katie has become an activist: she and her best friend have started an organization for young women to combat sexism. They go around to local high schools and raise awareness about sexual harassment.

Lucia joined Katie by sharing with her the skills and information necessary to take action. Taking action usually begins close to home, often at school. Many mothers take action on the part of their daughters by bringing their authority to bear on the school on behalf of their daughters. In the school that Claire's second daughter, Jessica, is attending, teachers punish children by making them sit in isolation and face a wall. Claire has told Jessica's teacher and the principal of the school that she won't allow that for Jessica. While Claire respects their need to discipline students, she insisted that this method would be counterproductive for her daughter.

While the conventional wisdom in the separation model of development implies that daughters will reject what their mothers embrace, recognizing that adolescence is traumatic for most girls implies a different course. While some mothers may avoid involving their daughters in what they care about for fear that such action will lead to rejection, the growing number of activist women whose daughters are following in their footsteps contradicts this conventional wisdom.

In a 1986 study in Waterloo, Ontario, Canada, entitled "Feminist Attitudes and Mother-Daughter Relationships in Adolescence," researchers explored 102 adolescent daughters' perceptions of their relationships with their mothers. The researchers found that "the majority of daughters who have a good relationship with their mothers see both themselves and their mothers as feminist." (The daughters do not attribute their good relationships to feminism alone.) But the minority of daughters who do claim to have a poor relationship with their mothers also attribute their problems to feminism: the mothers are not feminist. The girls are unhappy about their relationships with their mothers because their mothers are urging them to capitulate to traditional female roles, and these mothers disagree with their daughters about sexuality and freedom.

School, as the first major cultural institution that mothers and daughters come up against, often is the context for mothers to join their daughters in taking action to resist their daughters' disempowerment. Virtually every mother with whom we spoke had a story of intervening on her daughter's behalf. Zena, a former teacher, gave supplemental classroom materials to the overworked teacher in the poor school that her daughter attended. She wanted to enrich her daughter's school experience because her daughter was bored in the school and beginning to say that she hated it.

When fourteen-year-old Athena was hauled into the principal's office of her high school for punching out a boy who continually harassed her, Bonnie, her mother, went on the warpath (after asking Athena whether she needed her mother's help). Athena had done everything she possibly could to get the boy to stop, or to get someone in the school to intervene.

Finally, discouraged and frustrated, she had slammed him in the face after he had grabbed her. Bonnie was outraged, not because Athena had resorted to physical violence, but because the school administration wanted to punish Athena and the boy equally. When an assistant principal suggested that Athena be more ladylike, Bonnie was furious. "Don't listen to them!" she told Athena in front of the administrators. "If you can't create an environment where my daughter is safe from harassment, then you'd better expect her to take care of herself." Bonnie reminded them that Athena had sought their help to no avail, and then applauded Athena's bravery for fighting this bully.

Theta Reed Pavis-Weil, a journalist now in her twenties, recalls what she learned from her feminist mother, a pipe fitter in an oil refinery: "I had some teachers in Jersey City, where I grew up, who were racist and would scream at the kids who didn't speak English. I'd tell my mother, who would make a fuss with the principal and get the teachers in trouble. It was great. I was raised with the feeling you don't have to accept the way things are." Theta's mother was not reluctant to intervene in her daughter's school, but some mothers are. After all, the Fury insists, the school does know best. From within the silence of perfection, mothers doubt their own knowledge of their own children in favor of the judgment of a teacher or other authority.

Ruth Nemzoff, a psychologist, has studied the ways mothers of children with disabilities come to assert their knowledge and authority in the face of the authority of doctors, social service workers, and teachers. One mother refused to have her disabled daughter wear slipperlike shoes, and instead, the girl wore lace-up high tops. While the caseworker pointed to this as an example of the mother's undermining of her daughter's autonomy by making her dependent on her mother to tie her shoes, the mother was adamant and stood up to the doctors and social workers. All of her daughter's classmates wore high tops. She knew that for her daughter it was far more important to fit in than to be able to tie her own shoes every morning. She joined with her daughter to resist further marginalization.

Maria Corazon, a brilliant but illitcrate mother, saw clearly that the public school serving her housing development was a dangerous place where learning didn't happen. She took her oldest daughter to a Catholic school and argued that she was a good girl and smart, and that they should let her go to the school—for free. Maria was persistent and very persuasive, and her daughter received a scholarship. "I think that going to this school will save her life," she says. Neither class status nor literacy skills need prevent a mother from resisting what she knows to be bad for her daughter, from taking action on her behalf.

Taking action on behalf of a daughter, whether or not the action is effective, shows a girl that it is important and possible for a woman to have a strong public voice. Taking action demonstrates to a daughter that she, and her mother, are part of a larger, vibrant, powerful community of women who share her concerns. Judith Herman, in *Trauma and Recovery*, explains that, after suffering trauma, a woman experiences a shattering of her relational world and her sense of life's meaning. Herman notes that women who find ways of connecting to communities of women and who join with others to fight for a cause and resist the forces that harmed them stand a better chance for recovery.

On primary night in California during the summer of 1992, Barbara Boxer's daughter stands before a room bursting with women and pride. Her mother has just won an incredible victory and will be the Democratic candidate for the Senate (a seat she went on to win in November). Barbara Boxer's daughter talks to the crowd about how rich and exciting her life has been because she's grown up in a household surrounded by gatherings of women putting together the plans and organizations that have, over time, led to this night. Taking political action together is a powerful way of bearing witness to the power of women's voices in the world. Daughters see that women telling the truth and using their voices to make change in the public domain can effect change on personal and political levels. It is a straightforward way for a girl to see the advantages of keeping her voice.

Some mothers have raised their daughters from infancy in a climate of social change and political action. Remember Hila, who took her eight-year-old daughter, Rebecca, to a prochoice march in Washington (described in chapter 1)? Action outside the home, action on behalf of women and girls, can encourage girls and women to garner deeper support from within themselves. One mother remembers, "When I took my babies to anti-war or pro civil rights marches I knew I was putting them in the middle of radical things, but right things." Girls who stand with other women to "take back the night" (demonstrations to protest women's lack of safety on the streets) and hear women talk about problems of feeling safe in the world, girls who stand with women over choices to be made about their reproductive lives, and girls who march in support of civil rights are more likely to feel they can stand tall in their own homes and schools and raise their voices about the unfairness and injustice they experience there. While a daughter may still complain to her mother about unfair treatment, the daughter knows that—at home and in the world—she and her mother are joined, both are connected to other women, and both are actively resisting their mutual disempowerment.

For some women, however, taking action in the public arena of school or community is precisely the problem: it is public. But taking action need not begin with a public face. Taking action is not exclusively about marches and protests. Daughters benefit from the courage and the outrageous acts mothers perform daily in their homes. At the end of every speech, Gloria Steinem asks the audience to perform one "outrageous act" of everyday rebellion in the next twenty-four hours. She promises that if each person in the audience will perform such an outrageous act in the next twenty-four hours, she will also, and the world will be different. It doesn't have to be big or momentous, Steinem will say—you can simply tell your partner to pick up his own socks. For women, the smallest act of resistance is often experienced as outrageous. At the end of one speech, a small, meek-looking woman in the back of the auditorium raised her hand and said, "I often find that nailing his undershorts to the floor is quite effective."

Joining a daughter to take action on her behalf and on behalf of all women is not only a powerful way of connecting women and girls to their heritage and to the larger community of women but also a powerful way of healing the traumatized relational world of adolescent girls. When women join girls to resist separation and to take action in the world, they offer girls the hope that the world can be changed to allow women the safety and freedom to live fully. Mothers whose actions en-courage their daughters are women who deeply respect what their daughters want and deserve. Their actions tell daughters that the world can be changed to make room for a daughter's voice and desires. They engender their daughters' emulation, not separation.

7

The Power of Desire

Perhaps the best we can do in a bad situation is to speak the truths of both sides of the reality that we live in by speaking the truths about female sexual desire—both the pleasures and the dangers—and voicing the real experiences that girls and women have in their bodies.

Deborah Tolman
"DARING TO DESIRE"

Desire presents a huge dilemma for mothers and daughters. Throughout a girl's life, the dangers of desire make a mother her daughter's jailer and make it unsafe for a daughter to live freely in her own body. Desire—wanting, lusting, craving, longing, needing in all and every way— is critical to women's integrity and power. The power of desire is the root of a woman's power. Desire gives force to what she can and will do. It empowers her life and liveliness. Forbidding or compromising desire cuts off a girl's life force.

While we live in a culture that equates girls' expressions of desire with "asking for" sex, desire isn't just about sex. It is, as essayist and poet Audre Lorde has written, about the power of self-knowledge and of a self-love that moves outward to others. This desire, she says, "is an internal sense of satisfaction to which, once we have experienced it, we know we can aspire. For having experienced the fullness of this depth of feelings and recognizing its power, in honor and self-respect we can require no less of ourselves." Desire is both loving and the want of love, a movement of creation for oneself, with others, and in connection with the greater, abstract world through one's work. Lorde calls such feeling "the *yes* within ourselves, our deepest cravings."

But desire in this culture is shaped by men's wants. The cultural equation of power with dominance and superiority creates desire for control. Desire, rather than a lifeforce that guides from within, becomes experienced as the thrill of domination or a compelling drive to be safe. The system of desire that rules in this culture channels desire for relationship into romance and desire for pleasure into sexual sensation without feelings. This separation of relationship and pleasure distorts both. Within this distortion of desire, girls are identified either as "good" marriageable girls or "bad" sexual girls, and the distinctions are often unclear. What *is* clear is that, either way, girls are objects of desire.

Within a culture where sexual images leap out of every magazine cover and television commercial and where rapes and abductions of girls seem to be a fact of life, a daughter's new physical power to attract men and to bear children seems to be a justifiable cause for a mother's panic. Within such a context, desire is difficult for mothers and daughters. At adolescence the pressure on a mother to protect her daughter intensifies because a daughter's powers of attraction intensify. Adolescence, marked by the physical changes of puberty, is when children become capable of bearing children. A mother's love leads her to look for ways to protect her daughter as she travels through adolescence, so that she can enter womanhood with her options open and her soul still intact. Typical ways of protecting a daughter make sexuality shameful or bad. This makes a girl's body—her self—a source of shame.

A girl's dilemma parallels her mother's. A girl's "turn on" to sexual desire through the blooming of her powers of reproduction is an extension of the experience of desire that has motivated a girl's entire life. The pleasures and possibilities of sexual adulthood, edged round by the dangers, make negotiating the terrain of desire very difficult. Being openly desirous lands girls in a quagmire of physical, social, and psychological dangers. Many girls cope by "disembodying," that is, they lose the integrity and fullness of their desire by separating desire for pleasure from desire for relationship. When a girl disembodies from her sexual desire because it is too dangerous, she virtually unplugs her power by disconnecting from its vital, bodily source. Without it, girls lose their appetites for living and lose their inner sense of direction and meaning. They adopt definitions of desire that live in the world around them. With their desires split apart, girls enter the world of male desire that suffers from a similarly distorted split between idealized romance and "bad" sexual pleasure.

In the course of a woman's life, the culture provides three invisible institutions—womanhood, marriage, and motherhood—for her to enter and, supposedly, receive the blessings of male culture. Each time a woman crosses the threshold into one of these patriarchal institutions, she is asked to give up her body, her experience, her pleasure—the desiring parts of her self. Entering the patriarchal institution of the good woman at adolescence requires that a girl give up the desire that leads her to love herself, seek pleasure, and crave connection with others and the world. To fit in, she must become desirable, not desirous. Dalma Heyn, in *The Erotic Silence of the American Wife*, argues similarly about the patriarchal institution of marriage. Women who enter marriage give up their erotic voice, their sexual history, and their past to become the bland and non-sexually threatening mate. We would argue that the patriarchal institution of motherhood asks the same sacrifice of desire, of a woman's pleasure in herself and her connections. By the time a woman is mother to a daughter who is about to enter womanhood, this repeated sacrifice of self may feel so normal that preventing these sacrifices in daughters goes against what women have been taught as fitting and right.

Simultaneously, a daughter's budding procreative powers and her increasing power to create a life and a career for herself can raise conflicting feelings in a mother, feelings that point to a mother's own self-sacrifice, to her own dreams deferred. The separation of desire itself exists within a larger separation of desire into two worlds—the powerful public world of work achievement and the powerless private world of love. Many mothers, forced to choose between or to balance these separate spheres, have made painful sacrifices and compromises with their own desires. These sacrifices made by mothers can lead to feelings of competition and betrayal between mothers and daughters, particularly when a daughter has choices that a mother never had.

To understand these sacrifices, we need to explore desire as a life force that is far more than sexuality. We need to create new ways of understanding and exploring desire that don't get lost in limiting cultural scripts of male desire. At adolescence, girls dis-integrate as they realize it is not safe to live fully in their bodies. The absence of desire squashes passion for life and an ability to know one's heart's desire. Things become flat, colorless, and confused. Girls become easily manipulated by the ways desire is sold in the marketplace. Women's bodies are packaged to make products more desirable; and women are sold products to make their bodies more desirable. White patriarchy maintains its power in the public world by manipulating desire through the marketplace. Girls who explore their desires by mimicking the marketing of women's sexuality are in danger of contracting AIDS, becoming pregnant, or being harassed. How can mothers guide their daughters' exploration of desire during adolescence when the stakes are so high? We want to reclaim the word *desire,* to reappropriate it from its narrow sexual meaning. Until we do, girls will continue to be shaped by men's desires rather than their own. There are desirable ways for mothers to encourage their daughters' connection with their bodily desires and what they really want.

THE YES WITHIN US AND JUST SAY NO

In *Their Eyes Were Watching God,* the writer Zora Neale Hurston describes a girl's awakening:

> It was a spring afternoon in West Florida. Janie had spent most of the day under a blossoming pear tree in the backyard. She had been spending every minute that she could steal from her chores under that tree for the last three days. It had called her to come and gaze on a mystery. From barren brown stems to glistening leaf-buds; from the leaf-buds to snowy virginity of bloom. It stirred her tremendously. How? Why? It was like a flute song forgotten in another existence and remembered again. What? How? Why? This singing that she heard that had nothing to do with her ears. The rose of the world was breathing out smell. It followed her through all her waking moments and caressed her in her sleep. It connected itself with other vaguely felt matters that had struck her outside observation and buried themselves in her flesh. Now they emerged and quested about her consciousness.

Janie's awakening continues. "Oh to be a pear tree—*any* tree in bloom! With kissing bees singing of the beginning of the world! She was sixteen. She had glossy leaves and bursting buds and she wanted to struggle with life but it seemed to elude her. Where were the singing bees for her?" Janie's blooming as a woman speaks of a longing for life and for loving that captures all of her senses. She wants to know, "to struggle with life," to join in with something that connects her with the deepest meanings of life. Janie desires.

How many of us can say that the changes in our bodies at adolescence felt this way? It would be inaccurate to say that Janie's desire is simply about sex. It encompasses all of her, her ideas about herself, and her connection to the world. Janie's embodied longings and her questions for herself and her place in the world are deeply integrated. Janie has integrity, wholeness. Her example points to the difficulty of separating bodily desires from more intellectual desires about the future.

The problem that girls have, and that their mothers must negotiate with them, is that desire is wrongly equated with sex. Over time, as we said in chapter 2, girls learn that displays of life, of verve, are considered provocative. Within such a dangerous context, girls are schooled to "just say no" to those who desire them and, many times, say that to their own desires, as well. Some girls—often at great risk—try to play with their provocativeness or harden it and wear it as a shield. Many more girls monitor themselves so that they limit risk, but they have to disconnect their ideas of self from their bodily source of desire. But either of these strategies cuts girls off from the yes within themselves—the self-knowledge of what they want and what feels right to them. They become vulnerable to cultural scripts for their lives rather than being able to create their own stories for themselves.

As we mentioned in chapter 2, desire begins as a full-bodied (and often full-voiced) experience in young girls, who are passionate, desirous beings. "My three-year-old daughter wanted to watch—for the hundredth time—this cartoon about ducks," says Xiaoming. "I had to get to an appointment, so I had to say no. She jumped up and down, screaming, 'DUCK SHOW! DUCK SHOW! DUCK SHOW!!!' I was annoyed but amazed—what a voice, what passion!" The French novelist Colette also recalls the passions of girlhood: "Yes, passions, since I can find no better word for the compelling, fierce, secret rapport I had with the earth and everything that gushes from its breast." Young girls' full body slam of desire, where what they want is made piercingly clear, is vivid and immediate.

Girls' desire and self-love grow first out of girls' pleasure and confidence in their bodies. A strong self always begins with the body. Little girls' direct affection and feelings are an undiluted desire for love—of themselves and those close to them—and the sense that they deserve it. This is desire. And this desire, so often exhausting to adults, holds the force of a girl's embodied self-love—*I want, I need, I love.* This desire is a power source to be celebrated and valued. The greater a girl's connection to the "yes!" within herself, the greater a girl's ability to be autonomous, that is, to care for herself.

From the moment girls begin to watch television, the manipulation of their desires begins. While men usually control the finances in the household, women spend the money. We live in the most consumption-based culture ever. Through Barbie, originally billed as "the doll you love to dress," girls learn their role in the marketplace as consumers and their role in life as decorative objects. Their desires are directed toward becoming model middle-class consumers. Barbie lives in a Barbie Dream House—every little girl should want a dream house, too. Despite Barbie's new briefcases and Superwoman paraphernalia, Barbie's body, clothing, and boyfriends lead girls to spend their desires in the trappings of romance.

By middle childhood, girls often want to know more about the kinds of loving and desiring that they see around them. "When my Vera was eight, she used to play a secret game with her Barbie and Ken dolls in the bathroom," said Judith.

> Anytime she would play, she'd be very careful to clean everything up —and she's not the kind of kid who cleans up without a lot of reminding. One day, she was interrupted and ran out of the house without cleaning up. I went into the bathroom and found that she had taken tape and paper and made her dolls anatomically correct! I talked to my husband about it and finally we figured it out—she wanted information; she was struggling to figure out what goes on. My husband and I went to the library and got out every book that we could find for kids on sexuality and reproduction. She read them *all.*

A few months later, she dropped the whole subject and didn't speak about it for years.

Other mothers have similarly recalled that at about age eight or nine their daughters began to ask more direct questions about sex. Their desire to know develops both as they know more and as they feel new sensations in their bodies.

"You've got to be kidding" or "my parents would never do that" is the typical first response of grade-school girls upon learning about sexual intercourse. This first response focuses on other people—parents and other adults. "Oh my god," said Dara, at eleven, laughing in disbelief mixed with horror, "we have four kids in our family. My mom and dad must have done it *four* times!" But as girls' bodies change and the looks that they get for their looks change, they begin to realize that this is meant to happen to them, too.

What girls are most often told about desire (when desire is wrongly equated with sexuality) is "just say no!" Mothers often unwittingly and subtly sexualize girls' desire when they give girls messages to be quiet and demure. Michelle Fine, an activist and psychologist, found that girls' desire was missing from the school sex education curricula she studied. Within schools, where today probably more supervised discussion about sexuality takes place than in the home, girls are taught about the dangers of sexuality and the precautions they need to take before engaging sexually. While this is critical and lifesaving information, these messages also promote equations between sexuality and violence, sexuality and victimization, and sexuality and moral uprightness.

Sexual desire is discussed in these curricula as something that girls are at the receiving end of, but not as something that girls possess. Thus, sexual desire subtly becomes the terrain of boys, who place girls in danger of violence, victimization, and immorality. Michelle Fine heard the pleasures of sexual desire only as a whisper among girls, an "interruption," within health and sex education classrooms. But the dilemma is that girls who explore sexual desire in any way are at risk; girls who separate them-selves from it are also at risk—of losing their integrity as whole human beings and the power of their desires.

Unfortunately, the reality of the dangers of sexuality are all too pres-ent in girls' lives. In 1990, the Children's Defense Fund reported that "every 31 seconds an adolescent gets pregnant." The rates of sexually transmitted diseases are "higher among adolescents than any other age group; one-fourth of adolescents are infected with a sexually transmitted disease before graduating from high school." Teenagers are one of the fastest-growing groups for susceptibility to AIDS. In school, sexual harass-ment is rampant, and even though girls report such harassment, the au-thorities often ignore it. Violence against girls, from this harassment in schools and on the streets to rape and incest, exists to a mind-boggling degree. The consistent and persistent sexualized interpretation of girls' bodies and behavior, too, is a low-level violation of their integrity and lifeforce.

Faced with these pressures and dangers, girls can easily lose touch with the "yes!" within themselves. Psychologist Deborah Tolman spoke with thirty girls—girls of color and white girls, including a few lesbian and bisexual girls, from suburban and urban schools—about their experience of sexual desire. While slightly more than half of the girls described feeling sexual desire, many of the girls weren't sure or said that they felt desire but couldn't describe how it felt in their bodies.

Some girls aggressively hold on to their sexuality. They become "bad" girls. "You know this girl," writes Dalma Heyn, "she wears a lot of makeup, maybe; she is overtly sexual; she ridicules phoniness and talks about it out loud; she dares to look and dress and speak and do precisely as she wishes." (To white culture, this "badness" practically defines the Afri-can-American girl.) Yet these girls are in danger—not just of violence, victimization, and disease but of never being seen as other than their bodies and their sexuality. Access to good schools and to better work is often blocked for "bad" girls. Too often, too, these girls deny the degree of danger they are in. The power of their desires seems to become channeled into their defense of their sexual feelings.

For girls who have entered the patriarchal institution of "good girl-ness" (which is policed by women and girls), they lose integrity by split-ting real desire from internalized patriarchal ideas about their selves and, so, pull the plug on their power. Girls who split this way are no longer tapped into their desires, the deep and expressive source of their wanting. They hook into what is desirable in the market and begin to create new images for themselves from the outside in so that they can be chosen—and can be safe from the violence and uncertainty surrounding them. They lose their agency as autonomous people. They wait for their bodies to change to see how they will rate men's desires, and they wait for someone to activate their desire.

In several studies, Deb Tolman has noticed that adolescent girls rarely speak as the actors or initiators of sexual activity—it's "he kissed me," not "I kissed him." This causes an enormous drop in self-confidence, in their ability to feel that they can make their way in the world. Girls lose their certainty and enthusiasm. The echo in their speech of "I don't know" reflects that in very real ways, they *don't* know. Even Sigmund Freud noticed the link between the taboos on women's sexual expression and the constraints on their thinking.

Given the ever-present dangers, girls might easily rationalize a sacri-ficing or postponing of their sexual feelings. But the problem is that true desire, the "yes!" within, is a deep and joyous feeling that goes far beyond sexuality. The psyche cannot cut off one kind of desire without affecting another. When sexual desire is truncated, all desire is compromised—including girls' power to love themselves and to know what they really want. Knowledge of desire, of our capacity to live and feel fully, says Audre Lorde, is the touchstone for every aspect of our lives both in our relation-ships and in our work. Cutting off from or defending sexuality causes us to lose touch with our knowledge of what feels deeply right and true. When out of touch, girls begin to feel that they want a new hairstyle or new clothes—whatever the market tells them they want. Girls' desire for life and living becomes a consuming passion for desirable things. By losing embodied desire, girls become vulnerable to cultural scripts for women's lives because they no longer are in touch with what they truly want.

Recently, the dean of a prominent Ivy League school explained to an alumna, in confidence, why the school had no women Rhodes scholars, that is, recipients of the most prestigious fellowship granted to college students for advanced study. The school obviously had young women with excellent grades, athletic talent, and a record of social responsibility. But when the interviewers asked the candidates what they really wanted the Rhodes scholarship for, the girls were floored and had no idea what to say. Wanting had no place in their lives. These were champion "good" girls who had done everything right; they were accustomed to doing well and jumping through hoops. Although successful, they were disconnected from the desire that sprang from the "yes!" within them. In a study at the Harvard Project across three different schools, girls faltered when they spoke about what they wanted. Rather than owning what they want by saying, "I want . . . ," they would hedge by making their desire more general, "You want . . ."

By the end of the high school years, girls often appear clearer and more certain of themselves. But they are, sadly, neutered versions of themselves. And, unfortunately, this enables them to fit well into middle-class culture. Girls' malleability leads advertisers and marketers to target them as a blossoming market. Desire is subverted into a consuming passion—for clothes, shoes, cosmetics, hair-care products, CDs, jewelry, electronic gadgets, and more. Girls adopt desires from the outside rather than from the well of desire within them, and they gain an air of certainty by resorting to cultural scripts for desire and success that have been shaped by men's experiences.

RECLAIMING DESIRE

To reclaim desire, we can begin resisting the narrow definitions that have confined and sexualized our lifeforce and desires. A mother can begin to trace a heritage of pleasure—for herself, with others, and in work—as well as the history of her sexuality. Exploring survival strategies, women can begin to articulate how the ideals of true love and romance were false promises of salvation that led them into consuming passions. Enjoying a young daughter's vibrancy also allows a mother to reclaim her own desires and body.

Reclaiming begins with resisting and challenging our internalized equation of desire and sexuality. Joy and its cousin pleasure are the first points of departure for our reclaiming of resistance to the narrow, the conventional, the external ways of experiencing desire. Beginning with the present and moving back through life, each of us can collect joyful memories. "The first rays of sunlight over the hill on my first Girl Scout camping trip," laughs Carla. "I stood very still, beside a lake, while the whole wood became pink. I was so happy." Lisa's adolescent joy came through "tennis and sports." She says, "I loved to be running, moving, feeling myself as the wind. I felt exultant." Desire fulfilled is joy and is entirely unique to each woman. Touchstone experiences such as Carla's and Lisa's set our personal standards for living fully.

Linda remembers having had a touchstone experience when she was in the eighth grade in a private school. Linda's class was paired with an inner-city class to evaluate whether and how racial integration was working in the St. Louis school system. "And it was a really pivotal experience for me and I was really completely into it and really, I mean just completely turned on by it, and I remember, my mother thought it was a great thing I was doing . . . but . . ." But her mother didn't really listen to her thrill and pride at being involved in such a project. What Linda craved, and what she occasionally found among her parents' friends, was "just having someone else who was just wanting to know and who would sit there and listen because they were just as fascinated. I can remember how I would feel physically, I would just be like, it would just be this incredible relief and I would just be buzzing, you know."

Linda's experience of fulfilled desire touched her body and mind with the power of her ability to love, to connect with the wider world, through the work she was doing. Linda's sense of joy and fulfillment was rooted in her desire to live fully and meaningfully in the world. Linda's eighth-grade experience was a touchstone experience for work against which she measures other experiences: Do I feel as passionate, alive, here? Why not? This string of touchstones can form a lifeline to true desire.

Reclaiming our sexual histories is often less than joyful, less about pleasure. Teresa recalls the cheerful malevolence of boys snapping girls' bras or running their fingers down a girls' spine to taunt her, whether or not she was wearing a bra. Agnes remembers being chased by two boys in the swimming pool: when they caught her they tried to shove their hands down her bathing suit bottom. "I didn't understand why they were doing this; I was eleven at the most. But I felt strangely dirty."

Yet some women recall a surge of romantic longing at eleven or twelve. "I read a fragment of a novelette in which the hero applied his burning lips to the heroine's ripe breasts," writes Simone de Beauvoir in her *Memoirs of a Dutiful Daughter*. "This kiss burned right through me; I was both hero and heroine, and watcher, too; I both gave and received the kiss, and feasted my eyes upon it also." She ached for the only union that she knew was possible: "Desperately I would reckon: 'Girls aren't allowed to marry until they're *fifteen!*'" Yet, shortly thereafter, she was molested in a moviehouse by a man who smirked at her as she left. She was totally puzzled and had no idea what he wanted.

"My brothers would watch 'Bonanza' and 'The Big Valley' on TV after school," remembers Jean. "By the end of sixth grade, I found myself mesmerized by the kisses. I used to look very carefully—what were their mouths doing? Did they just press their lips together? That didn't seem right. I remember seeing my first open-mouthed kiss on TV—wow! I was

214

freaked out but fascinated. I would practice on my pillow at night, making up all kinds of adventure fantasies of the wild West."

Learning about intercourse and menstruating for the first time are often hallmarks of coming of age. "I was ten years old and I showed my mother the strange stains in my underwear," says Sara. "She slapped me across the face—not really hard—and laughed rather bitterly. 'Congratulations, you've just become a woman,' she said. It felt terrible." Memories of cramps and of struggles with sanitary napkins are often how women recall their entrance into womanhood. "I was only nine when I first got my period," remembers Dora. "I was so excited that I ran down to the kitchen with my underwear and showed my parents. I thought that it was so cool." But other girls who got their periods so early were mortified and hid all evidence for months and months.

Late bloomers have a different story to tell: "My mother was beginning to get worried because I was fifteen and no period," says Louise. "I lied to all of my friends. In swimming class, I would sit out once a month and pretend that I had my period. I was worried but secretly happy because I was very flat-chested, and I thought that if I got my period that would keep my breasts from ever growing. I think that was a superstition that I told myself to keep from feeling like a total freak." The established story of women's coming of age usually involves a focus on the body as a source of pain and discomfort or anticipation. By remembering what they were told about their bodies, sex, and love, mothers can see how their own desire and longing were shaped by the marketing of sexuality and romance.

For some women, the idyll of longing is followed by fear and a grim anticipation. Simone de Beauvoir remembers the difference between her feelings of longing at twelve and her feelings later on: "At the age of twelve, I in my ignorance had an inkling of what physical desire and hugging and squeezing meant, but at seventeen, though in theory I was much better informed, I didn't even know what the trouble was all about. I don't know whether there was a certain amount of self-deception in my ingenuousness: whatever it was, sexuality frightened me." Beauvoir's awareness of slipping into some sort of self-deception to keep her desire and her fear at bay typifies the loss of desire we have been describing.

Many girls find themselves confronted with knowledge about sexuality that is staggering. "My brother kept dirty books hidden in the clothes hamper in the bathroom," recalls Melissa. "My guess is that he would jerk off in the bathroom. I found *Candy* there, the porn novel. I was terrified and curious about all of the sick things that they did to that girl." Babysitting was often a source of sex reading. "I knew right where every one of my babysitting clients kept their secret books—in the nightstand, behind a row of books. One guy had an entire room three feet high with pornography," recalls Terri. "I wasn't supposed to go into that room but I peeked —boy, did I get an education in perversion. I couldn't stop reading although the magazines made me numb." Sheila recalls playing "dirty Barbies" with a friend in the eighth grade: Barbie would be her usual pretty self and find herself in sex trouble with Ken. "It was a nasty game where Barbie was pretty much humiliated," she says. "I remember having this tight feeling in my chest as we played—it was shame and anger at Barbie's stupidity. And Barbie's stupidity was later my own."

The memories of violence in women's lives—through exposure to pornography, catcalls, unwanted touches, cruel grabs, and defiling glances —are painful and frightening to reclaim. We encourage women to join with others in this process. As we saw earlier, our psyches have created elaborate rules to protect us from feeling the fear and dread that came with the realization of our sexual vulnerability. Remembering these moments can be a fear-filled experience. Realizing that we have survived and that there are women joined with us can free us to safely reexperience the fears and shameful feelings, and not just the incidents of abuse, that most of us have kept a lid on for so long.

For some women, memories of sexual abuse will surface in this process. "When I think about coming of age as a woman, I draw a blank," says Barbara. "But that's because I was raped by my uncle at the age of three. I became a woman at three. He robbed me of that." We encourage women who begin to recall such memories to seek the assistance of a professional, feminist therapist. Reclaiming those parts of ourselves that have been brutally taken from us gives us back the power and energy that we so deserve and need to live powerfully in the world.

Barbara also recalls that she spent her adolescence and early twenties run by her relationships with men. "I was a doormat, feeling desperately in love. I had learned at an early age how to relate sexually—to confuse it with love—and that's what I did." The flight into romantic, obsessive love —and often away from any sort of serious life planning or desire to live fully in the larger world—may be women's largest and most debilitating survival strategy. Even women who have powerful careers are not immune. Women self-immolate on the shrine of romantic passion, wasting their true desire and self-love. Teresa tells of living an increasingly meager life with a man "who I was desperately in love with but didn't even like. When he started to hit me, I said, 'I've got to get out of this.' " The confusion of love and fear, of romantic love and one's true desires, sets up an incredible mess for women to work through. Sex, when it comes from loss, is a desperate, blind grasping for another person in the misguided hope that the partner will give back what has been lost. But the other person can never do that. By validating all of these often messy relation-ships as the survival strategies that they were, we begin to free our true desire and our love, in its grandest sense. Until we reclaim this love, we will have difficulty guiding our daughters.

Holding the double strands of a heritage of desire and a sexual his-tory, seeing the consuming passions of romance as the vain survival strat-egy that it is, leaves women with a complicated, rich way of seeing desire in their lives. Women courageously persist in looking for the beautiful and searching for the joy, even amidst all of the fear and pain. Mothers, in seeking a source of resonance with their own pure desire, often find that interactions with their daughters are touchstones.

"Sometimes I hear my daughter skipping through our apartment and singing," says Belle. "I can't tell you what that does to my heart. 'She's happy here,' I think to myself. It gives me such joy." In these moments of connection to a daughter's joy and erotic lifeforce, a mother can reclaim her own—or at least decide that she deserves to feel such joy, too. "When I bathe my daughter," says Diane of her six-year-old, "I am almost taken aback by her openness with her body. It frightens me." Moving from fear at a daughter's open pleasure in her body to reclaim the source of those fears can be a powerful gift from daughter to mother, and from mother to daughter. For mothers of grown daughters, photographs of their daughters as children can be another source to help a mother recall and reclaim what passion and desire are like in a young girl. Without such reaffirmations, a mother who has been trained to fear the "yes!" within herself often has difficulty celebrating her daughter's body and desire, particularly as those change.

If a mother can hold fast to the string of these experiences in her own life, resisting both romance and a narrow definition of desire, she stands a better chance of being an authority from whom a daughter would want to learn. The power of the erotic and of women's desire is so strong that no girl wants to give it up. Her questions for her mother are: Will you help me to keep desire or to squelch it? Are you my jailer, or will you teach me about freedom? Only by knowing both pleasure and danger does a mother have the authority from reclaimed experience to teach lessons of true liberation.

DESIRING LESSONS

The presence of desire in a mother's life is the equivalent of operatic training for a daughter's voice. A daughter evaluates whether a mother can be trusted as a voice teacher on the basis of a mother's own life, her ability to tap into the deepest source of her power and pleasure. She judges whether her mother's life holds any valuable lessons. Are a mother's warnings of danger real, or are they sour grapes because she couldn't have what the daughter hopes to have? Two of the biggest blows to mother daughter relationships at adolescence are conflicts of desire: the conflict between a mother's fear for her daughter and a daughter's desire to explore her world and the conflict between a mother's perceptions of her own obsolescence in patriarchy and her daughter's wider opportunities.

How a mother negotiates these potential conflicts will affect how much a daughter will trust her mother through a dangerous passage. While adolescents have new thinking skills, those skills are dangerously coupled with limited life experience. Adolescents are reluctantly dependent on parents for guidance, but the first time that a parent is wrong, an adolescent is apt to generalize that the parent is completely unreliable. By teaching desire, a mother stands a better chance of maintaining authority in her daughter's life. And by looking to her own desires, a mother can avoid the subtle perils of competition with her daughter. Mothers can break the silence around desire and acknowledge eroticism when they listen and speak about menstruation, sex, and pleasure.

"My mother hates me," says Dora. "It's hard for me to believe but it's true. When I graduated *summa cum laude* from college—from the college that my father went to when she quit school to marry him—the look in her eyes was deadly. It was frightening." Dora's mother, a brilliant woman who is also agoraphobic, lived her life bound and frustrated by conventions that limited her own ambition and power.

Within the traditional cultural arrangements, mothers and their adolescent daughters often become smiling competitors. Who will be more attractive? Who is more popular? Who will get the attention of the man in the house or other interesting men? "I used to pore over my mother's high school yearbooks," remembers Lorelei, "because I was so jealous of her. She was the captain of the cheerleaders. Even though I was an athlete and played sports, I wasn't nearly as popular as she was. I hated her for that. But we never talked about it, talked about how different our experiences were."

As girls begin to see how and why resources and relationships are allotted and their mothers begin to see in their daughters the outlines of their own obsolescence, the rage of powerlessness—often covert—can seep into mother daughter relationships as competitiveness. Mothers who learned to negotiate the culture by playing out the romance story also learned that attractiveness and acquiescence were the keys to a happy ending. A mother and her daughter often compete with each other, using the rules of the consumer market to establish their relative desirability.

Many women, as their youthful attractiveness mellows into middle age, are confronted with losing what has given them their validation as women. When these feelings intersect with their daughters' blooming, mothers can find themselves enraged to the point that they cannot join with and celebrate their daughters' growth. "My mother used to take my two sisters and me shopping for school," recalls Golda with a pained laugh. "We'd come home with a few cheap things from some discount place. But my mother! Every time we went shopping for us, she would take us to the best stores and buy elaborate, exquisite clothes for herself."

"I remember coming home from school and finding my mother wearing the clothes that I had bought for myself," says Rhea. "It made me feel so strange—like she was trying to be me." A number of women and girls have talked about how their mothers would try on their clothes or flirt with their friends in ways that felt wrong and strange. While a daughter often will try on her mother's clothes as she approaches her full height and size as a young woman, this is an aspect of a daughter's growing edge, her excitement at reaching (literally) the heights that her mother has represented to her. Playing with a mother's clothes is a way of trying out being an adult. Playing with a daughter's clothes, unless invited by her daughter ("Try it on, Mom. Let's see how you look"), is experienced very differently by a daughter. A mother's power in her daughter's mind is usually too overwhelming to have that mother act like the daughter. And, too, a daughter needs her mother to be an authority, not an adolescent, so that she can grow into her own power and authority.

Mothers are expected to be the middle managers of patriarchy. In a classic study of life in business, *Men and Women of the Corporation,* sociologist Rosabeth Moss Kanter discovered that women had such bad reputations in business because they were typically middle managers—people given enormous responsibility and no real power. Kanter found that attributes blamed on women were attributes of all persons within the corporation who were powerless. When powerless, individuals tend to be competitive because they have so little that they can count on, petty because within the narrow scope of their power they have to guard against any infringement, and controlling because they couldn't afford to lose any of what they had. "Powerlessness corrupts," she writes, turning the familiar phrase upside down. "Absolute powerlessness corrupts absolutely." Given little power except through access to the greater power of the men in their lives, mothers are asked to shoulder the enormous responsibility of raising the next generation. Mothers who have accepted that their attractiveness to men, which goes beyond physical attractiveness, is what gives them security and power in the world can begin to be competitive, petty, and controlling with the daughters they see as so like themselves.

Daughters who have opportunities that belie a mother's survival strategies can feel threatening to a mother who has based her sense of herself in the world on the limited, reflected power within the romance legend. Not only do the daughter's opportunities raise questions about the necessity of a mother's choices, but the daughter's very different strategies can cause anxiety in the mother for the daughter. A mother's feelings about her daughter's life choices may, thus, become a very complicated mixture of anger, anxiety, and jealousy. These feelings (usually too terrifying to acknowledge) inhibit authentic connection between mother and daughter and guide a mother to act in ways that will feel competitive and hateful to a daughter. Likewise, these feelings will often confuse a daughter: Can she explore the world freely with her mother's blessing? Or will her success in the world be at the cost of her mother's love? Daughters are placed in a double bind of potential betrayal of themselves or their mothers when these thoughts and feelings are not acknowledged and brought into conversation. Daughters often want to tell their mothers, "Explore your own desires—'get a life.' "

VOICING DESIRE

When a woman lives life fully by seeking pleasure, she breaks the silence around desire that traps both mothers and daughters. By paying attention to sensual pleasures and joys, by sharing them with a daughter, a mother teaches and affirms a broader sense of desire. Allowing a daughter to know that physical passion is important to a mother's personal fulfillment but that this is not the only way women experience passion and desire is a powerful lesson. The example of a mother's passion and love for her work encourages girls to love outside of the text of romance. When a mother speaks of joy, pleasure, and desire—beyond that found in seeking sex or relationships with men or in shopping for things to make one more desirable—she tells her daughter that women's experience encompasses a range of desire.

Desire is silenced in women both by its absence and by its replacement with regimes of control. Those mothers who are caught in cultural expectations of perfectly selfless nurturance are cut off from self-love, from the joy within them that is deeply renewing. Freeing desire through activities that provide simple pleasure is a great start. The Fury in some mothers has compelled them to control themselves and their desires through exercise and other activities where the body is pushed increasingly beyond its limits. If movement doesn't give pleasure but is performed solely to meet a goal of fitness, weight loss, or beauty, then it is not about desire. Comfort and pleasure are the best guides.

In Dalma Heyn's exploration of women who have affairs within marriages they had not considered leaving, the women found that they got "themselves" back by transgressing patriarchy's boundaries so completely, so desirously. Some of the women even felt that their affair was good for their children because afterwards they were more confident, more rooted in the lifeforce of desire. Eleanor says,

> I mean look: Before I had the affair, I used to detach from my children because of my own insecurity and depression, buying the teacher's verdict about people I knew better than she—siding, in effect, with the authorities. It's a small issue, maybe, but now I see that as such a gross injustice, such a betrayal of the people I care about, such a betrayal of my own real feelings. It's as if something snapped into place in me and I can see now, and feel my own real feelings. As if I had manufactured feelings before—this is what a mother feels; this is what a wife feels. The affair has made me feel the feelings of the outsider, while still giving me the authority and concern of the insider. Me. I feel like me.

Other mothers have broken the silence of desire by insisting on what they want. "My daughter Audrey was really upset that I was thinking about applying to a Ph.D. program at the same place I had been commuting to for my master's," says Virginia. "We talked a lot about it. Then I told her, 'Hey, this is important to me to fulfill my dreams. And, you know, I think it's important for you that I do this, too. I think it's important that you see that it is possible to get what you dream of—and that you see that I can do it.' The conversation shifted there. I think she really got it."

Claudia, at twenty-one, describes how she was upset with her mother's decision to go to law school when Claudia was in high school. "All of the other mothers would pick their kids up after school. I felt deprived. But now I can't tell you how glad I am that she did it—for her and for me. It would have been awful for her to be in the house with nothing now that we're gone." Yes, these mothers say, it's important to want and to go after what you desire.

"My daughter, Cristina, was going through that tough time in early adolescence," remembers Claire. "She wasn't interested in any activities at school—despite my pushing. Finally, I asked her, 'What do you want? What turns you on?' When she said she'd like to swim, I told her that I would help her in any way that I could. I am a timer at her meets and took her to Florida for a competition last spring. She's changed. She's become much more confident." Cristina, fourteen, remembers deciding to take on swimming. "I didn't like the way I was; I didn't do anything. So, I liked swimming—I decided to really try. I wanted something of my own to be good in."

Listening for desire in a daughter, validating it, and helping her amplify it form an important set of lessons between mother and daughter. This is easier the earlier a mother begins. For Xiaoming and her lusty three-year-old, hearing her daughter's urgency as desire helps her to keep her daughter's desire alive. Giving little girls as much control as possible over their bodies, eating, food, and room decoration keeps them in contact with the "yes!" within themselves. Giving little girls accurate terms for their body parts—vagina, labia, clitoris—also gives them control. Translating a girl's "loudness" or "brashness" into passion and desire helps her to have a wide range of desiring experiences to carry into adolescence with her. "After my first parent-teacher conference when my daughter was in kindergarten," recalls Elba, "the teacher said to me, 'Your daughter has such passion!' I was taken aback. I would never have thought of it that way —I've always been called 'intense,' which sounds like too much of something. But, hell, it *is* passion!" Elba now looks for ways to celebrate her daughter's passion and applaud, rather than dread, her intenseness. Sometimes, changing the label on a behavior changes our relationship to it.

Also, listening to a daughter's voice of desire as she approaches adolescence, validating her own sense of timing and readiness, will help her to keep in touch with her desirous voice. Different girls mature differently. Edie, at eleven, tells about not having felt ready to go on a group date, one with a group of boys and girls. A student at a girls' school, she wasn't used to socializing with boys. Small and less mature than some of her friends, she wasn't sure she wanted to go. "I told my mother that I didn't want to, but she just laughed and told me that I should go, that I'd have a good time." While Edie's mother hoped to help her daughter along, Edie felt scared. "I just didn't feel ready. I didn't want to do it. It's not time for me to do it yet." Making this group date sound as though it were as big a step as intercourse, Edie felt that she shouldn't go. In the end, she did go. But, she reports, "I just talked to my girlfriends, so it was okay." A girl's desire might also tell her that she wants to be with girls, rather than boys. The strong cultural messages about heterosexuality lead many girls into painful, strange relationships with boys when they really love girls. Allowing a girl the space to hear her own voice of desire can save her years of torment.

By normalizing desire, a mother can normalize discussions of reproduction and sexuality. When *desire, pleasure,* and *passion* are common words in the house, then sex can be just one way to experience desire. Menstruation can be explained and celebrated as a phase shift in a girl's body that gives her access to a most sacred creative power. Some mothers are beginning to ask their women friends to form a circle of welcome and initiation when their daughters first menstruate. A joyful celebration of this new life-giving capacity provides a girl with a fitting entrance into womanhood.

Even when affection and desire are common in a household, discussions of sexuality have a very different meaning for a six-year-old and a twelve-year-old. Girls in early adolescence are often embarrassed by these conversations, as are mothers. Zena said that she would just keep talking about sexuality, recognizing her daughters' embarrassment or wish to shy away. Gradually, her daughters joined in the conversation and opened up. Initially, a mother may have to be gently persistent and keep on introducing the topic. To begin, she can speak of her own doubts and questions when she was her daughter's age. It is more than okay for a mother to talk with her daughter about sex and birth control. Nathalie Vanderpool, who has studied the available research on communication between mothers and daughters about sexuality, says of her conclusions:

> [They] made me want to shout from the rooftop (with a bullhorn): "Listen, all you mothers of young adolescent daughters—talking about sex with your daughter is *okay*. It won't cause her to become sexually active sooner, but if she decides to, these discussions with you will likely lead her to use birth control. It's *okay* if you don't know all the right language or get a few things mixed up. Do it your way; take a few guidelines from people like me and fit these into your own particular family values and lifestyle. And it's also *okay* to share some of the pleasurable aspects of sex too!"

A mother's willingness to speak about sexuality can help free a girl to discuss her own hopes, fears, and questions. For many girls growing up now, the sexual world seems more, not less, dangerous than it did for their mothers. These generational differences can lead to conflict, but just as often they can be a starting point for open discussions of the sexual world that girls face today.

A mother starts in exactly the right place when she starts from exactly where she is: with the truth about her own discomfort or excitement, or about the embarrassment she feels when discussing sex with her daughter. Mothers of girls with disabilities, even more than other mothers, seem to shelter their daughters from sexual knowledge in ways that can leave their daughters open to victimization. These mothers often need information from other women with disabilities similar to their daughters' or from doctors about their daughters' capacities for pleasure and reproduction. Today with AIDS and other dangerous diseases, a mother might want to go with her daughter to the library or the doctor or to Planned Parenthood to find out the latest information about reproductive health.

A mother can let the conversation flow with her daughter's desire. What does *she* want to know? What is *she* looking for from sexual experience? What does *she* desire from her first intimate relationships? Listening to learn gives a mother a clear sense of a daughter's struggle with desire and a greater ability to trust her daughter's thinking and have her daughter trust herself.

"When I was 'told' about sex as a teenager," remembers Teresa, adopting an exaggeratedly long face, "my mother and grandmother were *so* serious. They made it sound so deadly, so awful. Sex is funny. I want to tell my daughters that." Sex is often the way that adults play when they care about each other. (Work is the other adult forum for play.) Remembering the humorous side of sex can make the whole discussion lighter. When fun, desire, and love—which are what adolescent girls usually are hoping for from their first sexual relationships—are absent from discussions of sexuality, girls may ignore warnings and information because the situations described may not feel like the ones they are experiencing or are hoping to have. The sex-is-bad equation doesn't fit with the reality of girls' experiences with kissing and petting.

While each mother has to decide what she is comfortable with, talking with girls about how to seek pleasure, giving them permission to seek and to demand pleasure, can be a very important voice lesson. Some girls find themselves having "slam, bam, thank you, ma'am" experiences of sexual intercourse with boys for two reasons: first, they don't feel entitled to ask for pleasure and a more sensual experience; second, they don't know what other things bodies can do. Explaining to a daughter about touching and petting can give her new avenues for fulfillment that she might not have thought about. Mothers may want to avoid such discussions because the conversation could easily turn too personal. But a mother needn't say, "Honey, I love it when your father strokes my clitoris." Instead, she can talk about how important touch is to her own pleasure, and she can encourage her daughter to find out what kind of touch feels good to her.

"What does it feel like for the first time?" "How do you get a boy to do something that you want to do?" "Will anyone ever want to be with me?" These are a few of the questions that a group of young women with disabilities wrote and put into a hat for older women to answer. Their questions, perhaps more poignant given their disabilities, are universal ones and are probably the questions that most mothers wanted to know in adolescence. Just as mothers wanted them answered, so do their daughters. Truth telling, as we have said, is important. But there are many truths to speak. There is truth in speaking about one's decision not to speak. There is truth in making general, rather than specific, statements about pleasure. And there is truth in telling the stories of a mother's life without the high gloss of romance. (Romanticizing one's past only perpetuates the myths.) Speaking about personal experiences as an adolescent and about the first time or times for various sexual encounters gives a daughter the connection with her mother that she wants so badly. The most reliable guides are a mother's own feelings of comfort or discomfort and a daughter's readiness to know. In sexual discussions, at least at first, a mother will most likely have to initiate.

Many women live with deep silences in their lives about portions of their sexual history, places in their lives that have been too painful or shameful for them to even look at. Yet we have heard so many stories of daughters making "mistakes" virtually identical to their mothers', that we have begun to wonder whether the perpetuation of these silences doesn't also perpetuate the history.

Angela's mother and her grandmother both had their first child at the age of fifteen. Angela, the seventh child in this poor family, gave birth to her daughter, Vivian, when she was nineteen. Determined not to leave school, Angela married the baby's father, finished college (as only one other sibling was able to do), worked, and cared for her infant daughter. She stayed in the neighborhood but moved into middle-class housing. Clearly members of the middle class, both Angela and her husband had solid careers. Vivian was the first child in the extended family to be accepted at a college away from home and to be able to go. At age eighteen, Vivian left for college. At nineteen, in December, she returned home for break—with her first child. She had been five and a half months pregnant when she left home. "She won't talk about it," says Angela, unnerved that this pattern should be repeated in her daughter's life.

Other women have told of other patterns being repeated across the generations. "When I was pregnant and thinking of keeping the baby and sacrificing my hopes for a career, I called my mother—and I'm not sure quite why I did. Maybe to let her know that I was going to disappoint her," recalls Bethany. "She told me that the same thing happened to her at my age and in my circumstances. I was stunned. She had an illegal abortion—my mother, a devout Catholic!" Her mother's confession to her was a gift of grace, a dispensation. "I blurted out, 'But you are such a good woman—you would do anything for your children!' Suddenly, I realized that she was less than perfect, which gave me room to be myself, to do what I wanted to do." Unbeknownst to Bethany until this moment, she had equated her mother's self-sacrificing mothering with being a woman. Bethany's conflict about pursuing a career and not being more womanly like her mother played itself out in becoming pregnant.

Perhaps daughters tie the foundation of their womanliness to their mothers' reproductive histories. Whatever the reason, none of the mothers or daughters we have spoken to about these difficult intergenerational cycles engaged in an honest dialogue about their questions and choices before the pattern was repeated. Mothers who break this silence by telling the truth about their experiences might give daughters the consciousness with which to make real choices.

Athena, Bonnie's younger daughter, wanted to get birth control pills from her doctor. At fourteen, she hadn't had sex yet but was thinking about doing so. Bonnie and Alethea, Athena's older sister, sat down with Athena and asked her not to begin having intercourse. "Please wait," Bonnie remembers saying. "We don't think this is safe for you to do right now. Both of us have been through this and we really think that you are too young." With a shrug, Athena says that she decided not to pursue sexual intercourse. Why? "Because they asked me not to. It seemed to be a big deal to them, so I thought it must not be a good idea." The openness and forthrightness that characterize their relationship helped Athena make a decision in accordance with Bonnie's and Alethea's wishes.

A mother's discussion of her own life experience, encouragement of her daughter's exploration of pleasure through petting rather than intercourse, and establishment of an open communication about sexuality all help tremendously when a daughter is making decisions about her own sexual behavior. Sometimes a mother might feel uncomfortable with her daughter's choice of a companion and talk with her daughter about the basis for these feelings. If the mother has valid reasons and doesn't unfairly demand an ending of the relationship, her daughter may listen, even though she appears not to. But perhaps the most difficult thing that a mother has to realize is that, ultimately, a daughter will make her own decisions.

While we have focused almost exclusively on sexuality, we have done so because it is such a source of fear for mothers. The larger discussion of desire doesn't stop when sexuality begins—that would be buying into the desire-equals-sexuality equation. The discussion of desire continues, with sexuality as one component. The silence surrounding a mother's desire for meaningful work also needs to be broken through truth telling. What were a mother's dreams as a girl? How were her desires to act in the world diverted or realized? What made it difficult for a mother to work and to live fully in her desires and power? By telling these truths, a mother gives her daughter a deeper consciousness of how the culture forces women to make limiting choices, affirms another realm of desire, and encourages her daughter to begin shaping a life outside of the romance story.

JOINING IN DESIRE

Joining a daughter as she enters the patriarchal world of desire is a formidable task for a mother. Men's desires are so pervasive in shaping women's lives that knowing where to begin is hard. By entering patriarchy together, reinterpreting and broadening the standard male-based interpretation of desire, fostering girls' competence, and taking action against sexual violence, mothers and daughters join as a daughter negotiates her way through the labyrinth of men's desires.

The extraordinary power to carry another human life in one's body, to bring a child into the world, to become a mother—the awesome power that girls gain at puberty—is a sacred trust that women hold. Those who limit women attempt to contain and control that power. To enter patriarchy with daughters, mothers can teach girls the "appearance of conformity." Daughters need to be invited into an underground—not a psychological underground but an underground of resistance. In this underground, girls are taught to protect the power that they hold in their bodies by appearing to conform to outward conventions for women in their communities. Girls may maintain their autonomy by becoming secret agents disguised as nice girls. Rather than get caught up in the passion to consume, girls can learn that the standards of dress and outward behavior are costumes to put on and take off so as to slip in and out of male institutions, rather than desirable ways for a woman to be. A mother's irreverence for feminine conventions, her ability to play with them freely, gives her daughter an approach to entering patriarchy without being so transformed by its limits for women.

Most girls, depending on the standards in their schools and communities, want to be attractive to boys. While these standards change constantly, a mother has a tough path to cut between buying in to "boy pleasing" and leaving her daughter a social outcast. A daughter's pleasure, comfort, and sense of joy and fun are the best guides. "I want my daughters to understand that when a guy wants to change you, he doesn't love you," says Teresa. "I have plenty of life experience to share with them about how it doesn't work."

When a mother lovingly accepts her daughter as she is, a daughter learns to expect acceptant, affirming love from others. As girls enter the competitive world of dating boys, a mother can also encourage her daughter not to abandon her friends as girls trash each other. By letting a daughter know that keeping her commitments to girlfriends is important, a mother gives a daughter another way of thinking and behaving amidst the world of men's desires, which typically leaves girls defenseless.

We encourage mothers to join their daughters in learning self-defense. We cannot emphasize enough how important it is for girls to know how to defend themselves. At a Brooklyn, New York, self-defense program for girls, the teachers found that girls aged ten and eleven eagerly learned self-defense skills. Just before girls hit the wall but have some awareness of what is happening between boys and girls, they are aggressive and eager to be able to beat boys at their own game, so to speak. Afterward, girls' defensiveness and denial seem to leave them giggly in the face of instruction that asks them to act forcefully in their bodies. Self-defense enables girls to defend themselves physically before they have to create severe psychological defenses around desire.

The extraordinary nationwide program Model Mugging, for example, has special classes for mothers and adolescent daughters designed to give them back as much control as possible in situations of potential violation. Model Mugging helps women reclaim their anger and adrenaline so that they can respond intelligently and alertly to danger. Daughters who enter patriarchy by being able to defend themselves may have a slight psychological edge, which could enable them to stay in touch with their desire. While this individual solution to a systemic problem of male violence is not a real solution, it at least begins to recognize a daughter's vulnerability and gives her the competence to keep herself more safe.

When girls enter the world of men's desires, mothers can show their daughters how to reinterpret the prevailing messages. Classically, mothers have reinterpreted boys' nastiness to girls as a sign of affection: He teases you because he likes you, dear. Giving girls that knowledge is one thing, but more powerful is helping them to confront boys with this knowledge. In situations of harassment, a mother can explain why a daughter is being harassed—that such treatment is a way to keep her down, to make her afraid of being fully herself. Mothers can also explain to their daughters why some girls become "boy crazy"—that for some girls, being preoccupied with boys seems like the best way to survive in the world. Demystifying romance and encouraging a girl, instead, to know someone deeply and intimately are powerful acts of reinterpretation.

As a mother continues her echo of a daughter's desires and passions, she can suggest ways that her daughter might build competence from those desires. Girls have to struggle to figure out a life of passion that isn't just the romance story because they see and hear so few stories of women's full passion at work in the world. The media, movies, and popular stories collude in urging girls to secure their futures within the marketplace of desire. Sharing biographies of women whose power of desire led them to greatness can provide girls with new stories. To help a girl bear herself outward into the world, a mother can provide her with access to the skills and experiences that will carry her desire into the future. When Alyshea, twelve, expressed doubt and outrage over the AAUW study on the drop in girls' self-esteem (see chapter 1), Karen, her mother, went with Alyshea to talk with a psychology professor. This professor and Karen helped Alyshea begin prize-winning efforts as a psychological researcher—she has won two school science prizes. Alyshea is now considering whether psychology is a field she might want to pursue professionally. Alyshea is learning how to let her desire bear her outward into the world.

Much ado has been made of girls' love of horseback riding. For the women and girls we have spoken to, horseback riding is not a simple erotic exercise but an opportunity to develop a sense of mastery over something powerful outside themselves, which we mentioned in chapter 6. "When my daughter was eleven, I got her a horse," says Jane. "The man who ran the stable told me that I was making a good move—on horseback she would sail through her adolescence. On some level, it made sense." Her daughter, Corinne, says that riding a horse has given her new confidence, a sense of competence in herself because she knows that she can control and guide her horse. While horseback riding is expensive, bike riding and other sports activities provide girls with experiences of living fully in their bodies, and of becoming competent and masterful. For Latina and white girls in particular, sports activity is linked to enhanced self-confidence and self-esteem.

In chapter 6, we described two mothers who had joined their daughters to take action against sexual harassment. Mothers joining with daughters to protect women's rights to their desires and control over their lives and bodies is essentially what feminist activism is all about. Marches to "take back the night," prochoice activities, or actions to stop rape and violence against women are all exciting places to begin.

Guided by daughters' desires and concerns as expressed through an issue, mothers can join daughters by taking action within a school, a community, or the nation. A mother's passion and activism, expressed as a love of her daughter and a desire for freedom, is a powerful statement of joining. For a girl coming of age in a world of mothers who will take action on her behalf, the fear of being female in a violent world of men lessens in its traumatic impact. In such a world, a girl can begin to answer fully the "yes!" within her and to resist living through the survival strategies of the romance story and the consuming cult of beauty.

Mothers whose true desires were diverted by romance and motherhood can direct anger and disappointment away from themselves and their daughters and toward the culture to gain the energy for social action on behalf of themselves and their daughters. The divisions in this culture between private and public life, between work and love, keep women from easily being able to care for their children and to contribute to society outside the home. Women's love of work and love of their children are constantly at war in a culture that has been created out of men's desires, because women are expected to make painful compromises between work and love that undermine power and integrity. Mothers who work to change what limited them have less need to compete with their daughters. A mother's renewed sense of life purpose and connection outside the romance story gives her daughter the freedom to explore her potential and to affirm the power of her desires.

8

Body Language

The contemporary ravages of the beauty backlash are destroying women physically and depleting us psychologically. If we are to free ourselves from the dead weight that has once again been made out of femaleness, it is not ballots or lobbyists or placards that women will need first; it is a new way to see.

Naomi Wolf
THE BEAUTY MYTH

Billy, the heroine of Judith Krantz's *Scruples,* enters the romance hall of fame with a stunning transformation. From a 218-pound schoolgirl, Billy becomes a long-stemmed American beauty. "She was thin and she was beautiful, Billy told herself fiercely. . . . This new Billy could marry anyone she liked. No need for her to go to Katie Gibbs to study to become a dreary secretary." Billy was right. Her looks get her the boss and his $250 million.

Billy, like most women, knew what it took to become the perfect and desirable woman. What she did not know, or could not acknowledge, is that the entire cult of beauty—the emphasis on appearance and the drain of energy and money to make oneself beautiful—distorts women's lives because it so deeply distorts women's selves. Billy seems to have recognized, though, that beauty is the prime survival strategy for women within this culture.

Stories like Billy's can happen—perhaps one in a million times. Like lottery fanatics, women bet their lives on looking good to men as a way of getting the love, security, and fulfillment that they long for. Getting a new haircut, beginning a diet, joining a gym, and buying a new lipstick are all long shots that bring a woman a little closer to becoming the desirable woman and, just maybe, to a glamorous life. Beautiful and desirable women—real-life winners—attract rich and famous men: Cindy Crawford marries Richard Gere, Christy Brinkley marries Billy Joel, Jerry Hall marries Mick Jagger (but is replaced by a newer, younger model).

What is beautiful and desirable in a woman is narrowly defined by the image that calls to us from magazine covers, movie screens, and television sets. Like Cindy, Christy, and Jerry, a desirable woman is tall and thin with big breasts and long, shapely legs—not unlike a Barbie doll. Her hair is shiny and often long, her face is always clear skinned and wrinkle free, and her features are small and regular.

In the 1970s, many women—some of whom now have daughters—began to question this standardized vision of female beauty. Within and outside of consciousness-raising groups, they grappled with whether or not to wear makeup, shave their legs and underarms, pluck their eyebrows, wear high heels, dress fashionably, and, with considerably less angst, give up girdles. They compared themselves to the norm set by popular culture, as women often do, but not to see how *they* measured up. This time they were looking at how the standard measured up to them and were asking: Why doesn't the image of the desirable woman look more like us? In a country as diverse as ours, why is she invariably white, young, and upper-class?

Yet, somehow, after making only small gains, women gradually shifted their attention away from the politics of beauty. Other issues on the agenda of the mainstream women's movement were of greater importance—and less susceptible to ridicule. In an era of backlash against feminism, women were warned about man shortages and lonely, empty lives. Caught between ridicule and fear, women became increasingly susceptible to assurances of the benign role that beauty could play in their lives. Now *more* women have their desires caught in the consuming passion to be beautiful by dieting, running, walking, swimming, working out with weights, going to exercise classes, applying moisturizers or anti-aging creams or other cosmetics, and seeking out image and color consultants and plastic surgeons. Women work at beauty with an unquestioning dedication that author Naomi Wolf likened to religious fervor in *The Beauty Myth*. While the image of the desirable woman may change over time, the paramount importance of embodying that image seems to remain stubbornly ingrained in our culture and psyches.

In adolescence, our daughters are initiated into the cult of beauty. They struggle to strike some kind of bargain, usually an uneasy one, with the image of the desirable woman. Whatever the terms, in the process girls end up wrestling with difficult issues: power, violence, economics, sexual attraction, class, and race. Their lonely struggle shapes their identities as women in an environment of conflicting messages, competition, and women's silence or collusion.

LOOKING TO SURVIVE

At an early age girls begin learning painful lessons about the value placed on their appearance. Sara, an eighth-grader, tells the story of her best friend, who is in trouble:

> She's got a very low profile of herself. I mean, well, part of the reason is none of the boys like her . . . because of her, like she being so immature and stuff like that . . . and also because, you know, she's

got a pretty face and everything, but as it comes to chestwise, she's a little on the flat side, so [the boys] they're calling her flat-chested and they tell her she has no, and she hasn't started to fill out or anything yet. . . . And so, she's noticed that we've filled out except her. . . .

Sara joins with the boys in their contempt of her best friend's lack of curves, even though she understands that their contempt is one of the causes of her friend's low self-esteem. Barely out of elementary school, all of them—Sara, her friend, and the boys—are already buying into a romantic framework that values women because of their attractiveness to men.

In this framework, girls are reduced to their physical appearance and are cut off from each other by the competitive scramble for boys' approval. Boys enjoy a new source of social power: the authority to judge girls' attractiveness. The balance of power tips in boys' favor, and girls drop to an inferior position. After all, while girls may depend on boys' good opinion for status, boys do not depend equally on girls. Boys can rely on athletic and academic achievements in ways that girls simply cannot in most school settings. Led to believe they have no real choice, girls learn to trade on their attractiveness, comforted by its illusion of power and control.

What do boys find attractive? The girls in one study of eighth-graders identified three traits: a shapely body, a pretty face, and a boy-pleasing personality. With these traits, the girls described the phantom that haunts female adolescence: the perfect girl, the girlhood version of the desirable woman. Inevitably, girls search their maturing bodies and faces for signs of how closely they resemble her—a frequently disappointing quest.

Carrie, the mother of a ten-year-old girl, recalls with a mixture of pain and irony, "At thirteen and fourteen, I lay in bed at night, a 'Sleepless Not-Beauty,' praying—no, begging God to make my breasts grow, not to make me flat-chested." Only a few years earlier, at ten, Carrie had rejected the idea of God. "Now desperate, I put principles aside and offered all sorts of devout inducements to get 'Him' to save me, not from damnation, but from the hell of not having a body boys would find attractive."

Powerless over a body that can betray or save them, many girls wait anxiously, like Carrie, for breasts to grow, for hips to broaden, for their bodies to "fill out" and "get curves." Others wait to see when all the growing will finally stop. A shapely body is indisputably the most important aspect of attractiveness to boys. A pretty face, we know from Sara's story about her best friend, simply cannot make up for a lack of curves. But, apparently, a boy-pleasing personality, the ability to flirt, can at least spare girls public ridicule. Sara, still speaking about her best friend, explains:

> You know how girls like, usually flirt and guys just love it when girls flirt with them? [She] won't flirt. . . . She refuses. You know, she constantly calls me a flirt but she's dead jealous because I can flirt and she can't. And when she goes up to a boy, she starts talking to him, she'll usually hit him or something. . . . And so, you know, the boys are always telling her she's flat-chested and she has no body. She hasn't got a curve on her, really. . . . And you know, I don't mean to say it about my best friend, but she doesn't (laugh). . . . [O]ther girls who are flat-chested are really popular so they don't have to worry about it because they've got their popularity. And also, they know how to flirt, and that sort of thing.

Unable to flirt, Sara's friend cannot avoid boys' scorn like the more popular flat-chested girls. But none of them can avoid having boys look at their bodies and scrutinize certain parts, most commonly breasts, legs, and hips. Girls are reduced to being the object of boys' looks, which fragment them into pieces. What sense is Sara's friend to make out of being reduced to a flat chest and, then, to "no body" because of it? How is she to integrate this message into an emerging concept of herself as a woman?

Girls' feelings of powerlessness trigger their psyches to protect them.

With their newfound intellectual capacities, they begin to see themselves as they imagine others see them and internalize what they perceive to be male standards of beauty. Many girls react by looking at and judging themselves in the same ways that boys look at and judge them. In their competition for men and boys, women and girls are not just the victims but the enforcers of our cultural obsession with appearance.

Melanie, a college freshman, writes of being "trapped" at the age of thirteen in a girls' school "where physical beauty was the prime standard by which to judge and compare peers, and where the most complimentary adjectives were fashionable, trendy and slim." She has "vivid memories of nearly [her] whole class of thirty-two sitting in lines during lunch breaks comparing the merits of our shapely and shapeless legs." Reminiscent of beauty pageants, these schoolgirls rated each other on a scale of one to ten, giving each girl's legs two separate scores: one for length and a second for "general impression/shape." After careful deliberation, one of the girls decides, "I would give Victoria five out of ten for length and eight for shape, wouldn't you?" Another girl responds thoughtfully, "Yeah, I reckon so. She wouldn't do too badly with John you know; he likes short shapely ones. . . . And, what about Natalie—I'm afraid we're giving you only three for both marks. We have to be fair, you know." Natalie accepts her low scores with resignation and with anger at her mother: "That's right I suppose . . . I could kill my mom for giving me such horrible thighs." With each critical look, each wounding assessment, girls cut themselves off from each other and presage their future as women.

In a defensive maneuver, girls shift from feeling and experiencing their body to observing it—with the critical eyes of the Fury. Having internalized rigid, male-defined standards of beauty and perfection, they mercilessly scan their bodies, piece by imperfect piece. Missing the forest for the trees, girls like Irene, a seventh-grader, respond to compliments that "she has such a good personality and is so nice" with an emphatic denial in the self-critical voice of the Fury: "No, look at my nose, look at my legs, no." Girls' negative body images—their worry over and displeasure with how their bodies look—are familiar fixtures on the middle school and high school landscapes. In a recent survey of adolescent health, researchers in Minnesota found that 64 percent of the girls reported having a negative body image. And girls with negative body images are more likely to be depressed and suffer from eating disorders.

In contemporary culture, girls learn to equate beauty with slenderness. The current obsession with slender, toned bodies began at the turn of the century with the fashion and insurance industries. Couturiers introduced the new "slim silhouette" in the form of long, narrow sheaths, at the same time that American actuaries developed the first of the now-too-familiar insurance tables of "average," "ideal," or "desirable" weights. Doctors began weighing patients as part of routine medical examinations, so that women suddenly had objective numerical measures for judging their bodies. As if one such number were not enough, the newly burgeoning ready-to-wear garment industry introduced the concept of standardized sizes. In the past, women had sewed their own clothing or had relied on seamstresses, so such sizing didn't apply. With ready-made clothes, it did. Women's bodies were objectively and, perhaps irrevocably, standardized.

Modern dieting was inevitable, and the first best-selling diet book, *Diet and Health with a Key to the Calories,* published in 1918, found author Lulu Hunt Peters proclaiming, "How anyone can want to be anything but thin is beyond my intelligence." How, indeed? The definition of *thin* has fluctuated over the years (most visibly in the 1950s when a more voluptuous silhouette was in vogue), but, overall, "thin" has been getting thinner. Models, movie and rock stars, and even Miss America, whom emcee Bert Parks used to remind us is "our ideal," are now thinner. Despite an average height of five feet seven inches for Miss Americas, their average weight during the last thirty years has been a very thin 117.5 pounds.

Negative body image is a response to cultural messages that leave no doubt about what girls and women are supposed to look like and how important their looks really are. Our country's singular Barbie doll standard of female beauty is certainly oppressive for white girls but puts African-American, Latina, and Asian girls in an impossible bind. Playwright Ori Faida Lampley pointedly remarks of Barbie, "What a sweet toy for a little Black girl, a rubber-headed, relentlessly white woman with plastic torpedo titties, no hips, no ass, who needed a kickstand up her butt to stand because she was permanently poised on the balls of her feet. . . . Barbie's hair never had to be straightened. She had no burn scars on her tiny pink ears."

Feminist theorist and cultural critic bell hooks describes a friend's dark-skinned daughter as "just reaching that stage of preadolescent life where we become obsessed with our image, with how we look and how others see us." The child was angry. "And yet her anger had no voice. It could not say, 'Mommy, I am upset that all these years from babyhood on, I thought I was a marvelous, beautiful gifted girl, only to discover that the world does not see me this way." Echoing her pain, an art teacher in the New York City public schools describes the self-portraits of his Latina and Asian students: Wide noses are narrowed, full lips thinned, and Asian eyes rounded.

With greater hopes of success, white girls attempt to mirror the image of the desirable woman. They search the pages of *Seventeen* and *Sassy* for diets, exercise routines, beauty secrets, and the latest cosmetics and fashions. (Girls and women in America spend over $3 billion on skin care products each year; worldwide, women spend $20 billion on cosmetics annually.) Girls, like many of their mothers, also fantasize about makeovers. In the "Baby-Sitters Club" story *Mary Anne's Makeover,* the thirteen-year-old heroine is launched into her modern-day Cinderella story by finding the perfect hairstyle in *Seventeen* magazine. She decides to go for it: "My New Year's resolution was to be 'the best person in all possible ways' —and didn't that mean looking my best? Sure it did." Torn-out magazine page in hand, Mary Anne goes to a fashionable beauty salon to get her hair cut. Her new hairstyle and "an elegant makeup job" earn her the supreme compliment: "Darling, you look like you stepped off the cover of *Vogue*." With some new clothes, she is "sensational" (in her stepmother's words) and "gorgeous" (according to her father). Her boyfriend asks teasingly, "Who's the new girl?" At school, she tells the reader, "I felt like a movie star. Imagine, *me,* drab old Mary Anne! No one had ever fussed over my looks before. And now *everyone* was paying attention." Even her teachers respond differently to her.

Mary Anne is delighted with the effect of her makeover, and she learns an important lesson in women's survival strategies: beauty is women's wealth, "a commodity to be bartered" for power, money, safety, and security. Beauty and attractiveness are women's chief survival strategies. The "economics of beauty" rule the marriage market, and beyond. Like their mothers in the workforce, schoolgirls realize that beauty lends them some limited power. But relying on good looks to secure some small advantage or to deflect an abuse of authority at work or in school is an individual and short-term solution to a collective problem. The cult of beauty is a survival strategy that allows women to maneuver safely around, rather than threaten, men's privilege and power.

RECLAIMING OUR BODIES

"When I was ten I weighed 106 pounds. The family doctor said I had to lose twenty pounds and put me on a really strict diet. He handed my mother a mimeographed sheet and told her to bring me in once a week for a shot to help me lose weight." Linda ate what her mother gave her, occasionally managing to get her hands on a coveted candy bar. Every week, she went to the doctor's office. He would weigh her and then give her an injection in her arm. "I don't know what he was injecting me with and neither does my mother. All I know is that in a few months, I lost close to twenty pounds. I was thrilled." Linda also remembers changing in other ways. "I just started caring more about how I looked than I had. I fussed with my hair, and began paying attention to clothes. I wasn't a little girl anymore."

Through reclaiming, women uncover the ways they resisted cultural demands and the ways they succumbed. Generations of women in this country have succumbed to the cult of slenderness, a survival strategy with a deceptive veneer of resistance. Associated with youthful, even boyish, freedom and independence, slenderness masquerades as a protest against restricting traditional female roles. But this protest is played out on women's and girls' bodies, instead of in the political or social arena.

The obsession with slenderness, says philosopher Susan Bordo, "has to do, more profoundly, with a deep fear of 'The Female,' with all its nightmarish archetypical associations: voracious hungers and sexual insatiabilities." Or, as one woman described it, "I've often felt that I was *too much*—too much emotion, too much need, too loud and demanding, too much there, if you know what I mean." This woman's experience of herself as "too much" is reminiscent of a description of a healthy nine-year-old girl, but with a negative spin. Qualities that are tolerated, perhaps even celebrated, in a prepubescent girl provoke anxiety when found in a sexually maturing girl or a woman. At the onset of adolescence girls are encouraged to shift their attention from knowing and satisfying their desires to managing their appearance and controlling their appetites.

Since that first diet, Linda has dieted many more times. She isn't a fat woman, but she is always trying to shed those extra five or ten pounds. She is not alone. Although just one-fourth of the women in the United States are fat by any standardized measure, three-fourths think they are, and anywhere from one-half to three-fourths of women are on diets at any one time.

The cult of slenderness is a paradox of seeming resistance and painful collusion that diverts women and girls from their own desires and wears away at their self-esteem. True resistance, however, what psychologists Tracy Robinson and Janie Ward call "resistance for liberation," encourages women "to acknowledge the problems of, and demand change in, an environment that oppresses them." Most women and girls know of moments when they have resisted the lure of the cult of beauty. Late childhood, before adolescence, is usually a time in a girl's life when she likes how she looks just because it is how *she* happens to look. Liking herself, she likes her looks, or as nine-year-old Celeste answered after first agreeing that she was pretty and then being asked why she thought so, "Just the way I am is fine with me . . . because it's me."

Thirty-five-year-old Lorraine attended a workshop for women led by Carol Gilligan and voice teacher Kristin Linklater. Very tall and thin, Lorraine wears her straight, dark-blond hair chin length and brushed back from her face. In one of the exercises, Carol asked the women to draw pictures of themselves as girls. Lorraine is "no artist," as she told the group, but she still produced a creditable drawing of herself at nine or ten. Everyone was struck by the strong resemblance between the adult Lorraine and the girl she was.

Her eyes glued to the drawing, Lorraine told the other women, "I'm one of those people whose faces don't change. Even in baby pictures, you can tell it's me." Unable to pull her eyes from the drawing, she remembered how "happy and content" she was with her looks then. Saying that, something clicked for her. If she still looks the same, which she does, why shouldn't she be just as "happy and content" with her looks now? Smiling, at that moment she was. Lorraine used the connection she made that day to stay with that feeling, and something has begun to shift for her.

Nine- and ten-year-old girls enjoy an integrated sense of themselves. Bodies are not split off from minds to be observed and judged with the mean-spirited separateness and cold distance of the Fury. In photographs, girls this age are usually looking directly into the camera, hiding nothing. They hold themselves with careless grace and ease, yet they still look as if they could jump into action in a flash. Looking at family snapshots is one of the ways women try to recapture some sense of themselves at this age.

Anne, the forty-five-year-old mother of a nine-year-old girl, was surprised by what she saw, remembered, and felt. For most of her adult life she had not thought of herself as attractive. Yet, in a photograph of herself at nine taken at a family party, she seemed surprisingly unselfconscious. She was wearing a pale blue, white-and-gray striped party dress with silver threads and an artificial flower at the waist, which Anne remembered vividly. She had a crooked smile, and her big eyes stared out intently from behind blue-and-white speckled cat's-eye glasses. Her brown hair was pulled back into a ponytail high on her head. Reviewing each detail of the picture brought Anne a little closer to how she had felt about herself that day. She remembered being suffused with pleasure as she admired herself in the mirror in her parents' room.

When Anne turned to a photograph of herself as a young adolescent, she saw a very different image. She sat on a chair, trying to take up as little space as possible, her body caved in on itself. Her shoulders were stooped, her chin tucked in so that the face was bent down and a bit to the side. Her small smile did not part her lips or brighten the rest of her face as it had at nine. Anne remembered riding a public bus to school each day with two boys from her eighth-grade class, Stanley and Dennis, who teased her loudly about her weight and the pimples beginning to appear on her face. She remembered feeling angry when they first began bothering her, but over time she just felt ashamed and powerless. She would sit there silently each day wanting desperately to be perfectly pretty, so the torture would stop.

At nine her assessment of her appearance was firmly grounded in her sense of herself. By thirteen, the Fury in her criticized herself as brutally as did Stanley and Dennis. Anne had spent time and tears in therapy, exploring issues of self-esteem and feelings of inferiority about her appearance. Connecting with herself as a confident nine-year-old has strengthened her and her relationship with her daughter because, Anne says, "the girl in me remembers what the woman prefers to forget."

When we each recapture personal experiences from when we were a girl, memories of our mother's courage often surface. With those memories we begin to construct what Adrienne Rich calls "a strong line of love, confirmation, and example" to support ourselves and our daughters. Adele remembers special evenings with her mother and sister when her mother would dress up for nights out with her father. "My mom's an artist, not bohemian, but very much her own person. Most of the time, she dressed simply, didn't wear makeup, and just pulled her hair back with a clip." But Adele's father was a partner in a San Francisco law firm, so when Adele was growing up, her parents entertained clients and went to partners' dinners and firm parties. "For those nights out, Mom would knock herself out, but without taking it seriously. Dressing up was a game that she invited my sister and me to play with her. It was fun, and kind of silly. The fancy dresses, putting up her hair, doing her makeup, were all part of the game, . . . as if she were getting ready for a costume party." Adele's mother taught her daughters about the joy of adorning oneself, while subtly subverting the conventions that place too much importance on women's appearance.

By reclaiming both our pleasure in our younger selves and the survival strategies that we employed to play the beauty game, women break the hold of the Fury's voices. The joy of playing with our looks and of embracing our selves and our appetites gives women the freedom to celebrate a different, deeper beauty—more grounded in the pleasures of girlhood. The more continuous a mother's connection is with her own heritage and her own experience of pleasure in herself, the better she can teach her daughter to live beautifully in her body.

BODY LESSONS

With prohibitions and advice, mothers try to shape their daughters' appearance.

Pull in your stomach.
Fix your hair.

Get your hair out of your face.
Are you going out looking like that?
Put a little lipstick on.
Take your hands away from your face.
Stop picking at your face.
Stop biting your nails.
Stand up straight.
Don't slouch.
Sit straight.
Smile.

Sound familiar? Underlying each admonition is a cultural ideal of what is and is not attractive in a woman. Both the standard and the ways it is communicated undermine women and girls.

What does a girl understand when told, "Pull in your stomach"? To begin with, she understands that stomachs that stick out are bad, although this isn't actually said. Expected to correct this, she realizes that it is within her control and is her responsibility. By letting her stomach stick out, a girl is shirking her responsibility and should be ashamed. By sucking it in, she will fool others into believing that she doesn't have a stomach that sticks out, when in fact she does. Girls must choose between deceiving others or feeling guilty for being irresponsible. Either way, they won't feel quite right about what they are doing.

Adolescent girls are serenaded by the critical chorus of parents' admonitions, boys' comments, other girls' harsh judgments of their appearance, and their own unrelenting judgments. That critical chorus, coupled with the mass media, communicates the cultural messages responsible for the prevalence of negative body images among girls in this country. One less critical voice, her mother's, is a boon to a girl's shaky self-confidence in her looks. Silencing that critical voice is surprisingly difficult, despite the best of intentions. Accustomed to criticizing our own and other women's appearance, the words are out of our mouths before we realize what we are saying. Understanding the impact of those words and making a concerted effort certainly help us break the habit.

Luisa has two daughters, fourteen-year-old Amanda and nine-year-old Margarita. With a sheepish grin and sorrowful eyes, Luisa remembers, "When Amanda was about seven, I took her shopping for clothes at the Gap. I hurried her into a dressing room, so that she could try on a pair of jeans. I don't remember why we were rushing—we so often are—but we were and my attention was completely focused on helping Amanda take her clothes off quickly and put on the new jeans." Luisa, who had bent down to help Amanda, looked up and was startled by her own image in the dressing-room mirror. She muttered, "God! I'm ugly!" Amanda looked up from pulling on her jeans and said, "You aren't ugly, Mommy. You look just like me." She paused and added, "You're always saying that."

Luisa tried to make the best of it, telling her daughter that, yes, they do look alike, and yes, they are both pretty. She went on about what she had really meant, that she was just commenting on her messy hair and on how tired she looked. Finally, she told Amanda that she was right, that Luisa did say that too much, that she used to believe it was true, and that sometimes she forgot and acted as if she still did. Two things changed for her after that experience: "One, I don't say I'm ugly, even when I'm feeling that way, and certainly not in front of Amanda and Margarita. Two, when I do feel that way, I remind myself that I look like Amanda and I know she's lovely."

Because the culture equates beauty with thinness, girls' displeasure and dissatisfaction with their appearance centers on their weight. As one mother says, "I love Heather and I want her to have a successful, happy life and I think that if she tries to maintain her thinness and her attractiveness, she certainly is going to be accepted by those around her." Heather at first resists her mother's body lesson, "I say: Mom, why do you always need to work out? I mean, you're so skinny. You're too skinny." But her mother tells her no, "You can never be too thin or too rich." Heather learns from her mother and capitulates to the cultural standards that her mother hopes will protect her: "And so I use that expression now." Heather does more than use that expression; she has learned to be displeased with a body that can never be too thin.

Negative body image, the name given to that displeasure, increases the likelihood that a girl will suffer from anorexia nervosa and bulimia. Women who are in their thirties and forties now had never even heard of these eating disorders as girls or young women. Now women gaze at their daughters and their friends, nieces, friends' daughters, students, and all the other adolescent girls who pass through their lives, and wonder whether they will fall prey to these diseases. With this increasing concern, the symptoms of anorexia and bulimia are now more widely known. The anorexic suffers because of an intense fear of "fatness," a refusal to eat, a distorted body image, and a decrease in body weight by more than 25 percent. Identifying anorexia in its early stages is difficult because the early signs are synonymous with behaviors common to so many adolescent girls: depression, perfectionism, desires for independence and achievement, excessive dieting, and claims of being fat. The bulimic, more commonly an older adolescent or a young woman, binges on large quantities of high-calorie food, then purges herself through vomiting and the use of laxatives. Bulimia is now recognized as a separate disorder rather than just a symptom of anorexia.

First identified in the late nineteenth century, anorexia is part of "a long history of food-refusing behavior and appetite control in women dating back, at least, to the medieval world." In the twentieth century, particularly the last two decades, anorexia has reached epidemic proportions among white upper- and middle-class girls, largely because of the cult of slenderness and the pervasiveness of dieting in this country. Girls of color experience these disorders less often; they are more likely to suffer from obesity. (In the last twenty years, obesity has increased by 53 percent among African-American teenage girls.) Their vulnerability to anorexia and bulimia, however, does increase with their families' upward mobility —shifts in social class status are usually accompanied by stronger alignments with dominant cultural norms, like the cult of slenderness. This is not to say that anorexia and bulimia are exclusively cultural maladies; these eating disorders are clearly also psychological and physiological. The prevalence of these conditions now, compared to even thirty years ago, supports theorists who maintain that eating disorders are a "crystallization of culture" and "reflect and call our attention to some of the central ills of our culture—from our historical heritage of disdain for the body, to our modern fear of loss of control over our futures, to the disquieting meaning of contemporary beauty ideals in an era of female presence and power."

No guaranteed preventive measures for anorexia, bulimia, or obesity exist. Certainly, increased awareness is key. Among the most important measures mothers have available are efforts to change their own relationship with food and weight. Even if we don't succeed in totally reforming our own behavior, our increased awareness can keep us from perpetuating an obsession with food. Commenting on girls' weight, remarking about their size or eating habits, and suggesting diets only reinforce negative body images and chip away at girls' self-assurance. When women begin to explore their own feelings about weight and food, they are able to help themselves and their daughters move away from harsh self-blaming and from critical judgments about other women's and girls' appearance.

Leah is a slim woman in her thirties. As a child, Leah was fat and felt miserable about that. In late adolescence she lost weight and has managed to maintain her weight at an "ideal" level for most of her adult life. Ruth, her twelve-year-old daughter, has started putting on weight in the last year or so, and Leah found herself asking, "Are you sure you want to eat that?" when Ruth took another helping, snacked between meals, or ate dessert. Leah knew she should keep her mouth shut, but she couldn't always silence herself. The next time she caught herself doing it, she told Ruth what she thought was going on. "I told her that I was acting out my own anxiety about being fat as a child and fearing being fat as an adult. I didn't use those words exactly, but I let Ruth know that basically it had nothing to do with her. And, I asked her to remind me if I slipped and stepped out of line. It worked."

Supporting girls' resistance means that mothers refrain from mirroring society's preoccupation with their daughters' appearance. Girls are smart, persistent, funny, honest, compassionate, independent, strong, agile, artistic, athletic, musical, hardworking, and much more. Bodies do more than look good. Sixteen-year-old Alison, when asked what she thinks of her body, says, "In general I like the way I am. I'm stronger than most people. I have more stamina. I'm not great looking, but I'm not ugly either." She is happiest with how her body functions, its strength and endurance, rather than its appearance. A mother who resists the urge to comment on a daughter's physique and encourages her daughter's physical capacities to act and move powerfully and forcefully can help her daughter find joy and pleasure in her own body's functioning, rather than in the thought of becoming a beautiful object.

JOINING BEAUTIFULLY

The capacity to withstand the onslaught of the culture of romance and attractiveness to men is strengthened if girls possess a "full knowledge of its dangers, . . . a clear definition of their own principles, and . . . strong faith in their allies." These traits, identified by Judith Herman in *Trauma and Recovery* with regard to political prisoners, are more likely to develop fully in girls who are strongly connected with the women in their lives. Through such connection, the "community of women" welcomes girls with an invitation to share knowledge about the politics of beauty, pursue a joint inquiry into varied conceptions of beauty as they affect girls' and women's lives, and strengthen a commitment to supporting girls as they resist the culture of romance and attractiveness.

As girls develop and mature, their mothers can bear witness to their daughters' anxieties and concerns about appearance. "When my daughter was twelve, she was going through a, um, let's say, awkward stage," says Claire. "She grew I don't know how many inches in a very short time. She was really gangly." Claire noticed her daughter's changed appearance and never said anything. Neither did her daughter—until they were on vacation.

There, far from home, her daughter Cristina was teased by two boys about being skinny as she walked down the beach in her bikini. "I thought that no one would bother me here," she sobbed to her mother. Claire told Cristina that she knew how much it hurt and that she was powerless to change her and a world where a girl's looks matter so much. "I also told her that she was going through a growth spurt that was awkward, that she didn't look like the cute kid that she used to be. I knew that she would continue to change and come through this time—but I had no idea how she would look. While I knew it might not make her feel better, I told her some of the reasons why she was special and unique. I told her what I saw in her."

But Claire also recognized the reality of living in a culture where looks are important. She found out what was bothering Cristina most about her appearance and let her experiment with her hair and clothing. Cristina simultaneously decided to take up swimming and to invest energy in developing her strength and endurance. "I really appreciate my mom's helping me with how I look and for helping me think about it," says Cristina. "I felt she was really on my side."

Insisting that looks don't matter, when in fact they do, does not help girls. Instead, women can respectfully and compassionately listen to girls' concerns and affirm their experience of the misplaced importance put on looks in our culture. We can bear witness that this is how it is, while acknowledging the sexism and the purposes served by our national obsession with appearance. We can honor the feelings without condoning the system that provokes them.

What role should beauty play in our lives? What are alternative, empowering definitions of beauty? What is the connection between sexual attraction, beauty, and power? Gloria Steinem, in *Revolution from Within,* presents an extraordinary example of a woman who by conventional standards was not a beauty yet was dazzling to everyone she met: Margaret Mead. "Magnetic, sensual, and entirely herself," Margaret Mead was so beautiful "that even men who most disdained 'a lady intellectual' fell under her spell." Beauty isn't just skin deep; beauty is as beauty does. *Beauty* originally meant "what stirs the senses and mind at the highest level." What is beautiful, what attracts, is passion—for life, for ideas, for pleasure, for experience. Women can join girls with a foundation constructed of shared knowledge to examine, evaluate, and reinterpret their experiences.

Recently, tattoos for women were all the rage—not real ones inked in under the skin, but real-looking press-ons that lasted for two or three days. A few dollars purchased a sheet of intricate and colorful tattoos reminiscent of those from Coney Island tattoo parlors—hearts, roses, Chinese dragons, tigers, eagles. In Long Island, New York, ten-year-old Marysa received some tattoo sheets as a birthday present. Her forty-year-old mother, her father, an older brother, and two indulgent "aunts" (in spirit, if not in blood), also in their forties, and their twentysomething nieces joined in the celebration over a long summer weekend. One by one, all the women, following Marysa's lead, ended up with tattoos. Watching and talking with Marysa as she exuberantly chose and affixed her tattoos—one was not enough—everyone could see that her pleasure, not how she looked to others, was what mattered to her in this process. She was truly adorning herself for herself. Others were welcome to share in that pleasure and the beautiful result, but other people and their opinions were not the motivating force. To the old hands with makeup brushes and wands, the experts of disguise, this was a fascinating and unfamiliar approach. What if women were to put on makeup and dress up for the joy of adorning themselves, for their own pleasure, or to celebrate with others? What if women were to give up ranking and judging each other's looks?

When Aurea and her daughter go to the beach, they talk about the fun of swimming and the pleasure of the sun on their bodies. Aurea also uses it as an opportunity to teach nine-year-old Lizette something other than the shyness she learned through her female relatives' obsession with appearance.

When I was growing up, two of the aunts—my mother's sisters—lived in Puerto Rico and one lived in Brooklyn not far from us. Every few years the Puerto Rico aunts would visit us in Brooklyn, usually in summer. And, when they came, the whole family—aunts, uncles, first cousins, and a slew of second and third cousins—would go on a day-long outing to the beach.

We kids spent the day in the water, coming out only to eat lunch. When we did eat, they made us wait an hour before going back into the water. That hour was spent playing in the sand near the women's blankets and eavesdropping on their conversation. Sharing family news and hometown gossip, the sisters sat facing the ocean. As women walked by in their bathing suits, one sister or the other would stop midsentence, calling her sisters' attention to "that one." "Look at the stomach on that one, and in a two-piece!" "Now that one has nice legs, but her waist is so thick." "Look at the fat rolls on that one's back!" They made us laugh. But it was also confusing. One of the aunts was fat and so was I. When I was older, I was very shy about walking on the beach.

Aurea and her daughter talk about why the aunts, now old women celebrated for their sweetness, criticized strangers; why it mattered to them how these women looked; and how for years the memory of their words had stolen Aurea's joy in walking on the beach. Aurea helps her daughter understand the perils of focusing on appearance, our own and others', so that her daughter can walk a truer path.

With increased awareness that the cult of beauty is life-threatening, some girls are coming up with alternatives, antidotes to enforcing the code of romance and attractiveness and the isolation it fosters. At a New York high school, the Women's Issues Club members mounted their own public education campaign to fight eating disorders among girls at the school. Corridors were papered with student-designed posters identifying the warning signs of anorexia and bulimia, and condemning the cult of slenderness promoted by the media. Club members organized many small peer discussion groups in response to a growing demand, handed out flyers between class periods to girls and boys alike, and wrote articles for the school newspaper. With their efforts, a small band of girls pushed their large urban high school to name and recognize a problem afflicting many of their classmates. And an individual, private matter was turned into a public, collective concern. Taking action, the girls found, gave them a sense of a higher purpose and replaced isolation with camaraderie.

Jenny and Nicki, two southern eighth-graders, have been acting as a two-girl support system. Not long ago, they noticed that they weren't as hungry as they once had been. Having read about anorexia in a teen magazine and feeling concern for each other, they began "to get annoyed with each other when [they didn't] eat lunch or something." In fact, when Nicki tries to give away her lunch in the school cafeteria, Jenny tells her, "You're going to eat that." When Nicki insists she is not, Jenny repeats, "Yes, you are!" and Nicki finally does. With teasing and bantering, the two friends monitor each other's eating habits and help each other resist the allure of media images of skinny models. Nicki tells Jenny when she disparagingly compares herself to reed-thin *Seventeen* magazine models, "Oh, those models are horrible! Don't buy magazines; it's the first step to feeling better."

Both girls "hate it when people pick on people about the way they look because some things you can't help," and they try to disregard unfounded taunts from kids who "come up to just everybody and just say, 'You're so fat.'" Yet the defiance in their words—"those people don't bother me"—doesn't quite mask the dread in their faces. With great authority, however, they quote Jenny's mother, who explained to them,

257

"People who feel really bad about themselves have to pick on other people to make themselves feel better." Jenny and Nicki have held on to their connection to each other, and they rely on that to bolster their resistance. Faithful allies, they also view their mothers as allies in a conscious struggle to resist harmful, disempowering cultural norms.

Girls are grappling to resist the allure of beauty as a survival strategy. They need women to join with them. Women also need girls, with their irreverent way of thumbing their noses at—and playing with—conventions of beauty. Women and girls together can break out of what Naomi Wolf calls the Iron Maiden—a prison of stultifying routines for physical perfection.

Freeing women's spirits and energy, releasing their minds from the harpings of the Fury, allows women to take a wider look at a world that disempowers women and girls. Then they can also begin to explore opportunities for freedom and create new selves. But these opportunities will be unnecessarily limited unless women join with each other and with girls. The power of joint action is the most profound resistance to the cult of beauty that mothers can offer daughters.

THREE

A Revolution of Mothers

MARIE:

In 1977 in Buenos Aires, fourteen women went together from government office to government office carrying pictures of their children. Frantically, they beat on doors: "Where are our children? Where are the babies? Just tell us where they are. We don't know if they're cold or hungry. They were taken alive; we want them back alive." Receiving no information, they became desperate and staged a daunting act of resistance. Defying the military government's ban on public gathering, they formed a small circle in front of the primary square of the city, the Plaza de Mayo. Wearing white kerchiefs with the names of their children written on them, they assembled every Thursday and walked round and round in a circle. They carried signs with the names and pictures of their children on them. Other mothers whose children had "disappeared" came to watch. "The first time I came and sat in the Plaza and watched them," one mother said. "The second time, another woman came and sat by me. Finally, we both stood up and joined them."

All the while, in homes and on streets, young people continued to disappear. And every disappearance, every story of torture or death silenced people and weakened their resistance to the government's oppression. Friends were afraid to visit a home where a family member had disappeared. The country was paralyzed into silence by fear . . . all except the mothers who marched every Thursday. Little by little, those who had only watched and called the mothers the "crazy women of the Plaza de Mayo" became infected with their courage. The march of resistance and the naming of those who had disappeared swelled from fourteen women to a thousand and garnered worldwide attention.

These women became aware of the power of resistance—not as a story of self-sacrifice but as one about the power to name what was happening. They claimed the power to call public attention to an unspoken but public lie by voicing the truth. They risked everything but could no longer be silent; they took a stand for their children and, thus, for themselves.

The world is full of stories of women sacrificing themselves for their children. The substance of women's daily lives has often been a tale of self-sacrifice, if not outright self-betrayal. But the women of Argentina found that in resisting the injustice to their children, they found a voice in themselves they didn't know they still had, and in reclaiming that voice, they found a power. And with that power they joined with their children for the good of all.

In the mid-1980s I heard about the "Madres," as the "crazy women" of the Plaza de Mayo were called. Seeing a picture of these circling mothers touched something deep inside my own life and experience as a mother. Their courageous vigil brought up years of concern about the safety of my own children, particularly my daughters. The Madres evoked memories of marching angrily to schools or to political meetings to speak out against mistreatment or insensitivity, and feelings of helplessness at not being able to effectively protect my children from danger on the street or to assure that their lives would be easier.

In the 1970s my political friends and I circled each other. "We won't be taken seriously if we lobby ONLY on issues relating to us and our children," one camp argued.

"These are the only issues we are seen as knowledgeable about, and besides, they ARE serious issues," said another camp.

We were debating what still feels like a dilemma to women: If we speak as women who care about children and families, will we be discounted? If we speak as women who care about other issues, will we be dismissed, as Senator Patty Murray was, as "moms in tennis shoes"? Increasingly, it is a false dilemma.

These are the real dilemmas: Who do we consider family and how will these diverse families be supported? How do we expand the responsibility for raising children beyond family to the community? How do we create communities where *all* people are nurtured?

It is time to bring these issues, which have been relegated to the private domain of women, into the public plazas of patriarchy. It is time to mother a revolution about the truth of women's lives. We cannot wait until another generation of girls disappears into a society that does not welcome them for who they are. Chapters 9 and 10 are about this revolution.

9

Intimate Allies

It doesn't matter whether we call them testifying or soul sessions as in the civil rights movement; consciousness-raising or rap groups as in early feminism; covens, quilting bees, or women's circles as in women's history; or councils of grandmothers, "speaking bitterness" groups, or revolutionary cells as in diverse cultures. The crucial thing is that they are free, no bigger than an extended family, personal/political—and everywhere.

Gloria Steinem
REVOLUTION FROM WITHIN

The wall of our present culture appears impenetrable and unassailable. As the only reality we know, it seems immutable, just life. Motherhood, as it exists, is a part of that wall; it's a patriarchal institution that subverts women's power to bring life into the world. On closer inspection, though, the wall has cracks in it and places ready to crumble. We see mothering as a gap in the wall that women, through their resistance to cultural demands, can claim as a source of power. The first step is women teaching voice and resistance in mother daughter relationships. In the next step women move beyond this intimate pair and make allies, creating a revolution of mothers.

Author Elizabeth Janeway explains that power is a process, a "moving, dynamic relationship." Very few power relations are absolute, operating at "the ultimate level of total dominance and utter subordination." She identifies three powers that the oppressed have that prevent total domination by the powerful. Elizabeth Janeway ascribes women's progress in the last twenty years to our grasp of these three counterbalancing powers: distrust and disbelief, bonding, and joint action.

We encourage a healthy distrust and a disbelief in the prevailing "reality" of white male privilege and urge the nurturing of a bond between mothers and daughters based on truth and integrity. We have shown that through mother daughter relationships, both mothers and daughters learn from each other to keep their resistance strong and their vision clear. As bell hooks writes, "By courageously looking, we defiantly declared: 'Not only will I stare. I want my look to change reality.' " The transformation of cultural reality begins when daughters find their mothers are allies who support their resistance and resilience. Likewise, mothers find in their daughters guides back to clear sight and honest connection. But daughters will only explore their power and freedom when a community exists that offers an alternative to patriarchal reality. For this, women need to come together and jointly take action.

We want to explore ways for women to "find a good way of going" that can happen right in our own backyards. Revolutionary movements start small. During slavery, the underground railroad provided a loose link of freedom fighters who responded to a desperate situation by providing their homes and whatever they had on hand. All that was really required was their courage. Modern revolutionary movements began with people in small groups talking and learning from each other about their oppression. Revolution builds from there, from the political margins to the center of human life. In a mother daughter revolution, joint action also begins small —in a mother's immediate circle.

Like the interlocking circles of a wedding ring quilt, revolutionary cells are patterned out of a mother's life. The first cell is the family, the living context of mother daughter relationships. Making allies out of a daughter's father and brothers makes a daughter's home a safe house in the underground. "Othermothers" form the second cell. These women, (relatives, "fake aunts," godmothers) are mothers in spirit "who assist blood-mothers by sharing mothering responsibilities." They provide mothers with support and daughters with connection to other women. The third cell is a circle of mothers who organize for mutual support and joint action.

THE FAMILY AS SAFE HOUSE

Family provides a girl's first experience as a group member. In the intimacy of their homes, girls learn what it means to be a woman in our society—and first experience sexism. They come to accept male privilege out of their one-on-one interactions with the men and boys they love. The intimacy and love basic to the idea of family make the experience of sexism more intense than other equally familiar oppressions, such as racism and classism. These other oppressions are usually first experienced in the outside world at the hands of strangers, not at the hands of those we trust and love. Home and family are a refuge from racism and classism, a sanctuary from the pain and fear of oppression. To make family a safe house for girls, all the members of a family must struggle against sexism or run the risk of teaching girls to be intimate subordinates, a lesson they will carry with them into their private and public lives. Obviously, the prerequisite for the family to be a *safe* house is that it be safe from violence and abuse. The struggle against sexism needs to be taken on and pursued consciously. The choice for parents is simple: to replicate male privilege and dominance in the home, or to ally with each other and their children to struggle for equality.

Family holds the potential "to humanize, to transmit history, and to resist." In the family, children are socialized, and they learn to communicate, to develop their emotions, and how to live with other people. Important information is passed on from one generation to another: values and ethics, skills of all kinds, an understanding of the world we live in, appreciation of music and art, knowledge about politics and economics, and an awareness of sexism. A family's powerful capacity for resistance needs to be focused against reproducing male privilege generation after generation. In the words of feminist activist and author Letty Cottin Pogrebin, "The family can serve as *the* revolutionary cell in a repressive society, a place where nonconformity is validated and alternative values nourished. In short, an intimate agent of resistance."

Contemporary society provides any number of examples of families as "intimate agents of resistance." African-American families contradict racist messages and nurture the leaders of the civil rights movement. Working-class families inspire opposition to exploitation of workers and support union organizers. Immigrant families repudiate belittling stereotypes and motivate startling achievements. While a family cannot protect its members from excesses of power and force, barring extreme circumstances, the family can continue to seed change and shelter difference. This potential is available to women and girls in the struggle against sexism. Power relations in families engender power relations in the society. Fathers and mothers can refute limiting visions of womanhood and nurture strong, spirited girls through adolescence by taking action in this sphere of influence, in which they can exercise more power than outside their families. Change, social change, begins at home.

Despite the growing reality of different family forms, the culture still relies on the traditional nuclear family, a hierarchy where men enjoy greater authority and control than women, as the standard against which all families are judged. In this traditional family, the husband-father is firmly ensconced at the top—"the chief executive officer" of the "Corporate Model" of the family is an analogy Letty Cottin Pogrebin draws in *Family Politics*. "Mom, the operating officer, implements Dad's policy and manages the staff (children), who in turn have privileges and responsibilities based on their seniority."

While Mom now probably works outside of the home—two-thirds of married women do—in the home her role in the family hierarchy is much the same. Important family decisions, from where the family lives to how they use their resources, are still most often made by the husband-father. Despite their jobs outside the home, women still do most of the housework. After dinner, more likely than not, wives are doing the dishes, while husbands are sitting comfortably, reading the newspaper or watching television. "The modern individual family," wrote German socialist Friederich Engels over a hundred years ago, "is founded on the open or concealed domestic slavery of the wife. . . . Within the family [the husband] is the bourgeoisie and the wife represents the proletariat." Whether "chief executive officer" or "petty bourgeois," in the politics of family life, men wield greater power. But the family is changing.

The family is an institution in transition. Fewer and fewer families resemble the traditional family popularized in 1950s television shows. With almost half of all marriages ending in divorce and more single women choosing to have children, the number of single-parent families belies right-wing, family-values extremists' insistence on the traditional family as the only "norm." It just isn't. Families with complex networks of stepparents, stepsisters, and stepbrothers are too commonplace now to ignore and label as oddities. Extended families have always been the norm in African-American and Latino communities. Lesbian- and gay-parent families number over four million in this country. Being forced by change to rethink what is meant by *family* creates an opportunity to shift family power relations and to remake the family as a cell in the revolution of mothers. Recognizing the role of the family in reproducing sexism, women can enlist family members as allies in the struggle.

Girls glean women's reality in the world bit by bit as they watch their mothers maneuver through the daily politics of family life. "With the child's eye and ear for detail, the child's capacity for a frame-by-frame telling of human activity and relationship," write Carol Gilligan and Annie Rogers, "girls spoke to us in very matter-of-fact ways about the realities of women's lives—the tiredness and depression of mothers; the readiness of mothers to give in or compromise themselves in the face of disagreement; the readiness of men to resort to force in these situations."

Girls observe and question a mother's gender strategies, exactly how she deals with her husband and their father, and how he deals with her. If a mother adheres to the romantic fallacy that a woman is nothing without a man and places relationship with a man at the center of her life, depriving herself of her own importance, her daughter will know. The daughter will see that the price of romantic love for women is their own authority and power. In the family, then, romantic love buttresses traditional power relations. To shift those relations, women must undo romance's hold on them. Girls' keen observations and questions can help mothers to do just that. But in the process, girls' unvarnished truths may also be painful for mothers to hear, and even harder to answer.

Ana's parents both work. Her father, Angel, works longer hours and gets home later than her mother. Her mother, Julia, does all the housework, often staying up late into the night to finish the laundry or clean the house. She also does all the cooking and diligently has dinner on the table when Angel gets home from work. Each evening when the family sits down to dinner, Julia politely offers Angel each one of the dishes she has prepared. Just as politely, he answers yes or no and thanks her as she serves him his meal. During the meal, she notices when he finishes a particular dish and asks whether he would like another serving. She monitors his water glass and fills it before he empties it. Each time, he thanks her affectionately. Nine-year-old Ana watches this ritual with increasing interest.

One afternoon, Ana's brother, Luis, calls from the living room, "Mami, bring me some water." Julia turns to Ana, who is sitting at the kitchen table doing her homework, and says, "Ana, take your brother some water." "Why can't he get it himself?" "Ana, just get your brother some water." Incensed, Ana gets up, gets the water, glares at her mother, and says as she stomps into the living room, "Just because you do this for Papi, doesn't mean I'm going to do it for him. The lazy . . . creep." Ana's angry retort to Julia both acknowledges the mother's subordinate relationship with the father and announces Ana's intent to be different from her mother by refusing to accept a similar role with her brother. How is Julia to respond?

Mothers need not have perfect relationships with the men and boys in their families to provide their daughters with a safe house from sexism. But they do need to deal honestly with daughters, and themselves, about those relationships. Looking at herself in the network of relationships in the family, a mother may conclude that she does routinely acquiesce to her husband's demands or treat her sons differently. If she does, her young daughter will name these actions sooner or later. And despite good intentions, it will still be hard not to feel defensive in response to her daughter's clear-sighted, blunt statements of observed truth.

Acknowledging the discomfort that truth telling elicits is a good place for mothers to start in dealing with daughters. Simply telling a daughter, "I get defensive when you say that," gives a mother some space to find an honest, appropriate way to continue with the conversation. While a mother doesn't have to justify her life choices or confide in her daughter about her own struggles, a mother can give her daughter an honest response. Seeing the dynamics they take for granted through the eyes of their daughters, mothers may find that just allowing their daughters to share more perceptions is an effective response. It helps to remember that girls' observations in these instances reflect not only what girls see but also their fears for their own future with men.

When Barbara's teenage daughters point out her continual acquiescence to her husband, she admits that this is a place where she is struggling —having this man in her life is so important to her. But she is trying to resist. She is neither unaware of nor resigned to the subservience in her relationship with her husband. She also tells them, "This is my issue, not yours." Barbara doesn't deny the truth of her daughters' remarks, nor does she engage in apology or self-analysis with her daughters. She makes sure the burden of her issues with her husband is hers, and not theirs.

Given how easily families can fall into sexist patterns, mothers may need to look for opportunities to hear their daughters' voices. One mother realized that, unwittingly, she and her husband were treating their son preferentially at the dinner table. "When my older son was away at camp," says Isabel, "my husband and I found out things about my daughter that we didn't have a clue were a part of her personality. At dinner, she would do full-blown comedy routines. We loved it. When I asked her why she didn't do this when her brother was around, she just smiled at me and shrugged. We now look at her in a completely different way."

By enthusiastically welcoming a voice she hadn't heard from her daughter, Isabel supports her daughter's resistance more fully. Unable to control how boys will treat girls in the world at large, in families in which there are sons, parents can raise their sons' consciousness and affirm a daughter's voice by making space for her voice within the family.

Judith tells how her daughter Vera also "bloomed when Dennis, her older brother, was away at camp. I realized that he took up all of the space at the dinner table. When Dennis came back from camp, he had to fight Vera for space—things had changed when he was away and she wasn't going to let him just take over again." Judith's trust in her daughter's voice and in her son's integrity allowed her to tell her son that he would have to adjust. She then went a step further, enlisting him as an ally, another member of the revolutionary cell. Making space to listen to a daughter's voice within the cacophony of family life deeply validates her place in the family and the family's efforts to resist.

Despite the absence of a father in the home, mothers in single-parent families grapple with many of the same issues of gender power relations. Haunted by the idea of the traditional family headed by a man, single-mother families may have the experience of virtually holding a space open for the true head of the household, the ex-husband who was once there or the new man who will be there in the hoped-for future. Suffering from the ghostly presence of this missing man, single mothers' authority is undermined by the attitude, sometimes their own, that things would be better if only there were a man in the house.

Yet most often the daughters of single mothers enjoy some advantage in developing a sense of competence and self-esteem. In the absence of a man in the house, girls seem to trust their own authority more. Their mothers, most likely, do exercise more power in their households and their daughters' lives than mothers in traditional two-parent families. With greater control, single mothers are more able to resist sexism in their family's daily life. But this greater control does not extend to their daughters' relationships with their fathers.

In the aftershock of divorce, each family remakes itself, usually with little support and guidance from society. Parents negotiate new relationships with their children and each other. In a culture that fails to encourage responsible fathering, daughters may not see their fathers often enough; many girls don't. They run the risk during childhood of idealizing their fathers, and then, as women, they may painfully search for similar men in a romantic haze.

While a mother cannot control a daughter's relationship with her father, a mother can encourage it and, certainly, not interfere with it unnecessarily. Faith, for example, left her alcoholic husband six years ago when her youngest daughter was only six months old and the oldest was just a year and a half. Despite Faith's understandable trepidation, the two girls see their father two or three times a year (they live in different states) for lengthy visits. To ensure her daughters' safety, Faith insists that her wealthy ex-husband pay for full-time child care during their visits. She endures her daughters' worrisome visits to their father because she is convinced that denying them any relationship with him would be more harmful. His very real shortcomings might fade from memory without these regular visits.

Instead, Faith's daughters have some opportunity to test out their relationship with a man, to know the reality of who their father is, and to accept that reality. As they approach adolescence, knowing and being known by their father will be an increasingly important issue for them, as it is for most adolescent girls. Allowing girls to develop a sense of family and connection that extends beyond divorce and the walls of the home can be a powerful source of strength.

Girls' true connection to their family is one of the most important protections they can have against the problems that plague them in adolescence. To stay connected with girls, the family must embrace its capacity to resist and to become a revolutionary cell, a safe house through which girls can pass into womanhood. While the impetus for revolutionizing the family for a daughter's sake will often come from the mother, love for girls and commitment to their strength can mobilize every family member. The father's role is critical. By staying connected with daughters, fathers can learn to appreciate ways of being and feeling that they have been denied by themselves and by the culture.

FATHERS AS ALLIES

A daughter's relationship with her father is her first relationship with a man. How he treats her is a key lesson that a daughter carries into her future relationships with men. Her expectations about her place in the world are shaped by the place her father accords women in his world. Fathering a daughter is an opportunity for men to know and understand sexism in ways they rarely do. It is also an opportunity for them to struggle against sexism for their daughters' sake, and their own. As bell hooks reminds us, "Men are not exploited or oppressed by sexism, but there are ways in which they suffer as a result of it." Today's father chooses either to perpetuate sexism in his relationship with his daughter or to ally with her and the whole family in opposing it.

Sexism influences father daughter relationships even before girls are born. Researchers continue to find that fathers-to-be "overwhelmingly desire male rather than female off-spring with a degree of preference far exceeding that of their wives." Fathers prefer sons before a child is born and after. Two-year-old boys get twice as much attention from their fathers as two-year-old girls. And the amount of attention girls do receive from their father decreases as they get older. Even fathers who are "extremely attached" to their daughters as infants "are less close at nine, and less close, again, at thirteen."

Paternal neglect shapes the traditional father daughter relationship. In the traditional scenario, the father has little time or energy for his children, particularly girls. The daughter is cast in the role of "Daddy's Girl" or "Little Princess," and she is appreciated for her conventional femininity, her pretty appearance, her emotional warmth, her sweetness, and even her charming feistiness, but not for her competence, assertiveness, or independence. Outings with her busy father are special occasions when he charms and courts her. If she is Daddy's Little Princess, he is her prince. This romanticized relationship pushes girls toward the stifling feminine perfection valued in our culture. The Little Princess and the Perfect Girl are one. Both are really nice, good, cheerful, generous, loving, self-sacrificing, and, of course, pretty.

When father daughter relationships focus too intently on a girl as a romantic-heroine-in-training, downplaying the fullness of her being, the relationship takes on subtle but discomforting sexual overtones. Because of these overtones, the physical closeness a father enjoys with his young daughter may start to feel awkward for them both as she begins to develop womanly curves. Older girls routinely notice their fathers' pointedly *not*

274

noticing the sometimes dramatic changes in their bodies. While teenage girls want to be seen, they also don't want to be looked at intently. (One teenage girl reported that having people's eyes on her felt like "sandpaper.")

Negotiating this fine line is easier for fathers who truly know their daughters, and who resist the temptation to cast them in distorting stereotypes throughout their lives. By developing relationships with daughters that recognize and value a daughter beyond the constraints of conventional femininity—her lively mind, her sense of humor, her vivaciousness, her physical stamina and agility, or any of the other traits she may possess—fathers are rewarded by greater equanimity as their daughters mature.

The conventional femininity prized in traditional father daughter relationships is one of the well-trodden paths into patriarchy we named "paths of least resistance" in chapter 2. In this most recent wave of feminism, many parents, particularly white middle-class ones, tried to adopt gender-neutral child-rearing practices to avoid this path. Despite their good intentions, too often, gender neutrality translated into "girls will be boys," another path of least resistance. Fathers caught up in this approach insist that their daughters can—and perhaps should—do anything that boys can do. They tacitly promote male models of how to be and act in the world, without recognizing the cost to their daughters: betrayal of themselves and their connections with women. Appearing to treat girls equally by treating them as if they were boys affirms male superiority.

Moreover, girls typically aren't really treated equally with boys. Judith Levine, the author of *My Enemy, My Love,* found that fathers who engage in nontraditional activities with their daughters praise them for having fun and for being enthusiastic, but not for being competent, which is what they praise their sons for. Fathers' deep-seated belief that their daughters don't actually *need* to excel in these activities colors their behavior, and no doubt their daughters' performance.

As an ally in mother daughter revolution, a father purposefully struggles against leading his daughter down any of the familiar paths of least resistance—conventional femininity or "girls will be boys." Instead, motivated by paternal love and concern, he assumes his responsibility to unlearn and contradict sexism at home and in the outside world. Rejecting culturally sanctioned paternal neglect, he observes and listens closely to his daughter to find out who she is, particularly as she nears adolescence.

Most adolescent daughters insist that their fathers "just don't understand" them, in a foreshadowing of the common complaint between men and women captured in linguist Deborah Tannen's book, *You Just Don't Understand.* Tannen describes how men and women often miscommunicate. For women, "telling about a problem is a bid for an expression of understanding ('I know how you feel') or a similar complaint ('I felt the same way when something similar happened to me')." For men, it is an invitation to problem solve, and they are confused when their proffered solutions are rebuffed with impatience. Women and men are simply "talking at cross-purposes." As daughters start to become women, the ways fathers are accustomed to communicating with and treating women interfere with their relationship with their daughters.

Ellen, David's thirteen-year-old daughter, recently shared with him that her best friend was "being really mean" to her. The friend has been teasing Ellen, saying that she is "a baby" who doesn't know how to act with boys. David, seeing his daughter's hurt face, told her, "Just ignore her." He is puzzled when his daughter angrily walks away saying, "You don't understand anything!" Ellen wanted to talk about how *she* felt and about her relationship with her best friend, and her father responded with peremptory problem solving. The problem was clear to him and the solution even clearer. What he couldn't see was what his daughter wanted from him.

Observing adolescent girls with their families, psychologist Terri Apter was struck by the difference between girls' relationships with their fathers and those with their mothers. As girls go through adolescence, their relationships with their fathers grow less intimate and reciprocal, prompting Apter to conclude that "adolescent girls are not close to their fathers."

Girls begin to see and treat their fathers differently, and often express their feelings that their fathers do not know them. Fathers, girls insisted, had "no time" for, "no interest" in, "no patience" for girls' feelings and just didn't try to understand them. The girls focused on their fathers' inability or unwillingness to listen to and hear them.

Fathers and daughters, like men and women in general, often find themselves wary intimates. As parents, fathers bear the responsibility for overcoming the wariness and distrust by truly paying attention to their daughters, listening to what they have to say, and, most importantly, trying to understand what they mean. Opening the lines of communication is the foundation for creating the true relationship both daughters and fathers desire. By celebrating who their daughters truly are, instead of trying to push them into being who the culture insists they should be, fathers contradict sexism and act to break the cycle of cultural betrayal.

Mothers need not shoulder the responsibility for developing this true relationship between fathers and daughters. Enlisting fathers as allies is an empowering alternative to a tactic mothers often fall back on: acting as emotional go-betweens for fathers and daughters. By rejecting the temptation to do the emotional work of relationship for fathers, mothers encourage them to do it themselves and to come to know their daughters. Yet mothers often face the dilemma of not wanting to interfere with a daughter's relationship with her father but having to interfere to protect the daughter.

Rita, the mother of a sixteen-year-old, is having a difficult time resolving this dilemma. Recently, her daughter, Jeannie, wanted to go to an impromptu pajama party at a friend's house. Rita overheard from the next room, as Jeannie (timorously) asked her father for permission to go. The father, ordinarily a controlling man, had had a few drinks that evening. Like a cat playing with a mouse, he teased Jeannie, putting her through hoops, leading her on with the semblance of hope that he might let her go. Rita listened, pained by the exchange, knowing her daughter's desperation, and then anger, as it finally dawned on the girl that her father had no intention of letting her go anywhere. But Rita didn't intervene. Instead, she went to the family room where she has her study, sat in a chair, and felt the tears roll down her face. Moments later, her daughter came in, sat on the arm of the chair, nestled close to her mother, and sighed, "He's so mean, Mom." Rita simply answered, "I know."

Telling this story later, Rita confides that she felt trapped and confused. She didn't want to interfere with her daughter's efforts to work out an independent relationship with her father. She was also certain that if she had said anything to her husband it would only have provoked an argument, an argument about them and their relationship, and not about his relationship with their daughter. She was stuck and didn't know how to reconcile these concerns with her desire to protect her daughter. By allying with Jeannie as a sympathetic but equally powerless victim, Rita confirmed traditional power relations within her family, and therefore the world. What else could she have done? Certainly, confronting her husband about his emotional game playing would have been difficult, but as an adult, Rita is in a better position to weather that confrontation than her more vulnerable daughter. Regardless of her husband's response, she could model more powerful, active behavior for her daughter. She can join with her daughter in resistance.

If a father wants to be an ally in the revolution of mothers, and not the enemy, he must assume equal parental responsibility. Good fathering, like mothering, is a political act. Fathers must arm themselves with an awareness of how the culture exploits and oppresses women and girls. Fathers' reinterpreting of the world for daughters to expose sexism is a powerful rebuttal of the cultural messages girls routinely receive in school, the community, and the media.

A father, for example, who praises women for traits other than their appearance (ambition, physical stamina, assertiveness, humor, and intelligence, among others) and who refuses to evaluate women on the basis of their looks uses the authority and privilege he enjoys in the world as a man to oppose sexism. He is a convincing advocate, a responsible father. By taking action in the public arena against sexism—by protesting sexual harassment in schools, pushing for changes in curricula that discriminate against girls, participating in a prochoice march, or in any number of other ways—a father convinces his daughter of his commitment to fairness for women. His lived opposition to women's oppression is profoundly meaningful to a girl.

As an ally and a powerful member of the family as a revolutionary cell, a father strengthens his daughter's resistance with his own struggle against sexism. Fathers who join the resistance will not be able to eradicate their sexist training overnight. What is required is a willingness to be open to a process of learning, with its unavoidable uncertainty. As a father learns from an unexpected source, his daughter, he teaches her that masculine authority is not infallible and that she, too, is powerful. A father's active resistance is key to a family's transformation into a revolutionary cell, and his involvement moves the revolution beyond mother daughter relationships.

OTHERMOTHERS

At adolescence, writes Carol Gilligan, girls join Miranda in the *Tempest* by asking, "Why all the suffering? and where are the women?" This cry of adolescent girls echoes the often-unspoken question of mothers: Why am I so exhausted? and where are the women? "Tired, tired, and tired of being tired," one mother describes her life. "When I adopted my two children, I knew what it would mean for my life, and how it would change my work. What no one told me was about stamina." Motherhood is exhausting in our society. While it will continue to be exhausting until social policy changes, a change in women's personal policies could expand mothers' resources. Motherhood does not have to be the responsibility solely of biological or adoptive mothers living in the isolation of individual nuclear families. Much of the pain of mothering daughters and the possibility for betrayal grows out of mothers' sole responsibility for the outcome of their daughters' lives.

What if women were to reclaim the power of mothering from its patriarchal place? What if mothers could depend on other women to support their growing edge of self just as a mother does for her daughter? And who could second a mother's applause and offer daughters other perspectives and examples of being a woman? Joining mothers to reclaim authority and resist the role of "perfect motherhood," othermothers increase the likelihood of raising daughters who are resisters.

If, as researchers have documented, the presence of one caring adult with whom a girl has a confiding relationship reinforces her resiliency, why don't all women—mothers or not—take back and transform motherhood into a revolutionary network? Teachers, counselors, group leaders, church workers—all the women who touch girls' lives—hold the possibility for sustaining healthy resistance in girls. Reappropriation of the role of motherhood for all women reclaims mothering as a force for social change.

Motherhood as a patriarchal institution is built on the self-sacrifice of women. Mothering as a revolutionary experience holds the potential for conscious community and joint action. Reclaiming mothering is not a moral stance but a pragmatic one based in the very real power women have in their children's lives. Women in this culture are now divided into women who mother and women who don't, mothers who work and mothers who don't, mothers who can afford other women as caretakers for their children and mothers who take care of others' children instead of their own. Each of these divisions of women claims to hold the moral high ground, some using romanticized notions of women's nurturance and others asserting the right to equality of opportunity in order to punish each other. In these punishing separations, women fail to recognize the shared difficulties of being women in a system where, as Audre Lorde says, "we were never meant to survive. Not as human beings." Asking women to join each other as mothers to claim their ignored power from the sidelines of the culture creates an opportunity for solidarity among all women.

"For centuries," writes Adrienne Rich in *Of Woman Born,* "daughters have been strengthened and energized by nonbiological mothers, who have combined a care for the practical values of survival with an incitement toward further horizons, a compassion for vulnerability with an insistence on our buried strengths. It is precisely this that has allowed us to survive— not our occasional breakthroughs into tokendom, and not our 'special cases,' although these have been beacons for us, illuminations of what 'ought to be.'"

Within many African-American communities, women share the responsibilities of mothering within their communities. The complex interaction of West African traditions with the intentional destruction of families under slavery gives many African-American women a very different sense of communal responsibility for children than middle-class white women have. African-American othermothers speak of "our kids" and make it their business to know the children in their communities. As sociologist Patricia Hill Collins writes, "Black women's feelings of responsibility for nurturing the children in their own extended family networks have stimulated a more generalized ethic of care where Black women feel accountable to all the Black community's children."

Othermothers provide girls with more strategies for resistance. Othermothers, caring adults living outside the family story, love girls by choice, bring fresh eyes to mother daughter relationships, and teach voice by embodying different ways of being women than a daughter has available in her mother. Through close relationships with othermothers, girls come to know a range of options for their lives and, so, experience greater control in their own lives. Patricia Hill Collins sees this as central to resistance and empowerment: "In contrast to the isolation of middle-class White mother/daughter dyads, Black women-centered extended family networks foster an early identification with a much wider range of models of Black womanhood, which can lead to a greater sense of empowerment in young Black girls."

Othermothers often provide daughters with opportunities to build competence and skills—sometimes in surprising ways. Elsa adopted Jackie (an exchange-student friend of Elsa's mother) as an othermother even though Elsa lived in Denmark and Jackie in the United States. Despite the distance and language differences, the two developed a close bond. At eleven, Elsa surprised Jackie by confiding in Jackie that she had secretly taught herself English (from watching American soap operas!) to be able to write and speak with her. But Danish society frowns on individuals who stand out, who achieve ahead of their peers. Elsa decided to keep her knowledge a secret in school, where it would have caused a stir. Jackie supported her silence but placed it in perspective: "It's important for you to know that you're making a choice to do that, for your own reasons, but this is a major accomplishment." Jackie told Elsa's parents. While Elsa's parents were concerned that she had broken a silence required by Danish society, Jackie helped Elsa and her parents recognize Elsa's courage, intelligence, and persistence. Jackie, as an outside eye, gave Elsa another perspective on her experience.

Girls often approach othermothers to try out ideas and information they feel may be too risky to take straight to their mothers. Valerie became an othermother to her stepgranddaughter, Dalia. Valerie, knowing that her daughter (Dalia's stepmother) was anxious about talking to her about menstruating, wrote Dalia a letter about coming into womanhood. She asked her directly if she had gotten her period. Talking about the subject with Valerie allowed the girl to talk to her mother.

Sexuality and sexual abuse are often discussed and explored with othermothers first. Carmina's daughter told an othermother about her entrapment in an incestuous relationship with her own father, and this loving neighbor told Carmina. This othermother stood by both Carmina and her daughter as they gradually worked through their pain.

Othermothers not only often inform mothers of abuse but sometimes even prevent it.

"I wanted to have daughters so I could raise them differently, and I have," Monica said. Her daughters, now in their early teens, are confident young women. When asked what she thinks helped, she says, "I have a strong woman friend. My daughters see that it is possible to have powerful relationships with women as well as men. My friend boosts me in my own thinking about how to raise my girls. She challenges me when she thinks I'm not showing enough strength, and she provides my daughters with another model for being an adult."

Monica's friend also spends time in the home with the family, and her presence and importance in Monica's life models for her daughters that women are valuable and that men don't have to be the center of their relational life. But there are additional benefits. Monica continues: "When I told my friend that my husband was starting to get rough with me, she showed up at the house with other friends. They let it be known that they were witnesses, that it wasn't acceptable. It stopped him, just knowing that my friends were aware and watching."

Psychologist Mary Belenky worked with young mothers living isolated existences in rural Vermont. She broke their isolation by bringing them together in groups. Some of these women's husbands, who used violence to get their way, stopped their battering when they realized that their wives had witnesses and resources. Isolation enforces so much of the intensity and violence that strain families. Othermothers' presence in the home creates more resources and energy, and takes some of the strain off parents. Othermothers act to interrupt violence.

Othermothers are also important allies to mothers. Like the *madrinas* (godmothers) of Latino culture, they provide emotional and material support for girls and serve as *comadres* (co-mothers) with mothers. Othermothers encourage mothers to trust their expertise, to reclaim their authority, and to rely on their perceptions about mothering. By accepting a measure of responsibility for a daughter's well-being, othermothers join with mothers to build a revolutionary network of women where daughters can fearlessly exercise their power. Othermothers help women expand their power by creating community where mothers are deeply respected and valued.

"I have a lesbian friend who has no children, but her own tough growing up and surviving has made her a woman who trusts herself and isn't plagued by goodness," says Iris, in describing her *comadre*. "I grew up a good girl, and it's made it hard to stand up for myself as a mother. One of my daughters has really given me a hard time; she knows where I'm stuck and seems to brilliantly choose those areas to challenge me. I call my friend and cry and rant and rave. Together we talk about how I can be kinder to myself and trust my mothering."

Mothering in the places where a mother was never properly mothered is hard. A daughter often challenges her mother exactly at these vulnerable places in her mother's psyche. Othermothers can encourage a mother to care for herself in those "unmothered" places. With othermothers in a mother's world, she doesn't need to carry all the burdens, to be perfect. "I feel I can go in and allow the daughter to talk about the world in her terms, not in her mother's terms," says one othermother.

Othermothers validate a biological mother's perception and her expertise about her mothering. Patricia had a sense that her beautiful younger daughter, Elizabeth, was struggling with something that distracted her constantly and wordlessly. She had taken her to two different psychologists who simply saw a beautiful, charming girl. They doubted the mother, not this adorable child. Shelley, a friend of Patricia's, stayed with the family for a few days. She and Elizabeth hit it off and spent time talking about Elizabeth's hopes and dreams. Afterward, Shelley approached Patricia with the pattern that she saw in Elizabeth's behavior. "Shelley put together the missing pieces of what was troubling my daughter—Elizabeth spent years of her childhood in the hospital with a life-threatening disease. She was such a perfect kid through the whole ordeal," says Patricia. Shelley realized that Elizabeth's distraction and unusual attraction to risk taking was a way to conquer old fears that she hadn't dared to feel during illness.

While Shelley's analysis was helpful to Patricia, what Patricia valued most was having her perceptions validated, instead of being dismissed by experts. Othermothers teach mothers to trust their voices and knowledge of their daughters. As one woman complained, "Jane Goodall went into the woods and looked at apes and came out an expert. We look at our own daughters every day and aren't thought of as experts." Within the community of mothers and othermothers, women are the experts.

Othermothers' deep connections to mothers and children in their community give these women a tangible commitment to the ongoing life of the community as a whole. As Patricia Hill Collins observes, othermothering is a springboard for social action. The othermothers with whom we spoke described the power and pleasure they derive from their relationships with girls. "I identify with her," said Valerie, one othermother, about her "daughter." "By engaging with her, I am engaging in life, taking action, and it's very healing." Concerned about the everyday racism that her "daughter" had come to accept at school, Valerie, a theater critic, began a program to bring new plays by young African-American playwrights to public schools.

"Well, I have a dream," eleven-year-old Elsa tells her othermother, Jackie. "It's not just a nighttime dream," she goes on. "It's a dream where people are allowed to choose their own families. You could choose to be in each other's families and not just as friends, but by saying so, that you are actually family with them." Girls want real relationships with women, and they have much to teach us as women: how to value relationship, how to trust the power of women, how to be angry, how to fight and love fiercely. Women need to bring girls into their lives so that girls can resist disconnection by joining women who are joined, and so that women can heal the places in themselves where girls are still whole. "Sometimes Aida will run out of the room where I am with my friends," says Delia, smiling at her memory of her nine-year-old daughter. "She'll say, 'Bye, Mom, and Mom and Mom!' She loves to be with us. We take her seriously. She calls these women her friends. My friends, who don't have children, call her 'friend,' too." This mother and daughter both take joy in their small community of women and girl.

United in love and friendship, committed to resilience and resistance, a strong and unified community of women make a wedge in the wall. Only the union of mothers with othermothers can lift what has become "just life" for girls into moral outrage demanding that girls be allowed to live fully and safely. The first step is for all women to lock arms with mothers and join in the work of mothering. For the sake of the next generations of women, women have to stay linked to find noncompetitive ways to work together, while maintaining the integrity of their differences. Reappropriating mothering for all women transforms women's unique power to create life and shifts mothers' role from an exhausting transmission of limits to an opportunity to create new ways of living that redefine women's place in the world.

A CIRCLE OF MOTHERS

The contemporary feminist movement began with women who decided to meet and to share their stories—not theory, not extremist demands, just stories and the radical belief that women are human beings. Women's simple sharing of what had happened to them, of what they felt, and of what they were often afraid to say to themselves and to others created the beginnings of an analysis of the political conditions of women's lives. But in the last decade, the interweaving of the personal and political has unraveled. Rarely, these days, are personal support and political action combined into true solidarity. The mothers' groups that we know of came together for mutual support, and sometimes for joint action, but never explicitly for both. The most intimate details of our lives are shaped by power relations and, so, are political; every distant political action has deeply personal implications for who we are and how we are "supposed" to live. A circle of mothers, as we envision it, begins with the belief that mothering is powerful and political work and that, by developing a critical political awareness, we as mothers can claim and assert that power on behalf of ourselves and our daughters.

Isolation is one of the most powerful tools for oppression. By isolating women through shame, exhaustion, and fears of craziness and imperfection, patriarchy works its own special magic of separation and disconnection. The inner divisions created in women's collision with the wall isolate women's authenticity within ideals of the perfect woman, wife, and mother, and "girls will be boys" ideals of success. Women are also isolated from each other by the value placed on middle-class life and its accompanying expectations. Pressures of work and family life leave many women feeling as though they are standing astride two galloping horses like stunt riders in old wild West movies. Seeking support gets labeled "wimpy" in this culture when, actually, finding support and gathering the resources others have to offer is fundamental to our ability to be autonomous, to care for ourselves. Forming a circle of mothers is a powerful act that contradicts this isolation. For that reason it is as necessary as it may initially be uncomfortable (or inconvenient) to undertake.

"My daughter understands that part of being a woman," says Judith, "is meeting regularly with other women for support." Judith has met once a month with a group of women for support, some close friends and some not, for nearly fifteen years. Women have joined with each other for support around a variety of issues. Books like *Fat Is a Feminist Issue* and *Women Who Love Too Much* concluded with guidelines for forming support groups to tackle women's dependence on food and on men, respectively. Some twelve-step programs (such as Alcoholics Anonymous, Overeaters Anonymous, and so forth), particularly in variations that are more appropriate for women (such as Charlotte Kasl's *Many Roads, One Journey*), have given many women the safety to have their struggles witnessed and validated in nonpolitical versions of consciousness-raising groups.

Mothers, too, have joined each other for support, particularly in the early years of child rearing. Ruthellen Josselson, a clinical psychologist, decided to start a mother's group when the isolation of being a new mother hit her after the birth of her daughter. She called one of the women she liked from her childbirth class. They both agreed to find a few other new mothers and to meet. Their group, now composed of six women, has met for the past fourteen years. One of the original group members dropped out, another moved. "It was truly lifesaving to have this support," says Ruthellen. "We have talked about everything."

Lorri Slepian, the director of the recently formed National Association of Mothers Centers, recognized the pressing need for new mothers to have support and encouragement. This association loosely links 250 centers across the United States and in Germany. Slepian's office provides information and guidance for mothers to develop their authority and competence in community with other women. Slepian feels "a force out there" in mothers, a force that she believes is becoming increasingly savvy and politicized as mothers realize the power of their knowledge and skills and the ways they are discounted within the larger culture.

As word got out about the Harvard Project and AAUW research on girls' self-esteem, some mothers of daughters mobilized and formed groups to explore issues of gender equity. These mothers were particularly concerned about gender bias in the schools that their daughters were attending. One school in New York started a softball league for girls as a result of mothers' activism. The mothers of daughters in a Boston suburb organized a series of lectures and mother daughter events to bring greater awareness of girls' development into their school. In Texas, poor Latina mothers and their sixth-grade daughters came together in a program run by Josephina Villamil Tinajero, a Latina educator. These mothers and daughters meet in separate groups on a college campus to find ways to expand the girls' horizons despite apathetic schools. Research indicates that one of the reasons why girls, particularly girls of color, find it difficult to reach beyond the lives of their mothers is the threat to their relationships—by going to college, they would be in danger of becoming different and losing their protection from a hostile world. Not only did many of these girls go on to college, but a number of the mothers went back to school, too. The power of these mothers together created new programs and new opportunities for their daughters.

"We need to establish groups that supply safety, expertise, support and informed brass-tacks methods in order to address the feelings about our own adolescence and about theirs," argues Leslie McGovern, a psychotherapist who works with women to create such groups. She sees this work as the basis for addressing "an increasingly larger picture than just that of the relationship between ourselves and our daughters."

As Gloria Steinem says, "It doesn't matter where we begin the personal/political circle, but it matters desperately that we complete it." The circle of mothers we have in mind would form a complete personal and political circle to explore reclaiming, voice lessons, and joining. Essential to completing this circle is including women from diverse backgrounds. Only through engaging with the range of exploitation and oppression experienced by women of different classes and races can women come into a true understanding of sexist oppression and the ways that patriarchy thrives through racism, classism, and homophobia.

A circle of solidarity between different women thwarts the divisions imposed by the wall and develops the most radical perspective. Women from similar backgrounds can also explore the privilege and oppression that come from race, class, and sexual orientation. Every group of women will have differences to discuss—between mothers who work outside the home and those who don't, between single mothers and mothers with partners, and so forth. The combined creativity of women enhances our ability to draw political conclusions from our individual experiences. Through working together, Leslie McGovern observes, "We begin to think more clearly about the disempowerment our young women/daughters are battling each moment of their teenage years."

The work of a circle of mothers moves from reclaiming and learning from our daughters to learning from and joining with each other in action on behalf of our daughters. Reclaiming those parts of ourselves that were lost in the collision with the wall goes better in groups. The presence of other women who are daring to look for their prewall selves sparks our own remembering. At a workshop conducted by Carol Gilligan and voice teacher Kristin Linklater, women evoked the ambiance of their girlhood world by calling forth its sounds, scents, textures, games, and songs. One woman's memory would call forth another woman's memory. Women together can create new ways to access what they lost or forgot at the wall. Much of reclaiming the experiences of girlhood is playful and joyous. But remembering our collision with the wall calls forth the fears we faced then. With others' concern and attention we can face together as women what was overwhelming to us as girls. Reclaiming is a political act that reveals the structure of the wall and reconnects women with themselves. Developing a knowledge base about the wall from our personal experience allows mothers to be more present with daughters and more creative in developing strategies for their own lives and with their daughters.

There is no set program for circles of mothers. As Kathy Thurber, vice-president of the Minneapolis Park and Recreation Board, found out, taking part in social change for girls begins with women and girls doing what they know. Kathy began a Girls' Initiative in community parks to give girls a place in public space. She read every bit of research on girls from the Harvard Project and from the University of Minnesota in an effort to figure out how to work with girls. Worried that she needed to do more than she was doing (which was basically to ask girls what they wanted and to have them work with women to get it), she asked Carol Gilligan when she was going to develop curriculum guides. Gilligan explained that she had no intention of doing so. "You are doing it. You are listening to the girls, using the research, sharing it with others." Kathy said that she felt like Dorothy at the end of *The Wizard of Oz:* "You mean I've always had the power to go home?" By bringing girls together and finding out what they wanted, Kathy was doing it "right."

Mothers can begin a circle the "right" way by beginning with what most compels them. We suggest that mothers work through the process presented in this book, beginning with a discussion of mother blaming and sexism in the culture, and pick and choose from what is presented here to fit the group's needs. Each meeting of the circle could move through reclaiming, voice lessons, and joining, depending on the group's needs. The power of a circle of mothers comes from personal experience guiding political awareness leading to joint action.

The experience of many women has led to certain basic guidelines for working in groups. A first, organizational meeting for mothers (contacted through a daughter's school or a local newspaper) sets the initial ground rules: a strictly observed time to begin and end (two to three hours usually works well), the number of weeks (if the group wants to meet each week) or months (if monthly) that each member of the circle will commit to, and the location of the meetings (so that they are accessible and don't place a burden on anyone to play hostess). A circle works well with between six and twelve members who make a commitment to be part of the circle for the set amount of time. What women disclose about themselves in a circle is confidential. Leadership of the circle can rotate from meeting to meeting.

While the circle members can decide what they most want to explore, we suggest that each meeting move from the personal sharing of reclaiming to political insight and action. The Resources section at the end of this book contains different references that describe how to proceed in a small group like a circle of mothers. From these guidelines, we have culled a few that we feel are particularly important. At every meeting, each mother is asked to share her experience or to pass, if she doesn't want to speak at the time. Mothers speak from their own experiences—*I* feel . . . *I* think . . . *I* try . . . —rather than from others' opinion or theory. What is most important is sharing stories. Women don't give advice to each other or comment on another's experience except to relate experiences that another's experience may have called to mind. In this way, the circle allows each woman the dignity of her feelings and perceptions. After women have shared stories in reclaiming, the common and different threads of the experiences are drawn and connected to explore the political implications for women and their daughters. Joining can move from these implications into action.

Mothers in a circle learn voice in the process of creating a working, active group. A circle that works has room for humor and strong feelings, including anger between group members. The collision with the wall leaves many women vulnerable to bringing hopes based on loss into groups of women: hopes of perfect harmony and perfect attention to each woman's needs. The hope of being truly heard—and women's history involves not being heard—drives some women to bring that history of silence and pain to a group with unrealistic hopes for an audience. Some women are leery of joining with other women because, in their experience, group meetings of women become pain-letting or gripe sessions.

Fears of racism and the alienation of classism also prevent listening and joining. Critic bell hooks advises that "when women come together, rather than pretend union, we would acknowledge that we are divided and must develop strategies to overcome fears, prejudices, resentments, competitiveness, etc." Middle-class and upper-class white women's guilt and denial of privilege infuriate women who have neither the comforts of class nor a choice about working and who are denied recognition of their humanity by virtue of their skin color or ethnic background. Unfortunately, in mixed groups white women often infantilize their peers from different backgrounds and leap to defend themselves out of guilt. While guilt may be inevitable upon feeling the pain of those who are denied privilege, women of privilege can take responsibility for the ways in which they may act as oppressors and use this invaluable information for revolutionizing their consciousness. Responsibility and action, not guilt, move a revolution of mothers forward. A revolution in consciousness breaks the patterns of fearfulness rooted in an economy that forces people to compete for survival. It is a profound exercise in exploring freedom and in caring for authenticity.

There is no perfect group, no perfect circle of mothers. Educator

Judy Dorney worked with a group of teachers at the Laurel School as part of the Harvard Project's exploration of women teaching girls. Reflecting on their experience of community, Judy writes, "I struggle here not to fall into a common pitfall and say, 'But we were not a perfect community,' meaning we hadn't or haven't achieved a certain state or condition of existence or that there is somewhere a perfect embodiment of community. I see this to be as dangerous as falling into the belief that there is a 'perfect girl' or a 'perfect woman.' "

A circle becomes a community when its members can openly explore disagreement and reflect on their process with each other as they move toward greater knowledge and respect for themselves and each other, love, and meaningful joint action. The structure and purpose of the circle may change over time, but it remains grounded in member mothers' adoption of a critical perspective through sharing of experiences.

Judith Herman, in her brilliant *Trauma and Recovery*, explains that trauma results in a disconnection from the community that gives life warmth and meaning. When traumas enforce the very structure of the culture, they live unacknowledged and unknown except through the language of loss spoken through the grammar of the psyche from the psychic underground. Judy Herman argues that only with an active political movement can "the active process of bearing witness" keep from giving way "to the active process of forgetting."

Mothers must mother a revolution of all women that will bear witness to girls' courage and support daughters as they approach the wall. This revolution begins in women's intimate lives—in their families and among friends. A revolution of mothers calls to all women to claim and share the power and responsibility of mothering by becoming othermothers. And the revolution moves into the world through circles of mothers. These circles give women the opportunities for recognition and restitution that are essential for healing the rifts within themselves and in the community of women. Mothers mother a revolution by claiming power and by fostering transformation out of our deepest relationships.

10

From Betrayal to Power

Resistance is the secret of joy!

Alice Walker

POSSESSING THE SECRET OF JOY

What does it mean to love a daughter in a culture that is hostile to her integrity? In a culture where power equals dominance and superiority, men's control of public life—the world of political and economic power that shapes the desires of private life—places mothers in a double bind as their daughters approach womanhood. The common ways that mothers have of guiding daughters—what we call "the paths of least resistance" in chapter 2—ask girls to make deep psychological sacrifices to straddle the cultural division of work, in the "male" public world of politics and business, and love, in the "female" private world of home and family. As girls find that they cannot enter patriarchy fully and powerfully as themselves, they feel betrayed by their mothers. But mothers did not create the separate spheres of public and private life. It is this cultural betrayal of human integrity, which divides our wholeness into these separate spheres, that makes loving and raising a daughter political work.

The romance-into-mothering myth created in the mid-1800s told women that their true nature is best expressed in the home, in private life. When market-driven factory life in the Industrial Revolution consumed women's traditional work of producing food, clothing, medicine, and crafts, women were suddenly stripped of their expertise and authority. Rather than adopting a "rationalist" solution of admitting "women into modern society on an equal footing with men," male experts promoted the "romantic solution" of relegating women to the home, safe and separate from the capitalist forum of work.

Romance prevailed for some very unromantic economic reasons. The invention of motherhood as we know it, safely nestled in the nuclear family, ensured the increased consumption of goods necessary to a growing economy. Despite the reality that many women worked for pay on farms and in factories, it created the illusion that "true" women, and women who were truly loved, stayed at home with children. Working-class women were presented with a cultural ideal that they could never attain, thus dividing women along class lines. Girls at the edge of womanhood who were asked to embody this ideal of true womanhood suffered from hysteria.

Since this time, girls have suffered an increasingly widespread crisis as they enter the culture as young women. They face the choiceless choices of denying themselves public power or dividing themselves internally to balance these separate dictates for living.

Only now do we have the knowledge and power to transform girls' suffering. Girls *struggle* against making the devastating sacrifices called for by the separation of "male" public life from a "female" private world. Carol Gilligan first noticed this resistance. As she and Lyn Brown documented, young girls are clear-minded, courageous, and confident. Even shy girls know clearly what they want and think. At the edge of adolescence, though, girls see what is coming and they fight. But, without help, their courage is quickly turned into self-blame and self-doubt, which can often turn into depression, eating disorders, suicide, and other forms of self-abuse. In the most simple terms, they lose their self-esteem.

Revolutionary mothering en-courages girls' resistance; it is a practice of resistance. Revolutionary mothering rejects the myth of the perfect mother who is all-nurturing and encompasses more of women's personal and political heritage. Every mother has a personal heritage of courage and resistance that she can reclaim. As women, we can reclaim our collective heritage of resistance. Throughout the centuries, in every country, as Adrienne Rich reminds us, women have displayed a "vital toughness and visionary strength" in their struggle for freedom. Through the process of reclaiming the courage to resist, mothers begin to join daughters to change a mother's relationship to her daughter from perceived betrayer to corevolutionary.

Transforming betrayal into power begins at home in the intimacy of mother daughter relationships and through the transformation of families into revolutionary cells. But the power of women's reclaimed voices must move into the public world. When we reclaim our connections with each other, we transform mothering from an act of selfless nurturance confined to private life to a political act of solidarity that creates a community for our daughters to join. A revolution of mothers joins all women in the political act of mothering the next generation of girls, as biological or adoptive mothers or as othermothers. By fully claiming and sharing the power of mothering, we radically change the role of "mother" from middle manager of patriarchy into visionary and activist.

When the dynamic of betrayal no longer haunts women's relationships with each other, women become free to lead powerfully and to support powerful leaders. On all fronts the revolution begins to claim the work of love and the love of work to be equally important and necessary to bring together. A revolution of mothers brings the separate spheres of work and love together so that daughters are not faced with choiceless choices, the either/ors, that divide women from themselves and each other.

Transforming mother daughter relationships begins with voice lessons that encourage resistance; a mother daughter revolution begins with public speaking that resists cultural systems of separation and dominance. Naming for ourselves and speaking to each other about what we are not supposed to know or see are the first steps in transforming betrayal into power. Taking power back from betrayal begins with knowledge. The familiar adage "knowledge is power" happens to be true. Knowledge of our heritage and history, the politics of our psyches, our common differences, and ways to begin to take action gives us the power to know more clearly what options for living and loving we can create.

This power of knowledge creates a desire for more than what we are offered in the supermarket of the culture. What do we truly want for ourselves and for our daughters? Clearly, not just what money can buy. As a revolution of mothers, we begin reclaiming our power as women by asking these hard questions of ourselves and each other within the supportive context of our revolutionary cells—the safe houses of families, in concert with othermothers and in circles of mothers. We can bring our questions into public life in every contact with the institutions of the culture—schools, government, business.

The process of revolutionizing society by tearing down the oppressive walls of the culture and the division between public and private life will continue for generations. Creating a world where our daughters are truly safe and able to live fully certainly will not happen during their childhoods and probably will not happen in their lifetimes. No quick fixes exist for problems that are part of the very fabric of the culture. There is no simple mother-for-success formula that cuts a clear path into the unknown.

The answer is continuing resistance: a process, first, of bringing into knowledge and, thus, power what has been unspoken and unnamed between mothers and daughters, among women, and between women and men; and, second, a resistance that brings mothering into public life by organizing at every level of society—from circles of mothers to politicized networks of women who love girls. What our daughters need to know is that women are serious about making the world a place where they can dare to be whole, true, and powerful.

We can create a community of women for them to join. When women resist the guilt and seduction of private life, the true betrayal—the betrayal of girls and women by a culture created by men—can be transformed into greater potential and ways of living fully for daughters and sons, women and men of all classes and races. This is leadership: taking responsibility to bring this vision into reality through our words and actions. A revolution of mothers calls all women into leadership on behalf of the next generation of women.

PUBLIC SPEAKING

What would it mean for women to speak the truth in public? Truth-telling mothers challenge the public world to be responsible to our daughters, ourselves, and each other. Like young girls, revolutionary mothers sound the alarm that life is not fair. Revolutionary mothers join daughters' voices to argue for fairness and compassion in public policy and the world of work. These women talk their talk in community centers, at school meetings, in the halls of legislatures, on television, and with their votes. The call to revolutionary mothering invites women to tell the truths of their lives and to redefine the purpose of public life. The boundary between public and private, work and love, disappears as mothers speak and lead from home to capitol. Only then can girls join the culture without giving up part of themselves.

When women speak in public, separations in the culture get caught in women's throats. As we discussed in chapter 2, the most common routes for women into patriarchy, the paths of least resistance, provide the options for public speaking: either to embrace traditional feminine roles and speak a language of nurturance or to adopt the "girls will be boys" or "one of the guys" approach and think, and speak, "like a man." Feminist public speakers have different voices, but these voices are also distorted in a male-voiced culture. Women in public life are simply in a bind: if they speak "like a man," they are charged by other women with selling out; if they speak for "women," their concerns are marginalized because these discussions take place at the edges of public life, not at its center. So far, none of women's public-speaking voices successfully articulates the full truth of women's experience; none embraces the integration of women's work and love. A primary task of a revolution of mothers is to create new public-speaking voices that transform public dialogue itself. To do so, we need to know how women's truths and voices have been distorted within the existing dialogue.

Women's public speaking, like women's lives, has been framed in the public/private split in the culture. When women speak of the issues that most press on them as they try to balance work and family, their concerns are labeled "women's issues," which, by definition, place them outside the deepest concerns of male culture. Few men speak out about the so-called women's issues of child care and parental leave. The burden of family and children falls on women who are, at the same time, denied cultural authority to voice these concerns. Women, thus, find themselves betrayed both by not being taken seriously on the issues that most directly affect their lives and by being told in a variety of ways to stay in the private sphere.

We live in a culture where speaking of love in public life is still shameful. Those who show feeling and compassion in the masculine world of public life are considered weak and feminine. "Acting like a girl" in public is grounds for ridicule and dismissal. A revolution of mothers claims that love is worth bringing into the work of public life. If we, as a culture, do not exist to encourage the growth and joy of all of our children, then our culture betrays us as well as our children. The love of a revolution of mothers is not maternal self-sacrifice and idealized nurturance. The love of a revolution of mothers is a politicized love, born out of knowledge and understanding of our common differences. Voices of truth that speak out of this love for our daughters have the power to break through the betrayals that have separated us.

In the recent past, activist women have struggled to articulate women's concerns and perspectives and be taken seriously. Through the 1970s, these activists spoke in two predominant voices: the *voice of equality* and the *voice of victimization*. The voice of equality is a demand for rights spoken in a language understood by male culture. Equality speaks of contractual exchange—this equals that—which is the foundation of market relations and the legal system.

Speaking in this voice has had the unintentional effect of legitimizing the legal system created by privileged men to protect their interests. The call for women's right to equality with men was made and answered predominantly by white, middle-class women. As bell hooks asks, since all men are not equal to each other in this country, "which men do women want to be equal to?" For too many women at this stage of the women's movement, the answer was fairly clear: privileged white men. These women, in effect, asked to compete with men on the terms that men had defined. As these women protested to be able to move from the world of love to the world of work, their goals, at best, idealized work and, at worst, sought to give white women the privileges of upper-class white men. This approach inadvertently continued the race and class divisions among women that were created in the middle-class ideal of "true" womanhood.

As many women in the women's movement of the 1970s began speaking with the voice of equality, another voice could be heard in its echo. The voice of victimization attempted to bring the personal plight of many women's pain and powerlessness into public light. This voice has broken the silence around rape, battering, poverty, and the sexual and physical abuse of children. It has caused a deep shift in public awareness. Yet it also distorts women's reality. This voice presents a simplistic polarization of human beings as victims or victimizers. Women's strength and resilience were left out of the equation. For women whose lives were hard but who lived bravely, being cast in the role of victim felt like a betrayal.

By the early 1980s, these voices were joined by a different voice, the *voice of care*. By listening to women describe their experience and ways of understanding themselves and the world, the feminists who first articulated this voice in public speaking attempted to name women's strengths and vulnerabilities *in their own terms* rather than in comparison with men. Those who used the voice of care talked about the primacy of relationship in women's lives as a virtue that becomes subverted by women's intimate subordination. Psychologists such as Carol Gilligan and Jean Baker Miller and philosophers such as Nel Noddings and Joan Tronto spoke of the potential power of such a voice. The voice of care asked for a re-ordering of cultural values; it broke a silence in public discourse concerning issues of human connection and interdependence. Care expresses values that cannot be bought and sold in fair-market exchange. The voice of care asserts that the values assigned to private life are *also* values for public life. These values, speakers of the voice argued, were critical to the future of civilization itself.

To some women, the care voice sounded very similar to the romantic, traditionalist voice—the voice of the patriarchal woman. This traditional voice argues that women are different from men because women are specially called to nurturance. Women are viewed as special and better than men, not simply different because their life experiences are different from men's. Naming differences between men and women has historically been dangerous to women. In the nineteenth century, women insisted that their moral superiority as nurturers should give them the right to vote. After the vote was granted, women almost summarily were sent back home—where they said they belonged. Women's current status as the voting majority has yet to be translated into political power.

Differences between men and women continue to be used to keep women at the margins of the culture. As Susan Faludi documented in

Backlash, in the 1980s the traditionalist voice of nurturing, supported by business and the media, subverted the voice of care with the intention of pushing back the gains made by women in the 1970s. The voice of care was distorted into the lullaby of traditional femininity, which reinforces the betrayal of women through their exclusion from public life. The media told story after story of women, worn out by the grind of work and family, yearning for a more traditional life of 1950s motherhood. And for women who were not working outside the home, the traditionalist voice gave them a new opportunity for self-respect. The appeal of such a traditionalist voice, as Faludi also shows, is only a lingering romantic fancy for most women. This voice utterly denies women's practical, economic reality and conjures up the guilt of working women as inadequate caretakers, while pointing to the feminist movement as the source of the problem.

The feminist voice of care has not been able to articulate a way of public speaking that addresses the political concerns of women. It does not speak to the systemwide betrayal of women in discriminatory laws and practices. Within a culture that is so divided between public and private life, this voice is rarely heard as the critique of public life that it is. While it is a voice that transgresses the boundary line between public and private life by raising "private" concerns in "public," it is often considered to be a voice that keeps women out of public life because it doesn't sound like the public-speaking voices we are used to hearing and, so, it can be too easily subverted by traditionalists.

Hillary Rodham Clinton wants to "build a society based on love and connection, a society in which the bottom line would not be profit and power but ethical and spiritual sensitivity and a sense of community, mutual caring and responsibility." But she says that "the right language remains to be invented." For instance, when she tried to translate these ideas into policy, she and social commentator Michael Lerner wondered, "Would the press kill us on this?" And indeed, a prominent reporter did deride these ideas as "unintentionally hilarious."

What would new public voices for the revolution of mothers sound like? We cannot say exactly. We do know that the voices of equality and care must be brought together with a recognition of our different experiences of oppression and exploitation and our extraordinary capacities for joy, resistance, and power. The voice of equality that insisted on women's equal treatment with men must be revolutionized by caring about the particulars of women's situations. Equality of outcome, not equal treatment under the law, is what is fair to redress historical discrimination. Equal rights may have been an important strategic demand in the first phase of the contemporary women's movement. But our issues and concerns are far more complicated than those allowed by a blanket insistence on rights.

By holding together the complexity of our lives and experiences, we, and what we care about, are not split into pieces that then fragment our unity as women. The demand for abortion as a simple right, for example, was an important strategy. Women's right to choose when or whether to become mothers, and how often, is fundamental to our ability to be responsive and responsible human beings. Perhaps the prolonged struggle for women's reproductive freedom is a result of the inadequacy of speaking only in a rhetoric of rights that glosses over women's power to bring life into the world—and all of the emotional and psychological complexity that that power brings.

The voice of care humanizes the abortion debate and seems to present a more accurate reading of the choices that women confront in deciding whether or not to have a child. This voice articulates women's sense of responsibility and desire to have the means necessary to do right and care well for themselves and their children. Including this voice is necessary for the debate to become less polarized.

It is also important to realize that while the debate rages over whether or not women will have the right to make this choice for themselves, poor women, particularly women of color, are being sterilized at an appalling rate. Over one-third of all Puerto Rican women have been sterilized; these Latinas have the highest rate of sterilization in the world. Pregnant women who are poor or are not white have been told that unless they agree to sterilization or abortion, then no doctor will deliver their babies. Sometimes women are asked to sign away their wombs while in the pain of labor. Abortion and sterilization have been used against these women in ways that alienate them from middle- and upper-class white women's insistence on abortion as a right. An unspoken and underlying theme in the debate over women's reproductive freedom is that the state, the instrument of the male public world, wants to control which women reproduce children. Women's separation by race and class prevents us from developing a comprehensive understanding of issues that deeply affect all of our lives.

Within a revolution of mothers, the new voice for public speaking forges a *radical*—meaning, literally, "to the root"—consciousness of the divisions that we have accepted in our lives. Only through our commitment to a radical solidarity of women can we speak in ways that move women, and their allies, to meet the challenge of leadership. There is no essential "women's" experience but an evolving understanding of sexist oppression and how it is compounded and manipulated through other forms of oppression. A revolution of mothers calls each woman to join in the struggle for solidarity across our differences.

FIGHTING FOR SOLIDARITY

A revolution of mothers resists the betrayals of the culture by calling on women to exercise leadership through struggle toward solidarity. When women are denied access to political and economic power, except through the indulgence of men, we betray each other by competing for what little security we can find. Rather than allying with male culture's hierarchies of dominance, we women need first to ally with each other to create other options out of our combined power. Yet this alliance cannot simply solicit from each of us a long-suffering support that idealizes our victimization. The true revolutionary potential of mothers is realized as women join to

end the interrelated forms of dominance that separate women from each
other and perpetuate patriarchy in the process. Audre Lorde argues that
all forms of "human blindness"—sexism, racism, classism, homophobia
—"stem from the same root—an inability to recognize the notion of
difference as a dynamic human force, one which is enriching rather than
threatening to the defined self, when there are shared goals." Our shared
goal of changing the world for our daughters calls us together to fight for
connection through difference.

Just as mothers can risk imperfection and learn to fight for connection with their daughters, revolutionary mothers can fight for solidarity
across difference. This is difficult. As girls, we learned that our safety rested
with men and their systems. We have difficulty trusting each other because
our deepest betrayals came from the women we loved most. Our history as
women has done little to dispel these fears. To create true solidarity among
women, we begin by understanding and exploring the effects of our betrayal at the wall on ourselves and on women whose experience differs
from our own.

Within the last hundred-plus years, white women have repeatedly
opted to exercise their race privilege in order to gain an advantage in the
competitive public world. The fledgling coalition of white and African-
American women fighting for suffrage was violently torn apart when it
became clear that Congress was seriously considering granting suffrage to
men of color and not to women at all. White women argued that they,
because of their race, should be granted the right to vote before men or
women of color. This betrayal, white women's shame, leaves a bitter taste
in the mouths of African-American women even today. Most women of
color have justifiably internalized a deep suspicion and mistrust of white
people. Women of color were not heard or considered an integral part of
the last phase of the women's movement. Tired of educating white women
about their racist assumptions, many women of color have given up on the
possibility of speaking across race. White women can begin to educate
themselves about the privilege they assume.

The pressure of the class hierarchy that structures the culture has led middle- and upper-class women to act in ways that other women have felt as betrayal. In the 1970s, magazines glorified middle-class women in glossy cover photos and named them "Superwomen." But the working-class women who had always been stretched between work and family named them the "suits." Working-class women, writes bell hooks, "knew that new jobs would not be created for those masses of white women seeking to enter the work force and they feared that they and men of their classes would lose jobs." For middle-class women's right to enter the upper echelons of the existing power structures, the greater solidarity of women was lost.

Perhaps the deepest challenge to women's solidarity comes from the ultimate threat to male dominance: lesbianism. As girls, we both deeply loved and eventually felt betrayed by the women we loved: mothers, teachers, and other girls. Reluctantly, girls turned to men for protection. As payment for protection and power, patriarchy demands that men be placed at the center of women's lives and loyalties. Loving women, keeping women at the center of our lives, is the ultimate act of disloyalty to male dominance. As a result, homophobia, the fear and loathing of lesbians and gays, is the most elegant weapon for keeping male dominance in place. The fear of being branded a lesbian—a woman who loves women and, in a world of false dichotomies, is therefore supposed to hate men—is terrifying to women. Lesbians are all too accustomed to exclusion by heterosexual women who fear guilt by association. Such disloyalty carries the threat of being completely cut off from men's power and protection.

While much of the fear of lesbians can be attributed to our society's general ambivalence about sex, who sleeps with whom is not the issue. Choosing to love and value women is the real transgression in patriarchy. Any woman who does so in any way is vulnerable to being named "lesbian." Gloria Steinem showed she understood how homophobia buoys sexism when, in the middle of a particularly intense lesbian-baiting incident among national leaders, she suggested that all women declare themselves lesbians and diffuse the power of this poisonous division.

By unraveling our confused questions of loyalty, we can make a serious commitment to creating solidarity among women and a community for our daughters to join. Loving women does not mean hating men, and being loyal to women is essential not only for our daughters but also for our sons. If women can stay joined with women and affirm love for women, perhaps men will eventually question their own unnecessary losses and the need for boys to cut off from mothers and nurturance as the price of being male.

Speaking across cultural divisions is a painful and frightening process that inevitably puts at risk our self-protective strategies. But for the sake of the next generation, we must. This fight for solidarity among women can be a dialogue without blame and guilt, denial and reproach. We have so much to learn from each other. Listening to learn from each other about what we know and feel, naming the dynamic of oppression among us as it happens, creates powerful ways of working together that are not dependent on dominance. Just as listening to a daughter in her own terms is an act of love, listening across culturally inscribed divisions between women is equally an act of love. This love is as necessary in transforming mother daughter relationships as it is in transforming society for daughters.

Mothers' courage to create solidarity among all women for the sake of their daughters transforms girls' experience of entering the culture. Only women united across race, class, and sexual orientation can end the systems of dominance that divide us and cost our daughters. The love that this requires is a radical love, not the idealized love of the romance story. This greater, radical love is forged in the fire of difference.

Out of our love for our daughters, revolutionary mothers fight for connection with daughters by acknowledging the differences between them. By fighting for connection across our differences as women, we can bring this love into the world. This work, hard and painful and exhilarating, brings us into deeper connection with each other and with ourselves.

It is an ongoing process of resistance to easy commonalities and unbridge-able differences. A radical love speaks the truth even when it hurts. This love works to know others' struggle toward wholeness and to identify where we each collude with powerlessness and where we have opportunity for growth.

Through loving, we can work through the betrayals that have divided women from each other. Such love is a process of truth telling that lives always at the edge of what we can recognize as our truths. Through loving our daughters, each other, and ourselves enough to speak our truths in forging a solidarity against dominance, we create a reality that resists co-optation. When women can trust the women they learn from, and, there-fore, trust themselves, women will conspire to increase each other's power. Only the power of women united, joined by allied men, can create an alternative to patriarchal oppression. Our daughters cannot experience their power fully without the cultural transformation made possible by such solidarity.

A CONSUMING PASSION FOR COMMUNITY

For the sake of our daughters, we can reclaim the power of our desires for a truthful connection with them and greater connection among us all. How do we expend our desire now? The public world of business culti-vates a consuming passion within our private lives: perfect women have an endless array of products and fashions to shape themselves. Perfect mothers have an endless list of experiences and things that their children must have to live a good life. Breaking away from these cultural survival strategies is difficult, but far from impossible.

Breaking away begins by asking what we truly want for ourselves and for our daughters. What does happiness mean to us? What brings us joy? Our daughters are good guides for us: girls want the warmth and challenge of real relationship and connection. The *things* of life only become neces-sary as girls learn from the media, from us, and from their peers that these things are what matter. Breaking away also begins with the courage to figure out the first steps we can take, no matter how small, to integrate the divisions in our lives and to create a community for our daughters to join without having to make the same divisions in themselves.

The radical love that brings mothers and daughters and all women together is a practice that redefines what caring for ourselves means and a continually unfolding process. Where is the end point? As Audre Lorde has said, we can use the "yes!" within us as our guide to expanding our capacity for experiencing and sharing joy. We learn to listen to ourselves as we listen and learn from others. Caring for ourselves is a practice of freeing ourselves from the fears of being isolated if we're different and the assumptions built on fear that push us into an acceptance of the status quo. We don't know how women born and raised outside of the culture of dominance would look, act, or feel. By freeing our desires from fearful or resigned acceptance of what now is, we see our deepest desires more clearly. By testing what we want and what we need against who we are told we are and what we must have, we exercise self-care and freedom. We exercise the power to create new selves, new ways of being in the world. As we feel the power of our desires, we can begin to create new ways of living together.

Until we begin, our desire—for connection, for work that is interesting and valuable, and for communities in which we are safe and nurtured —will continue to be channeled into *things*. Our culture has created unlimited *wants* by linking products with the promise of "everything and anything—from self-esteem to status, friendship and love." A cycle of "work-and-spend," as economist Juliet Schor names it in *The Overworked American*, consumes working people and eclipses meaningful participation in public life.

This exhausting cycle, which has seduced all classes, has created a society that is increasingly fragmented and competitive. Earning and spending money becomes one of the few expressions of personal power that individuals hold. Meaning is sought exclusively in the private sphere, rather than in work or through participation in the public world and political community. We are urged to find true satisfaction from the luxuries of private life—the more a family has, the more satisfied its members should be.

Changes in the meaning and relation of love, work, and reward are key to our reweaving of the social fabric. Early labor activists wisely resisted losing leisure in exchange for more money to buy things. They knew that self-esteem cannot be purchased through material goods. What does success mean if we experience little meaning in what we do for work? What does success mean if work keeps us from creating fulfilling relationships in community with others? Breaking the addictive work-and-spend cycle becomes possible only as we find other alternatives and other sources of satisfaction.

Creating more community-based and communal practices of working is one way to find satisfaction. Creating greater community through new living arrangements is another. The violence and danger in our communities not only keep our daughters from living freely but keep us locked inside our individual homes, isolated from potential communities. Building safe communities is the work of mothers, othermothers, and men who are allies. Expanding our psychic and structural definitions of family and community, we create the possibility of creating contexts where daughters can thrive.

Community, however, is neither simply flexible work nor new living arrangements. True community is an integration of work and love, public and private life, through a restructuring of society. A revolution of mothers will eventually integrate these so-called separate worlds. Even by resisting the language of "balancing work and family," because of its legitimizing of the unnecessary separation of these parts of our lives, we begin to envision lives lived more fully in balance. Creating ways of living in work and in love where we can come to know and to trust each other will make a profound difference for us and our children. For daughters, every act of joining love and work is proof of our commitment to ending the possibility of betrayal in their lives.

PERSONAL AND POLITICAL CHANGE

"Change is what people want most, and fear most desperately," says activist Catlin Fullwood. "That's what accounts for the forward mobility and backtracking that all change efforts experience." Whether personal or political, change is at best more of a spiral than a straight line. Those of us who have struggled to create new selves from troubling pasts have learned how often we remember and then lose the insights we have gained through our hard work. We disintegrate under stress. Our stories about ourselves and who we are constantly evolve. We dance through our lives doing the two-step: two steps forward, two steps back, side to side, in an energized but ambivalent set of movements.

The dance of social change is also the two-step. The flurry of activity in the 1970s was followed by the backlash against women documented by both Naomi Wolf in *The Beauty Myth* and Susan Faludi in *Backlash*. Both in psychological and political change, when we are on the verge of transformation, we feel a strong pull, like a dangerous undertow, to stay as we were. But backlash itself is a sign of progress, a signal that at a personal, relational, or societal level, we are changing enough to cause alarm. It also tells us that we can expect more pressure to turn back with each step forward.

With each step, each change we make in how we mother, we will experience discomfort or the feeling that we just can't do it. To oppose the status quo, to betray the culture that expects us to raise daughters who hold men at the center of their lives, to confront the myths of perfection, self-sacrifice, and separation that hold sway for mothering a daughter will not be comfortable. Change almost always feels dangerous and uncomfortable. While it is important that we acknowledge and experience these feelings, they are not always our best guide to action. If we listened to them, we would never move forward. A circle of mothers and a community of women are essential to us in testing strategies and behaviors, sorting out feelings, finding confirmation for our authority, and making choices about where and when to act differently. At a societal level, only true solidarity—ever larger circles of mothers—can claim the power of mothering and begin to build communities where girls' losses are truly unnecessary.

Even with support and validation, change is a voyage into the unknown. Even when our minds and hearts say that change is for the better, change requires that we let go of who we are and of our deepest assumptions about life. In between living as we were and realizing the new, we hang suspended in midair like trapeze artists waiting to be caught. The patterns of our selves have been forged out of fear: we created them to protect us from being overwhelmed as children. The patterns of our cultural life are similarly forged out of fear. The deliberate psychological manipulation of our fears by advertising and business have created an enormous anxiety about having enough. No matter how much money or resources we have, we're urged to feel that nothing is enough. When we are each incited to consume and consume to achieve security, we become competitive and mistrustful of one another. What we fear most in others is often a clue to what we fear most for ourselves. Competitive individualism leads us away from each other and the possibility of community. To question this dangerous cultural pattern frightens us because consumerism has been billed as our ticket to survival.

Our survival strategies as women and mothers teach us compliance and imprison us in a fear-filled perfectionism. The approach described in this book requires that we risk imperfection and acknowledge the inevitability that we will make mistakes in an area where we care deeply: the way we love and teach our children. For that reason these changes require courage, speaking our minds by telling all our hearts, often moving toward what we want—and fear—most.

Each generation of women has wanted a better life for their daughters. The changes that have already been made for women have been dearly paid for at both personal and political levels. If these changes were easy, life would be different right now. The proliferation of mother blaming and women blaming assures us that our daughters will not love or trust us for our compliance or for demanding theirs at the cost of the lifeforce of their deepest desires. By engaging in continuing resistance to oppression and commitment to solidarity for liberation, we mother a revolution in life as we know it.

American life, argue Robert Bellah and his colleagues in *Habits of the Heart,* has been an experiment in separation and individuation. American culture, archetypally modern, broke with traditional European authority to create a nation of individualists. Now, these authors argue, America is at a crisis that sounds surprisingly like the crisis faced by adolescents who have been encouraged to separate. Loosely linked through mass culture and consumerism into a competition among individuals and between groups, American culture looks remarkably like a teen culture that separated from the "parental" authority of Europe. Consequently, our exaggerated separateness and individualism "must be balanced by a renewal of commitment and community if they are not to end in self-destruction." Psychological models of separation and individualism are inadequate for the creation of a complete model of human life at either an individual or a cultural level. To meet the challenge of its adolescence, to decide upon its identity, American culture needs to recognize that renewal through personal commitment within communities "is indeed a world waiting to be born if we only had the courage to see it."

What would a world in which daughters were not betrayed by the culture look like? We don't pretend to see this new world clearly. A world of all women and children and men living committed to radical love and solidarity is the vaguest of utopian ideas. Our ever-changing understanding of who we are and what living means alters what we find possible to envision. The theories that we present are working theories, not absolute truths. They are to be tested and explored, refined and expanded, and perhaps eventually discarded. This book could not have been written before now. Recent shifts in thinking about the psychological implications and politics of the traditions that structure the private and public world have created the possibility for our bringing forth this knowledge. No one of the three of us could have written this book alone. Our writing, like the process of solidarity that we have described, required that we work across our differences to create something new.

We ask you to join in solidarity with us. Transforming betrayal into power is a continuous process of resistance: we have attempted to bring forward knowledge and practices to aid in resisting psychological and political oppression. Through practices of resistance, we free our hearts and minds from traditional betrayals. We ask you to join in posing hard questions about mother daughter relationships and about our relationships with each other as women. Leadership begins by laying claim to the important questions, by beginning a public discourse that erases the divisive boundaries in our lives, by seeking partners who challenge our assumptions. Every woman can mother a revolution in her own life and join in mothering a revolution in the world for the next generation. Just as we were asked to join the resistance, we are asking you to join with us. The power of a mother daughter revolution waits to be born.

Notes

INTRODUCTION

xix. "Carol Gilligan's working theory . . .": This five-year longitudinal study of girls ages six to seventeen took place at the Laurel School for Girls under Lyn Brown's direction. Carol Gilligan was the principal investigator. Funding for this study came from the Cleveland Foundation, the George Gund Foundation, the Lilly Endowment, and the Spencer Foundation. Brown first analyzed these girls' development—which has provided the cornerstone of the Harvard Project's findings about girls' development—in her unpublished doctoral dissertation, "Narratives of Relationship: The Development of a Care Voice in Girls Ages 7 to 16" (Harvard University, Graduate School of Education, 1989). Lyn Brown and Carol Gilligan have published these findings in *Meeting at the Crossroads: Women's Psychology and Girls' Development* (Cambridge, Mass.: Harvard University Press, 1992).

xx–xxi. "That which does exist . . .": The first study, "Understanding Adolescents At-Risk," was directed by Jill MacLean Taylor with Deborah L. Tolman, assistant project director, and Janie Victoria Ward, consultant. The Boston Foundation funded the study. The second study, "Strengthening Health Resistance and Courage in Girls," was directed by Annie Rogers with Normi Noel, consultant. Funding for the research came primarily from the Lilly Endowment. Carol Gilligan was the principal investigator for both studies.

PART ONE: UNNECESSARY LOSSES

3. Quotes in Idelisse's story: Joanna Russ, "Russalka or The Seacoast of Bohemia," in ed. Jack Zipes, *Don't Bet on the Prince* (New York: Routledge, 1987), pp. 91, 94.

1: THE CROSSROADS

7. "According to several . . .": See Ms. Foundation for Women and Center for Policy Alternatives, "Women's Voices," Report on jointly sponsored project (New York: Authors, 1992); "1990 Virginia Slims Opinion Poll," (The Roper Organization Inc., 1990); The Yankelovich Clancy Shulman poll (October 23–25, 1989, for *Time*/CNN).

"Recent large-scale studies . . .": See B. Allgood-Merton, P. Lewinsohn, and H. Hops, "Sex Differences and Adolescent Depression," *Journal of Abnormal Psychology* 99 (1990): 55–63; A. Whitaker, J. Johnson, D. Shaffer, J. Rapoport, K. Kalikow, B. T. Walsh, M. Davies, S. Braiman, and A. Dolinsky, "Uncommon Troubles in Young People: Prevalence Estimates of Selected Psychiatric Disorders in a Non-Referred Adolescent Population," *Archives of General Psychiatry* 47 (1990): 487–96; Minnesota Women's Fund, *Reflections of Risk: Growing Up Female in Minnesota, a Report on the Health and Well-being of Adolescent Girls in Minnesota* (Minneapolis: Author, 1990); P. Gjinde, J. Block, and J. Block, "Depressive Symptoms and Personality during Late Adolescence: Gender Differences in the Externalization-Internalization of Symptom Expression," *Journal of Abnormal Psychology* 97 (1988): 475–86; M. Demitrack, F. Putnam, T. Brewerton, H. Brandt, and P. Gold, "Relation of Clinical Variables to Dissociative Phenomena in Eating Disorders," *American Journal of Psychiatry* 147 (1990): 1184–88.

8. "Researchers have described . . .": Linda Harris, Robert W. Blum, and Michael Resnick, "Teen Females in Minnesota: A Portrait of Quiet Disturbance," in *Women, Girls and Psychotherapy: Reframing Resistance,*

ed. Carol Gilligan, Annie Rogers, and Deborah Tolman (Binghamton, N.Y.: Haworth Press, 1991), pp. 119–35.

"Reports indicate . . . seriously": See Greenberg-Lake Analysis Group, *Shortchanging Girls, Shortchanging America: A Nationwide Poll to Assess Self-esteem, Educational Experiences, Interest in Math and Science, and Career Aspirations of Girls and Boys Ages 9–15* (Washington, D.C.: American Association of University Women, 1991); Myra Sadker, David Sadker, and Susan S. Klein, "Abolishing Misperceptions about Sex Equity in Education," *Theory in Practice* 25 (1986): 219–26; Wellesley Center for Research on Women, *The AAUW Report: How Schools Shortchange Girls* (Washington, D.C.: American Association for University Women, 1992).

9. "Girls' silencing and their internalization . . .": See Harris, Blum, and Resnick, "Teen Females in Minnesota," p. 119.

"Second, the differences . . .": See Dana Crowley Jack, *Silencing the Self: Women and Depression* (Cambridge, Mass.: Harvard University Press, 1991).

"The supposed 'riddle' . . .": See Carol Gilligan, *In a Different Voice: Psychological Theory and Women's Development* (Cambridge, Mass.: Harvard University Press, 1982).

10. Schonert-Reichl and Offer quote: Kimberly Schonert-Reichl and Daniel Offer, "Gender Differences in Adolescent Symptoms," in *Advances in Clinical Child Psychology,* vol. 14, ed. B. Lahey and A. Kazdin (New York: Plenum, 1992), p. 28.

"The Michigan Board . . .": Michigan State Board of Education, Office of Sex Equity in Education, 1991. *The Influence of Gender-Role Socialization on Student Perceptions: A Report Based on Data Collected from Michigan Public School Students.*

"sixty percent of elementary . . .": Greenberg-Lake, *Shortchanging Girls.*

11. AAUW report quote: Greenberg-Lake, *Shortchanging Girls,* p. 6.

12. "Carol Gilligan has spoken . . .": Carol Gilligan, "Teaching Shakespeare's Sister: Notes from the Underground of Female Adolescence," in *Making Connections: The Relational Worlds of Adolescent Girls at Emma Willard School,* ed. Carol Gilligan, Nona Lyons, and Trudy Hanmer (Cambridge, Mass.: Harvard University Press, 1990), pp. 6–29.

"As Gilligan puts it . . .": Carol Gilligan, "Joining the Resistance: Psychology, Politics, Girls and Women," *Michigan Quarterly Review* 29 (1990): 501–36.

13. Alyshea quote: Christina Kelly, "Why You Liked Yourself Better When You Were 11," *Sassy,* July 1991, p. 77.

"The following year . . .": Personal communication. This research won Alyshea Austern a science prize.

Rogers quote: Annie G. Rogers, excerpted from "The Development of Courage in Girls and Women," an earlier version of "Voice, Play, and a Practice of Ordinary Courage in Girls' and Women's Lives," *Harvard Educational Review* (Fall 1993).

14. "By twelve . . .": J. M. Tanner, "Sequence, Tempo, and Individual Variation in Growth and Development of Boys and Girls Aged Twelve to Sixteen," in *12 to 16: Early Adolescence,* ed. J. Kagan and R. Coles (New York: W. W. Norton, 1972), pp. 1–24.

15. "By paying close attention . . .": Lyn Brown, "Narratives of Relationship."

"Girls poised at the edge . . .": Brown, "Narratives of Relationship."

16. hooks quote: bell hooks, *Black Looks: Race and Representation* (Boston: South End Press, 1992), p. 116.

"Many African-American . . .": Nancie Zane, *In Our Own Voices* (New York: Project on Equal Education Rights, 1988). See also Greenberg-Lake, *Shortchanging Girls,* for more on differences in girls' self-esteem by race.

17. Story about Lorde: Audre Lorde, *Zami: A New Spelling of My Name* (Freedom, Calif.: Crossing Press, 1982), pp. 58–65.

19. "As they move through adolescence . . .": Greenberg-Lake, *Short-changing Girls.*

20. " 'the notion of difference . . .' ": Audre Lorde, *Sister Outsider* (Freedom, Calif.: Crossing Press, 1984), p. 45.

Ehrenreich and English quote: Barbara Ehrenreich and Deirdre English, *For Her Own Good: 150 Years of the Experts' Advice to Women* (New York: Anchor Books, 1979), p. 4.

21. " 'the expert looms larger . . .' ": Ibid., p. 212.

22. "This strength then becomes . . .": see Jean Baker Miller, *Toward a New Psychology of Women* (Boston: Beacon Press, 1976).

23. Apter quotes: Terri Apter, *Altered Loves: Mothers and Daughters during Adolescence* (New York: Fawcett Columbine, 1990), pp. 14, 16, 18.

25. Walker quotes: Alice Walker, *Possessing the Secret of Joy* (New York: Harcourt Brace Jovanovich, 1992), p. 18.

Ehrenreich and English quote: Ehrenreich and English, *For Her Own Good,* p. 227.

Surrey quote: Janet Surrey, "The Mother-Daughter Relationship: Themes in Psychotherapy," Audiotape of work in progress (Wellesley, Mass.: Wellesley College, Stone Center).

26. " 'The indictment of mothers . . .' ": Smith, 1990, cited in Surrey, ibid.

27. "In fact, after the Korean War . . .": Ehrenreich and English, *For Her Own Good,* p. 235. See also Betty Friedan, *The Feminine Mystique* (New York: Laurel/Dell, 1963/1983).

28. "Historians have shown . . .": Judith Lewis Herman and Helen Block Lewis, "Anger in the Mother-Daughter Relationship," in *The Psychology*

of Today's Woman, ed. T. Bernay and D. Cantor (Cambridge, Mass.: Harvard University Press, 1989), pp. 142–158.

"The skills of fitting in . . .": See ibid.

29. "Psychotherapists report that . . .": Irene Stiver, "Beyond the Oedipus Complex," in *Women's Growth in Connection: Writings from the Stone Center,* ed. J. Jordan, A. Kaplan, J. B. Miller, I. Stiver, and J. Surrey (New York: Guilford Press), p. 109.

Arcana quote: Judith Arcana, *Our Mother's Daughters* (London: The Women's Press, 1981), p. 105.

30. Rich quote: Adrienne Rich, *Of Woman Born: Motherhood as Experience and Institution* (New York: Norton, 1986), p. 236.

32. " 'Love, according to . . .' ": Valerie Saiving, "The Human Situation: A Feminine View" in *Womanspirit Rising: A Feminist Reader in Religion,* ed. Carol P. Christ and Judy Plaskow (San Francisco: Harper & Row, 1979), p. 26.

34. "As Susan Faludi documented . . .": Susan Faludi, *Backlash: The Undeclared War Against American Women* (New York: Crown, 1992), pp. 80–81.

"Psychologist Phyllis Chesler's research . . .": Phyllis Chesler, *Mothers on Trial: The Battle for Children and Custody* (New York: McGraw-Hill, 1986).

"Women have . . . loves them": See Linda Gordon, *Heroes of Their Own Lives* (New York: Penguin Books, 1988).

37. Brown and Gilligan quote: Lyn Brown and Carol Gilligan, *Meeting at the Crossroads,* p. 232.

2: FROM POWER TO BETRAYAL

39. Viorst quote: Judith Viorst, *Necessary Losses* (New York: Simon & Schuster, 1986), pp. 15–16.

40. Foucault quote: Michel Foucault, *Power/Knowledge: Selected Interviews and Other Writings, 1972–1977,* ed. Colin Gordon, trans. Colin Gordon, Lee Marshall, John Mepham, and Kate Soper (New York: Pantheon, 1980), p. 59.

41. Herman and Lewis quote: Judith Lewis Herman and Helen Block Lewis, "Anger in the Mother-Daughter Relationship," p. 149.

44. "Approximately 5 percent . . . 'are incestuously involved' . . .": Ibid., citing Russell, 1993, p. 151.

    "One girl out of three . . .": Judy Herman, *Father-Daughter Incest* (Cambridge, Mass.: Harvard University Press, 1981), p. 12.

    "Amazingly, before the early 1980s . . .": Herman, *Father-Daughter Incest, passim.*

    " 'surveillance of the daughter's . . .' ": Herman and Lewis, "Anger in the Mother-Daughter Relationship," p. 151.

45. Herman and Lewis quote: Ibid., p. 150.

46. " 'Susan, who has suffered . . . dinner ready?' ": Quoted in Dana Jack, *Silencing the Self,* p. 111.

    "When a little girl realizes . . .": Herman and Lewis, "Anger in the Mother-Daughter Relationship."

    Rich quote: Adrienne Rich, *Of Woman Born,* p. 249.

47. Morrison quote: Toni Morrison, *The Bluest Eye* (New York: Pocket Books, 1984), p. 62.

    "When asked, children of both sexes . . .": Jerome Kagan, *The Nature of the Child* (New York: Basic Books, 1984).

48. Jessie's story: For a fuller discussion of Jessie and of self-authorization, see Lyn Brown, "Telling a Girl's Life: Self-authorization as a Form of Resistance," in *Women, Girls and Psychotherapy: Reframing Resistance,* ed. Carol Gilligan, Annie Rogers, and Deborah Tolman (Binghamton, N.Y.: Haworth, 1991).

49. Brown and Gilligan quote: Lyn Brown and Carol Gilligan, *Meeting at the Crossroads,* p. 43.

50. "Carol Gilligan suggests . . .": Carol Gilligan, "Teaching Shakespeare's Sister," p. 17.

    "As Brown and Gilligan explain . . .": Brown and Gilligan, *Meeting at the Crossroads,* p. 47.

51. " 'the sugary buzz . . .' ": Susan Ferraro, "Girl Talk," *New York Times Magazine,* December 6, 1992, p. 62.

    "Girls come to believe . . .": Brown and Gilligan, *Meeting at the Crossroads,* p. 99.

    "For many middle-class girls . . .": Lyn Brown, "Narratives of Relationship: The Development of a Care Voice in Girls Ages 7 to 16" (Ed.D. diss., Harvard University, 1989).

53. "Seeing the framework . . .": Brown and Gilligan, *Meeting at the Crossroads,* p. 160.

54. "Because what girls . . .": See Carol Gilligan, "Joining the Resistance," pp. 501–36.

55. Ritu's story: Carol Gilligan, "Revision," Invited address by Division 24, Theoretical and Philosophical Psychology, American Psychological Association Annual Conference, San Francisco, August 1991, p. 25. Ritu was part of the "Strengthening Healthy Resistance and Courage in Girls" study directed by Annie Rogers, Carol Gilligan, principal investigator, and Normi Noel, consultant.

56. "the underground city . . .": Carol Gilligan, "Teaching Shakespeare's Sister," p. 17.

57. Brown and Gilligan quote: Brown and Gilligan, *Meeting at the Crossroads,* p. 185.

58. "Trauma is . . .": See Judith Herman, *Trauma and Recovery* (New York: Basic Books, 1992).

59. Rita quote: From Signithia Fordham, "Racelessness as a Factor in Black Students' School Success: Pragmatic Strategy or Pyrrhic Victory?" *Harvard Educational Review* 58 (1988): 68.

" 'raceless personae' " . . . " 'eternal . . . community' ": Fordham, "Racelessness as a Factor," p. 73.

"Girls' most traumatic . . .": The AAUW study reported that boys and girls both view the changes in boys' bodies as positive. Boys and girls both see boys' advantage in not getting pregnant or menstruating. African-American girls expressed the most concern about these "bad things" about being a girl. High school girls were three times as likely as elementary school girls to mention the greater physical strength and advantages of boys as a reason why boys are lucky to be boys.

60. "In a recent study . . . 'scareder every day' ": Nan Stein, Nancy L. Marshall, and Linda R. Tropp, *Secrets in Public: Sexual Harassment in Our Schools—A Report on the Results of a* Seventeen *Magazine Survey.* (Joint project of NOW Legal Defense and Education Fund and Wellesley College Center for Research on Women, March 1993).

61. "Of girls who have been . . .": For modal age of sexual abuse, Judith Musick, personal communication. See also Herman, *Father-Daughter Incest.*

Herman quote: Herman, *Trauma and Recovery,* p. 61.

"As many as one-third . . .": Barrie Levy, ed., *Dating Violence: Young Women in Danger* (Seattle: Seal Press, 1991), p. 4.

"Within sex education courses . . .": Michelle Fine, "Sexuality, Schooling, and Adolescent Females: The Missing Discourse of Desire," *Harvard Educational Review* 58 (1988): 29–53.

62. "As Deborah Tolman discovered . . .": Deborah Tolman, *Dilemmas of Desire* (Cambridge, Mass.: Harvard University Press, in press).

"Girls, much more than boys, . . .": Linda Harris, Robert W. Blum, Michael Resnick, "Teen Females in Minnesota: A Portrait of Quiet

Disturbance," in *Women, Girls and Psychotherapy,* ed. Gilligan et al., p. 123.

64. "By denying or walling off . . .": Anne Petersen, "Adolescent Development," *Annual Review of Psychology* 39 (1988): 583–607.

65. Brown quote: Lyn Brown, "The Conventions of Imagination" (Unpublished manuscript, July 1992), pp. 30–31.

66. Herman and Lewis quote: Judith Lewis Herman and Helen Block Lewis, "Anger in the Mother-Daughter Relationship," p. 156.

Apter quotes: Terri Apter, *Altered Loves,* p. 172.

67. Jack quote: Jack, *Silencing the Self,* p. 109.

"While men create the dangers . . .": Herman and Lewis, "Anger in the Mother-Daughter Relationship," p. 144.

"their mother's integrity . . .": *American Heritage Dictionary,* 2nd college ed. (Laurel, N.Y.: Houghton Mifflin, 1983), p. 362.

Smith quote: Beverly Jean Smith, "Raising a Resister," in *Women, Girls, and Psychotherapy,* ed. Gilligan et al., pp. 137–138.

68. " 'A decisive 94.5% . . .' ": G. Joseph and J. Lewis, *Common Differences: Conflicts in Black and White Feminist Perspectives* (Boston: South End Press, 1981), p. 94.

" 'Most notably, three-fourths . . .' ": See Carol Gilligan, Jill McLean Taylor, Deborah L. Tolman, Amy Sullivan, Pamela Pleasance, and Judith Dorney, "The Relational World of Adolescent Girls Considered to Be at Risk," final report to The Boston Foundation for the project "Understanding Adolescents: A study of urban teens considered to be at risk and a project to strengthen connection between girls and women," July 1992, pp. 234–235. (The quoted section of the report was authored by Jill McLean Taylor and Amy Sullivan.)

69. " 'anger is loaded' ": Audre Lorde, *Sister Outsider*, p. 127. " 'Girls, astute observers . . .' ": Annie G. Rogers, excerpted from "The Development of Courage in Girls and Women," p. 46.

70. "White women, Latinas . . .": Gloria I. Joseph, "Black Mothers and Daughters: Traditional and New Perspectives," in *Double Stitch: Black Women Write about Mothers and Daughters,* ed. Patricia Bell-Scott, Beverly Guy-Sheftalle, Jacqueline Jones Rayster, Janet Sims-Wood, Miriam DeCosta-Willis, and Lucille P. Fultz (New York: Harper Perennial, 1993), p. 96.

71. Miller quote: Jean Baker Miller, *Toward a New Psychology of Women,* p. 11.

Jack quotes: Jack, *Silencing the Self,* pp. 104–7.

72. "These girls wanted . . . 'one of the guys . . . men' ": Michelle Fine, *Disruptive Voices: The Possibilities of Feminist Research* (Ann Arbor: University of Michigan Press, 1992), p. 176.

73. " 'Many of these guy-girls . . . are still girls' ": Michelle Fine, personal communication.

"Our growing national awareness . . .": Herman, *Trauma and Recovery,* pp. 28–32.

74. Collins quote: Patricia Hill Collins, "The Meaning of Motherhood in Black Culture and Black Mother-Daughter Relationships," in *Double Stitch,* ed. Bell-Scott et al., p. 54.

3: THE STORIES WE LIVE BY

77. Segal quote: In Dalma Heyn, *The Erotic Silence of the American Wife* (New York: Signet/Penguin Books, 1993), p. 12.

"Anthropologist Peggy Sanday . . .": Peggy Sanday, *Female Power and Male Dominance: On the Origins of Sexual Inequality* (Cambridge: Cambridge University Press, 1981).

78. "The hallmarks of loss . . .": Carol Gilligan, "Joining the Resistance."

79. Campbell quote: Joseph Campbell, *The Hero with a Thousand Faces* (Princeton, N.J.: Princeton University Press, 1968), p. 3, emphasis added.

80. References to Freud: Freud's perspective is articulated most clearly in his *Civilization and Its Discontents,* trans. and ed. James Strachey (New York: Norton, 1961).

82. Miller quote: Jean Baker Miller, *Toward a New Psychology of Women,* pp. 11–12.

  "Miller questions whether . . .": Ibid., p. 26.

84. Silhouette Romance quotes: From Silhouette Book's guidelines for aspiring romance book authors, circa 1981.

85. " 'pubertal anecdotes . . .' ": Sharon Thompson, "Search for Tomorrow: On Feminism and the Reconstruction of Teen Romance," in *Pleasure and Danger: Exploring Female Sexuality,* ed. C. Vance (Boston: Routledge & Kegan Paul, 1984), p. 351.

86. Haug quote: Frigga Haug, ed., *Female Sexualization: A Collective Work of Memory,* trans. Erica Carter (New York: Routledge Chapman & Hall, 1987), p. 276.

87. Lorde quote: Audre Lorde, *Sister Outsider,* p. 58.

  " 'the threat of discipline' " . . . " 'jeans are mostly . . .' ": Susan Faludi, *Backlash,* pp. 194–95; see especially chapters 6, 7, and 8.

88. "In sociologists Dorothy Holland . . .": Dorothy Holland and Margaret Eisenhart, *Educated in Romance: Women, Achievement and College Culture* (Chicago: University of Chicago Press, 1990), p. 52. The study in England was by Sue Lees, *Losing Out: Sexuality and Adolescent Girls* (London: Hutchinson, 1986).

  Patty quote: From Linda Christian-Smith, *Becoming a Woman through Romance* (New York: Routledge, 1990), p. 108.

"Many of the girls to whom . . .": Ibid., pp. 99–100.

89. "A survey of 13- to 17-year-old girls . . .": Mindy Bingham and Sandy Stryker, *Women Helping Girls with Choices: A Handbook for Community Service Organizations* (Santa Barbara, Calif.: Advocacy Press/Girls Club of Santa Barbara, 1989).

"In a 1992 study . . .": Girls Count, *In America's Future, In Tomorrow's Workforce, In Colorado's Classrooms* . . . (Denver, Colo.: Author, 1992).

"Educator Beverly Jean Smith . . .": Beverly Jean Smith, "Raising a Resister," in *Women, Girls and Psychotherapy,* ed. Carol Gilligan et al., p. 144.

"The African-American girls in a study . . .": See Carol Gilligan et al., "The Relational World of Adolescent Girls," pp. 234–235.

92. "As Frigga Haug observes . . .": Frigga Haug, *Female Sexualization,* p. 130.

" 'speaks with a moralistic . . . I should' ": Dana Jack, *Silencing the Self,* p. 94. Jack calls this voice the "Over Eye."

"Negating girls' personal . . . 'truths beyond question' ": Ibid., p. 119.

93. " 'Good' as it . . . keep to herself": Dalma Heyn, *Erotic Silence,* p. 65.

" 'Because the tie . . . link affects children' ": Ibid., p. 210.

94. " 'practice self-love as . . .' ": bell hooks, *Black Looks,* p. 20.

" 'undefined work of freedom' ": Michel Foucault, quoted in Alexander Nehamas, "Subject and Abject: The Examined Life of Michel Foucault," *New Republic,* February 15, 1993, p. 33.

4: RECLAIMING

101. "But Carol Gilligan offers 'five psychological truths' ": Carol Gilligan, "Joining the Resistance," pp. 501–36. This is Gilligan's synthesis of basic psychology as theorized by Sigmund Freud and other psychodynamic theorists, by John Bowlby and other attachment theorists, by Jean Piaget and other cognitive developmental theorists, and also as narrated by Shakespeare, Chekhov, Virginia Woolf, Toni Morrison, and other recorders of the human scene.

102. Steinem quote: Gloria Steinem, *Revolution from Within: A Book of Self-esteem* (Boston: Little, Brown, 1992), pp. 36–38.

103. "The associations made . . .": Sigmund Freud's process of dream interpretation was a way of exploring images in dreams, following an image to first one associated memory and another and another until the chain of associations was exhausted and the underlying riddles of the dream were revealed. See Freud, *The Interpretation of Dreams* (1900; reprint, New York: Norton, 1955).

   "Judy, a thirteen-year-old . . .": Quotations from Lyn Brown and Carol Gilligan, *Meeting at the Crossroads,* pp. 133–34; interview analyzed by Elizabeth Debold.

105. Simone quote: In Judith Herman, *Trauma and Recovery,* p. 40.

106. "According to one recent study . . .": Jacqueline White and John Humphrey, presentation at the Annual Meeting of the American Psychological Association, as reported in *New York Times,* August 17, 1992.

108. "Gloria Steinem wrote . . .": Steinem, *Revolution from Within,* pp. 5–6.

   Terr quotes: Lenore Terr, *Too Scared to Cry: Psychic Trauma in Childhood* (New York: HarperCollins, 1990), pp. ix–x.

112. Rogers quotes: excerpted from Annie G. Rogers, "The Development of Courage in Girls and Women," pp. 43, 30.

113. "These 'outlaw emotions' . . .": Alison M. Jaggar, "Love and Knowledge: Emotion in Feminist Epistemology," in *Gender/Body/Knowledge,* ed. A. Jaggar and S. Bordo (New Brunswick, N.J.: Rutgers University Press, 1989), p. 161.

114. "Two African-American girls responded . . .": Michelle Fine, *Disruptive Voices,* p. 182.

116. " 'Code of Goodness' ": Claudia Bepko and Jo-Ann Krestan, *Too Good for Her Own Good: Breaking Free from the Burden of Female Responsibility* (New York: Harper & Row, 1990).

117. Robinson and Ward quotes: Tracy Robinson and Janie Victoria Ward, " 'A Belief in Self Far Greater Than Anyone's Disbelief': Cultivating Resistance among African American Female Adolescents," in *Women, Girls and Psychotherapy,* ed. Carol Gilligan et al., p. 89.

122. Elizabeth would like to acknowledge that her understanding of fear, of how it works and how to work through it, comes from therapist Peter Martynowych, who has developed unique ways of working with clients on fear.

Pogrebin quote: From Paula Caplan, *Don't Blame Mother: Mending the Mother-Daughter Relationship* (New York: HarperCollins, 1989), p. 1.

123. Rich quote: Adrienne Rich, *Of Woman Born,* p. 224.

Caplan quote: Caplan, *Don't Blame Mother,* p. 13.

125. Rich quote: Rich, *Of Woman Born,* p. 225.

126. Rich quote: Ibid.

128. Rich quote: Ibid., p. 249.

129. "a place to share fears . . .": Carolyn Heilbrun, *Writing a Woman's Life* (New York: Ballantine, 1989), p. 43.

130. Hall quote: From Brown and Gilligan, *Meeting at the Crossroads,* pp. 220–22.

131. "Within the safety and power . . .": See Herman, *Trauma and Recovery*.

5: VOICE LESSONS

132. Kingston's story: Maxine Hong Kingston, *Woman Warrior: Memoirs of a Girlhood among Ghosts* (New York: Vintage Books, 1970), pp. 198–200, 205.

134. " 'Their courage seems . . .' ": excerpted from Annie G. Rogers, "The Development of Courage in Girls and Women," p. 45.

135. " '. . . that a woman can give too much . . .' ": Valerie Saiving, "The Human Situation," p. 37.

137. "One in four adolescent girls . . .": Minnesota Women's Fund, *Reflections of Risk;* Christine Renee Robinson, "Working with Adolescent Girls: Strategies to Address Health Status," in *Women, Girls and Psychotherapy,* ed. Carol Gilligan et al., pp. 241–52.

139. "Yet these codes, too, . . .": See Valerie Saiving, "The Human Situation."

140. "June describes . . . 'was my answer' ": Dalma Heyn, *The Erotic Silence of the American Wife,* p. 44.

141. " 'The art of playing . . .' ": excerpted from Annie G. Rogers, "The Development of Courage in Girls and Women," p. 48.

Cleage quotes: Pearl Cleage, *Mad at Miles: A Blackwoman's Guide to Truth* (Southfield, Mich.: Cleage Group, 1990).

143. Brown and Gilligan quotes: Lyn Brown and Carol Gilligan, *Meeting at the Crossroads,* pp. 12, 15–16.

145. Herman and Lewis quote: Judith Herman and Helen Block Lewis, "Anger in the Mother-Daughter Relationship," p. 144.

146. "The classic breathiness . . .": see Susan Brownmiller, *Femininity* (New York: Fawcett, 1985), who describes the anatomical differences, and Kristin Linklater, *Freeing the Natural Voice* (New York: Drama Books, 1976), who argues that men's and women's voices both can reach a three-octave range.

" 'She really listens . . .' ": Carol Gilligan and Annie Rogers, "A Paradigm Shift in Psychology: Reframing Daughtering and Mothering," in *Daughtering and Mothering,* ed. Janneke van Mens-Verhulst (London: Routledge, in press), p. 7.

148. Apter quotes: Terri Apter, *Altered Loves,* pp. 118, 126.

151. " 'mothers with their mouths open' ": Ibid., p. 19.

Apter quotes: Ibid., p. 116.

152. Apter quote: Ibid., p. 128.

" 'I'll ask my daughter . . .' ": Ibid., p. 247.

153. Apter quote: Ibid., p. 129.

154. Atwood quote: Margaret Atwood, *Cat's Eye* (New York: Bantam Books, 1989), p. 125.

156. Apter quote: Apter, *Altered Loves,* p. 134.

157. Brown quote: Lyn Brown, "Narratives of Relationship," pp. 196–97. There are few programs that work with girls to develop their sense of authority and self-authorization. One of those that does—and with enormous success—is Discoveries, a program for teens directed by Leslie McGovern of The Alliance Project in Seattle, Washington.

163. "Young girls know that fighting . . .": See "Strengthening Healthy Resistance and Courage in Girls: A Prevention Project and a Developmental Study," final report to the Lilly Endowment. Carol Gilligan, Principal Investigator, Annie G. Rogers, Project Director and Editor. With Kathryn Geismar, Amy Grillo, Sarah Ingersoll, Naomi Noel, Kate O'Neill, Heather Thompson. Draft dated June 23, 1992.

164. Rogers and O'Neill quote: Annie G. Rogers and Kate O'Neill, "Mapmaking: Exploring the Landscape of Girl's Psychological Development," in ibid., p. 9.

Smith quote: Beverly Jean Smith, "Raising a Resister," p. 147.

165. Apter quote: Apter, *Altered Loves,* p. 117.

169. Rich quote: Adrienne Rich, "Women and Honor: Some Notes on Lying," in *On Lies, Secrets, and Silence* (New York: Norton, 1979), p. 188.

6: JOINING

182. Apter quote: Terri Apter, *Altered Loves,* p. 170.

183. " 'oppositional gaze' ": bell hooks, *Black Looks,* p. 116.

Rich quote: Adrienne Rich, *Of Woman Born,* p. 252.

Cleage quotes: Pearl Cleage, *Mad at Miles,* p. 44.

185. See Catherine Steiner-Adair, "The Body Politic: Normal Female Adolescent Development and the Development of Eating Disorders" in *Making Connections: The Relational Worlds of Adolescent Girls at Emma Willard School,* ed. Carol Gilligan, Nona P. Lyons, and Trudy J. Hanmer (Cambridge, Mass.: Harvard University Press, 1990), pp. 162–82.

186. Steinem quote: Gloria Steinem, *Revolution from Within,* p. 120, citing Linda T. Sanford and Mary Ellen Donovan, "If Only We Had Learned Differently: The Impact of Formal Schooling," in *Women and Self-esteem* (New York: Anchor/Doubleday, 1984), pp. 177–96.

187. Rich quotes: Adrienne Rich, "What Does a Woman Need to Know?" in *Blood, Bread, and Poetry: Selected Prose 1979–1986* (New York: Norton, 1986), p. 2.

Jane Margolis calls the process of learning to think and to speak in patriarchal terms cultural "voice lessons." She is writing a book on the subject.

Lerner quote: Gerda Lerner, *The Creation of Patriarchy* (New York: Oxford University Press, 1986), p. 3, as quoted in Steinem, *Revolution from Within,* p. 127.

188. Rich quote: Rich, "What Does a Woman Need to Know?" p. 2.

193. " 'were more likely than their nonathletic . . .' ": The Women's Sports Foundation Report, "Minorities in Sports: The Effect of Varsity Sports Participation on the Social, Educational, and Career Mobility of Minority Students" (New York, Author, 1989), p. 5.

194. Rich quote: Rich, "What Does a Woman Need to Know?" p. 2.

195. "Virginia Woolf in 'Three Guineas' . . .": Virginia Woolf, *Three Guineas* (New York: Harcourt Brace Jovanovich, 1938).

Lerner quote: Lerner, *Creation of Patriarchy,* p. 225, quoted in Steinem, *Revolution from Within,* p. 125.

197. "In a 1986 study in Waterloo, Ontario, . . .": Cited by Marilyn Webb, "Our Daughters, Ourselves: How Feminists Can Raise Feminists," *Ms.,* November/December 1992, p. 34.

198. Pavis-Weil quote: In ibid., p. 32.

7: THE POWER OF DESIRE

203. Lorde quotes: Audre Lorde, *Sister Outsider,* pp. 54, 57. What we are calling "desire," Lorde calls the "erotic." While we love and appreciate Lorde's reappropriation of the word *erotic,* we felt that the word *desire* was less specifically sexual in its general connotation.

204. "Dalma Heyn . . . threatening mate": Dalma Heyn, *The Erotic Silence of the American Wife.*

206. Hurston quote: Zora Neale Hurston, *Their Eyes Were Watching God* (Chicago: University of Illinois Press, 1978), pp. 10–11.

207. Colette quote: Colette, *Earthly Paradise,* ed. Robert Phelps (New York: Farrar, Straus & Giroux, 1966), p. 4.

208. "From the moment girls . . .": Since the 1980s when television programming was deregulated, children in this country have been exposed to feature-length commercials created by toy companies to sell products —an unheard-of situation in other countries. Recent attempts to stop the rampant marketeering in children's programming resulted in new laws that provide a weak compromise and little change.

"We live in the . . .": Juliet Schor, *The Overworked American: The Unexpected Decline of Leisure* (New York: Basic Books, 1991), p. 107.

209. "Michelle Fine, an activist . . .": Michelle Fine, "Sexuality, Schooling, and Adolescent Females," pp. 29–53.

210. "In 1990 . . . 'from high school' ": Both quotations from Christine Renee Robinson, "Working with Adolescent Girls: Strategies to Address Health Status," in *Women, Girls and Psychotherapy,* ed. Carol Gilligan et al., pp. 244–45. In the second quotation, Robinson cites the National Institute on Allergies and Infectious Disease Study Group "Sexually Transmitted Diseases Summary and Recommendations" (Washington, D.C.: United States Department of Health, Education, and Welfare; National Institutes of Health, 1980).

"The Children's Defense Fund reported . . .": Children's Defense Fund, "S.O.S. America: A Children's Defense Budget" (Washington, D.C.: Author, 1990).

"Teenagers are the fastest-growing . . .": An estimated 40,000 teens contract HIV each year. In addition, babies born with HIV are now beginning to reach adolescence. See Charles Kaiser, Op-Ed in *New York Times* November 30, 1992, A15:15; and in *New York Times,* July 12, 1992, XIII-LI, 6:4.

"In school, sexual harassment . . .": See Nan Stein, Nancy L. Marshall, and Linda R. Tropp, *Secrets in Public: Sexual Harassment in Our Schools* (Wellesley, Mass.: Wellesley College, Center for Research on Women, 1993).

"Violence against girls . . .": See Barrie Levy, ed., *Dating Violence: Young Women in Danger* (Seattle: Seal Press, 1991).

"Psychologist Deborah Tolman . . .": Deborah Tolman, *Dilemmas of Desire.*

Heyn quote: Heyn, *Erotic Silence,* p. 81.

211. "In several studies Tolman . . . 'I kissed him' ": Deborah Tolman, "Just Say No to What: Adolescent Girls' Sexual Subjectivity in Sexual Decisionmaking Narratives." Paper presented at the American Orthopsychiatric Association, Miami, Florida, April 1990.

"Even Sigmund Freud . . .": Sigmund Freud, " 'Civilized' Sexual Morality and Modern Nervous Illness," in *The Standard Edition,* vol. 9, ed. and trans. James Strachey (London: Hogarth Press, 1908), p. 179.

212. "In a study at the Harvard Project . . .": Unpublished three-population study conducted by Elizabeth Debold with Anne Elizabeth Blais and Martina Verba, Harvard Graduate School of Education, 1992.

215. Beauvoir quotes: Simone de Beauvoir, *Memoirs of a Dutiful Daughter* (New York: HarperCollins, 1974), pp. 100, 163.

221. Kanter quote: Rosabeth Moss Kanter, *Men and Women of the Corporation* (New York: Basic Books, 1977), p. 164.

222. Eleanor quote: Heyn, *Erotic Silence,* p. 333.

225. Vanderpool quote: Nathalie Akin Vanderpool, "Communication between Mothers and Adolescent Daughters on Issues of Sexuality: A Review of the Literature" (Qualifying paper, Harvard University, November 1991).

231. "appearance of conformity": Leslie McGovern, the director of The Alliance Project in Seattle, has worked with adolescent girls to "appear to conform" in an empowerment program called Discoveries. She has developed one of the few successful programs in the country that gives girls the skills to maintain their knowledge and assert their authority while appearing to conform to the conventions that so badly damage girls when they are not consciously resisting. We are indebted to Leslie for this concept.

234. "For Latina and white girls . . .": The Women's Sports Foundation Report, "Minorities in Sports."

8: BODY LANGUAGE

236. Quotes from *Scruples:* Judith Krantz, *Scruples* (London: Futura Books, 1978), cited by Wendy Chapkis, *Beauty Secrets* (Boston: South End Press, 1986), p. 95.

238. "In an era of backlash . . .": Susan Faludi, *Backlash.*

" 'Sara, an eighth-grader, tells . . . no body' ": Joyce Canaan, "Building Muscles and Getting Curves: Gender Differences in Representations of the Body and Sexuality among American Teenagers" (Unpublished paper, University of Chicago, 1984), p. 8.

239. "The girls in one study . . .": Ibid., p. 6.

240. Sarah quote: Ibid., p. 14.

241. "Melanie, a college freshman, . . .": Andrew Garrod, Lisa Smulyan, Sally Powers, and Robert Kilkenny, *Adolescent Portraits: Identity, Relationships, and Challenges* (Boston: Allyn & Bacon, 1991), pp. 19–40.

"Missing the forest for the trees . . .": Deborah L. Tolman and Elizabeth Debold, "Living an Image: A Problem of Body in Female Adolescence," presented at the American Psychological Association's 99th Annual Convention, San Francisco, Calif., August 1991, as part of a panel entitled "Resisting Silence: Women Listening to Girls." To be published in revised form as "Conflicts of Body and Image: Female Adolescents, Desire, and the No-body Body" in *Feminist Perspectives on Eating Disorders,* ed. Patricia Fallon, Melanie A. Katzman, and Susan C. Wooley (New York: Guilford Press, 1994).

242. "In a recent survey of adolescent health . . .": Minnesota Women's Fund, *Reflections of Risk.*

"In contemporary culture . . .": Joan Jacobs Brumberg, *Fasting Girls* (New York: New American Library, 1988), p. 231.

Peters quote: Ibid., p. 241.

"Despite an average height . . .": "Statistical Miss America," *Allure,* September 1992.

243. " 'What a sweet toy . . .' ": Oni Faida Lampley, "The Wig and I," *Mirabella,* March 1993, p. 146.

hooks quote: bell hooks, *Black Looks,* p. 3.

Mary Anne's Makeover quotes: Ann M. Martin, *Mary Anne's Makeover* (New York: Scholastic, 1993), pp. 25, 48, 53, 64, 66.

244. " 'a commodity to be bartered' ": Linda K. Christian-Smith, *Becoming a Woman through Romance* (New York: Routledge, 1990), p. 44.

245. Bordo quotes: Susan Bordo, "Anorexia Nervosa: Psychopathology as the Crystalization of Culture," in *Knowing Women: Feminism and Knowledge,* ed. Helen Crowley and Susan Weit Himmel (Cambridge: Polity Press, 1992), pp. 100, 103.

"Although just one-fourth . . .": Brumberg, *Fasting Girls,* p. 32.

Robinson and Ward quote: Tracy Robinson and Janie Victoria Ward, " 'A Belief in Self Far Greater Than Anyone's Disbelief,' " p. 89.

248. Rich quote: Adrienne Rich, *Of Woman Born: Motherhood as Experience and Institution* (New York: Bantam Books, 1977), p. 249.

249. "What do girls understand . . .": Frigga Haug, ed., *Female Sexualization: A Collective Work of Memory* (London: Verso, 1987), p. 127.

251. "The anorexic suffers . . .": American Psychiatric Association, *Diagnostic and Statistical Manual of Mental Disorders*, 3rd ed. (Washington, D.C.: APA, 1980; rev. 1987).

"Identifying anorexia in its . . .": For information on warning signs for both disorders, contact the American Anorexia and Bulimia Association, 418 E. 76th Street, New York, NY 10021. The work of Catherine Steiner-Adair is also particularly helpful in exploring the roots of eating disorders. Her work has been published widely in academic journals and may also be found in *Making Connections: The Relational Worlds of Adolescent Girls at Emma Willard School*, ed. Carol Gilligan, Nona P. Lyons, and Trudy J. Hanmer (Cambridge, Mass.: Harvard University Press, 1990).

"First identified . . . 'long history' ": Brumberg, *Fasting Girls*, p. 2.

"Girls of color . . ." Robinson and Ward, p. 88.

252. "The prevalence of . . . 'reflect . . . power' ": Bordo, "Anorexia Nervosa," p. 92.

253. Herman quotes: Judith Herman, *Trauma and Recovery*, p. 81.

255. Steinem quote: Gloria Steinem, *Revolution from Within*, pp. 225–26.

" 'what stirs the senses . . .' ": *American Heritage Dictionary*, 1st ed. (New York: Houghton Mifflin, 1983), p. 117.

9: INTIMATE ALLIES

265. Janeway quote: Elizabeth Janeway, "Women and the Uses of Power," in H. Einstein and A. Jardine, *The Future of Difference* (New Brunswick, N.J.: Rutgers University Press, 1980), pp. 328, 330.

hooks quote: bell hooks, *Black Looks*, p. 116.

"find a good way of going": Judith Anderson Dorney, " 'Courage to Act in a Small Way': Clues Toward Community and Change Among Women Teaching Girls" (Ed.D. diss., Harvard University, 1991).

266. "Like the interlocking circles . . .": Patricia Hill Collins, "The Meaning of Motherhood in Black Culture and Black Mother-Daughter Relationships," in *Double Stitch: Black Women Write about Mothers and Daughters,* ed. P. Bell-Scott et al. (New York: Harper Perennial, 1991), p. 47. Collins has taken the term *othermothers* from the work of Rosalie Riegle Troester in the same volume.

"Family provides a girl's . . .": Janeway, "Women and the Uses of Power," p. 332.

"These other oppressions . . .": bell hooks, *Feminist Theory: From Margin to Center* (Boston: South End Press, 1984), p. 36.

267. " 'to humanize . . . to resist' ": Letty Cottin Pogrebin, *Family Politics* (New York: McGraw-Hill, 1983), p. 30. Written ten years ago, this book presented a liberating vision of the family that remains valid.

Cottin Pogrebin quote: Ibid., p. 34.

268. Cottin Pogrebin quote: Ibid., pp. 213–14.

"While Mom now probably works . . .": Juliet B. Schor, *The Overworked American,* p. 25.

Engels quote: Friedrich Engels, *The Monogamous Family,* as quoted in Angela Barron McBride, *The Growth and Development of Mothers* (New York: Harper Colophon Books, 1973), p. 137.

"Lesbian- and gay-parent families . . .": Daniel Goleman, "Studies Find No Disadvantage in Growing Up in a Gay Home," *New York Times,* December 2, 1992.

269. Gilligan and Rogers quote: Carol Gilligan and Annie Rogers, "A Paradigm Shift in Psychology: Reframing Daughtering and Mothering," in *Daughtering and Mothering,* ed. Janneke van Mens-Verhulst (London: Routledge, in press), pp. 5–6.

272. "Yet most often the daughters . . .": Greenberg-Lake, *Shortchanging Girls.*

274. hooks quote: hooks, *Feminist Theory,* p. 72. "Researchers continue to find . . .": Michael Lamb, Margaret Tresch Owen, and Lindsay Chase-Lansdale, "The Father-Daughter Relationship: Past, Present and Future," in *Becoming Female: Perspectives on Development,* ed. Claire B. Koff (New York: Plenum, 1979), p. 98, cited in Judith Levine, *My Enemy, My Love: Man-Hating and Ambivalence in Women's Lives* (New York: Doubleday, 1992), p. 192.

"Two-year-old boys . . .": Miriam Johnson, "Fathers and 'Femininity' in Daughters: A Review of the Literature," *Sociology and Social Research* 67 (1982): 4–5, cited in Levine, *My Enemy,* p. 192.

"Even fathers who are . . .": Levine, *My Enemy,* p. 90.

"Older girls routinely . . . 'sandpaper' ": Terri Apter, *Altered Loves,* p. 8.

275. "Judith Levine, the author of . . .": Levine, *My Enemy.*

276. Tannen quotes: Deborah Tannen, *You Just Don't Understand: Women and Men in Conversation* (New York: Ballantine Books, 1991), pp. 52–53, 49.

Apter quote: Apter, *Altered Loves,* p. 87.

277. "Girls begin to see . . .": Ibid.

279. Gilligan quote: Carol Gilligan, "Teaching Shakespeare's Sister," in *Making Connections,* pp. 6–29.

280–1. Lorde quote: Audre Lorde, *Sister Outsider,* p. 42.

281. Rich quote: Adrienne Rich, *Of Woman Born,* pp. 253–54.

281–2. Collins quotes: Collins, "Meaning of Motherhood," pp. 49, 54.

288–9. "Research indicates that . . .": Judith S. Musick, "The High-Stakes Challenge of Programs for Adolescent Mothers," in *Adolescence and*

Poverty: Challenge for the 1990s, ed. Peter Edelman and Joyce Ladner (Washington, D.C.: Center for National Policy Press, 1991).

289. "Not only did many of these girls . . .": Josefina Villamil Tinajero, Maria Luisa Gonzalez, and Florence Dick, *Raising Career Aspirations of Hispanic Girls* (Bloomington, Ind.: Phi Delta Kappa Educational Foundation, 1991).

Steinem quote: Gloria Steinem, "Helping Ourselves to Revolution," *Ms.,* November/December 1992, p. 29.

" 'We need to establish . . .' ": Leslie McGovern is a therapist and director of The Alliance Project in Seattle, Washington. Leslie has worked extensively with mothers and daughters relating to girls' empowerment.

292. hooks quote: bell hooks, *Feminist Theory,* p. 63.

"Responsibility and action . . .": Peter Martynowych, a therapist who conducts workshops on classism, finds that guilt and the defense against feeling guilt are the most significant barriers to creating a productive solidarity.

Dorney quote: Judith Anderson Dorney, " 'Courage to Act in a Small Way': Clues toward Community and Change among Women Teaching Girls" (Ed.D. diss., Harvard University, 1991), p. 235.

293. Herman quote: Judith Herman, *Trauma and Recovery,* p. 9.

10: FROM BETRAYAL TO POWER

295. "The romance-into-mothering . . .": See Barbara Ehrenreich and Deirdre English, *For Her Own Good.*

296. " 'vital toughness and visionary strength' ": Adrienne Rich, "What Does a Woman Need to Know?" p. 7.

300. hooks quote: bell hooks, *Feminist Theory,* p. 18.

301. "As Susan Faludi documented . . .": Susan Faludi, *Backlash.*

302. " 'build a society based . . .' ": Michael Kelly, "Hillary Rodham Clinton and the Politics of Virtue," *New York Times Magazine,* May 23, 1993, pp. 63, 66.

303. "We do know that the voices . . .": In the last chapter of *In a Different Voice,* Carol Gilligan suggested that maturity in adulthood would combine the moral voices that she identified—the voice of justice and the voice of care.

"The voice of equality that insisted . . .": See, for example, Martha Albertson Fineman, *The Illusion of Equality: The Rhetoric and Reality of Divorce Reform* (Chicago: University of Chicago Press, 1991).

"The voice of care humanizes . . .": See, for example, the abortion study in Carol Gilligan's *In a Different Voice,* pp. 66–127.

"Over one-third of all Puerto Rican . . .": Eugenia Acuna-Lilli, "The Reproductive Health of Latinas in New York City: Making a Difference at the Individual Level" (Paper presented at the 1989 Third World Women's Conference, New York, N.Y., 1989).

305. Lorde quote: Audre Lorde, *Sister Outsider,* p. 45.

306. "But the working-class women . . .": The term *suits* was used by working-class women in the 1992 Women's Voices focus groups. They used the term casually and freely, suggesting its common usage. See Linda Williams, "Ending the Silence: The Voices of Women of Color," *Equal Means: Women Organizing Economic Solutions* 1 (Winter 1983): 13. According to Williams, "Blue-collar white women were emphatic in pointing out that they had the least in common with 'professionals,' 'the kind of women who wore suits,' and appeared in American Express ads. Throughout the focus groups, class and lifestyle, not race, were the main dividing points."

307. "Loving women, keeping . . .": For a similar and more in-depth analysis of these points, see Suzanne Pharr, *Homophobia: A Weapon of Sexism* (Little Rock, Ark.: Chardon Press, 1988).

309. " 'everything . . . and love' ": Juliet Schor, *The Overworked American*, p. 119.

"A cycle of 'work-and-spend' . . .": Robert Bellah, Richard Madsen, William M. Sullivan, Ann Swidler, and Steven M. Tipton, *Habits of the Heart: Individualism and Commitment in American Life* (New York: HarperCollins, 1986), pp. vii–viii.

310. "We are urged to find . . .": See Schor, *The Overworked American;* note particularly "The Creation of Discontent" in chapter 5, "The Insidious Cycle of Work-and-Spend," pp. 114–17.

"Early labor activists wisely . . .": Ibid., p. 120.

313. "American life, argue . . .": Bellah et al., *Habits of the Heart,* p. 277.

Resources

STORIES OF GIRLS' AND WOMEN'S LIVES

Allende, Isabel. *The Stories of Eva Luna*. New York: Bantam Books, 1992. Also by this author, *Eva Luna,* New York: Bantam, 1989.

Allison, Dorothy. *Bastard Out of Carolina*. New York: Dutton, 1992. (A girl's struggle with a stepfather who sexually abuses her and a mother who avoids seeing it)

Alvarez, Julia. *How the Garcia Girls Lost Their Accents*. New York: Plume, 1992.

Angelou, Maya. *I Know Why the Caged Bird Sings*. New York: Bantam Classics, 1983. (Autobiography of the poet's early life)

Anzaldua, Gloria, ed. *Making Face, Making Soul: Creative and Critical Perspectives of Women of Color*. San Francisco: Aunt Lute Foundation Books, 1990.

Atwood, Margaret. *Cat's Eye*. New York: Bantam Books, 1989. (Young girls' cruelty toward one another, told as a flashback from the perspective of a woman painter)

Augenbraum, Harold, and Ilan Stavans, eds. *Growing Up Latino: Memoirs and Stories*. Boston: Houghton Mifflin, 1993.

Barry, Lynda. *The Good Times Are Killing Me*. New York: HarperCollins, 1991. (Friendship between a black girl and a white girl and what happens as they come to understand what race means in America)

Bateson, Mary Catherine. *With a Daughter's Eye*. New York: Washington Square Press, 1985. (Memoir of Margaret Mead's daughter)

de Beauvoir, Simone. *Memoirs of a Dutiful Daughter*. New York: HarperCollins, 1974.

Brontë, Charlotte. *Jane Eyre*. New York: New American Library/Dutton, 1960.

344

Brown, Rosellen. *Before and After.* New York: Farrar, Straus & Giroux, 1992. (A family grappling with their son's murder of his girlfriend, and a young daughter's holding to the truth)

Calderón, Sara Levi. *The Two Mujeres.* (Trans. by Gina Kaufer.) San Francisco: Aunt Lute, 1992. (On the Mexican best-seller list)

Cameron, Anne. *Daughters of Copper Woman.* Vancouver, British Columbia: Press Gang Publishers, 1981. (Native American tales of creation and coming of age)

Chopin, Kate. *The Awakening.* New York: Avon Books, 1972. (Nineteenth-century story of a woman's awakening to her desires and to the constraints of being a woman in a sexist culture)

Cisneros, Sandra. *The House on Mango Street.* New York: Vintage, 1991. (Lyrical vignettes of a Mexican girl growing up in an American city) Also by this author, *Woman Hollering Creek.* New York: Random House, 1991.

Cofer, Judith Ortiz. *Silent Dancing: A Partial Remembrance of a Puerto Rican Childhood.* Houston, Tex.: Arte Publico Press, 1990. (An extraordinary weaving of memory and myth; great reading for women and for adolescent girls)

Conway, Jill Kerr, ed. *Written by Herself, Autobiographies of American Women: An Anthology.* New York: Vintage Books, 1992.

Cook, Blanche Wiesen. *Eleanor Roosevelt: Volume One, 1884–1933.* New York: Washington Square Press, 1985.

Dorris, Michael. *Yellow Raft in Blue Water.* New York: Warner Books, 1988. (Intergenerational story of three Native American women)

Dragu, Margaret, Sarah Sheard, and Susan Swan, eds. *Mothers Talk Back: Momz Radio.* Toronto, Canada: Coach House Press, 1991. (Interviews with mothers about mothering)

Duras, Marguerite. *The Lover.* New York: Harper & Row Perennial Library, 1986. (Chilling story of a girl who uses her budding womanhood to get her family out of Vietnam)

Flagg, Fannie. *Fried Green Tomatoes at the Whistle Stop Cafe.* New York: McGraw-Hill, 1988. (A great movie, too)

Frank, Anne. *The Diary of Anne Frank: The Critical Edition.* Netherlands State Institute for War Documentation Staff, comp. and trans. Arnold Pomerans. New York: Doubleday, 1989. (The version that Anne wrote—not the sanitized version approved by her father and a priest)

Frazer, Sylvia. *My Father's House: A Memoir of Incest and of Healing.* New York: Perennial Library, 1987.

Gibbons, Kaye. *Ellen Foster.* New York: Vintage Contemporaries, 1990. (Hilarious and heartrending story of a white girl growing up in the South)

Gómez, Alma, Cherrie Moraga, and Mariana Romo-Carmana, eds. *Cuentos: Stories by Latinas.* Latham, N.Y.: Kitchen Table/Women of Color Press, 1983.

Kincaid, Jamaica. *Annie John.* New York: New American Library, 1983. (A West Indian girl growing up and away from her mother) Also by this author, the sequel, *Lucy,* New York: NAL-Dutton, 1991.

Kingsolver, Barbara. *Animal Dreams.* New York: HarperPerennial, 1990. (A young woman reclaiming her past)

Kingston, Maxine Hong. *Woman Warrior: Memoirs of a Girlhood among Ghosts.* New York: Vintage Books, 1977. (Autobiography of growing up Chinese in America)

Lightfoot, Sara Lawrence. *Balm in Gilead: Journey of a Healer.* Reading, Mass.: Addison-Wesley, 1988. (Memoir of her mother's life)

Lorde, Audre. *Zami: A New Spelling of My Name.* Freedom, Calif.: The Crossing Press, 1982. (Autobiographical story of this poet's growing up)

McCullers, Carson. *Member of the Wedding.* New York: Bantam, 1985. (A classic story of a white girl struggling to understand what it means for her to become a young woman in the South)

Markham, Beryl. *West with the Night.* San Francisco: Northpoint Press, 1983. (A white girl growing up motherless in Africa)

Marshall, Paule. *Brown Girl, Brownstones.* New York: Feminist Press, 1981. (A complex portrait of a daughter growing up and butting heads with her mother) Also by this author, *Daughters,* New York: Macmillan, 1992.

Miller, Sue. *The Good Mother.* New York: Dell, 1987. (Also made into a film)

Moraga, Cherrie, and Gloria Anzaldúa, eds. *This Bridge Called My Back: Writings by Radical Women of Color.* Latham, N.Y.: Kitchen Table/Women of Color Press, 1984.

Morrison, Toni. *The Bluest Eye.* New York: Pocket Books, 1984. (Three young African-American girls learning to see themselves through the distortion of white culture) Also by this author, *Beloved,* New York: NAL-Dutton, 1988, and *Sula,* New York: NAL-Dutton, 1987.

Munro, Alice. *The Lives of Girls and Women*. New York: New American Library/ Dutton, 1974. (A girl becomes a young woman in the backwoods of Canada)

Neale Hurston, Zora. *Their Eyes Were Watching God*. Chicago: University of Illinois Press, 1978. (Amazing story of growing up and loving)

Olsen, Tillie. *Tell Me a Riddle*. New York: Dell, 1989. (Short stories—especially notable, "I Stand Here Ironing," about a working-class mother's thoughts on her daughter's growing up)

Payne, Karen, ed. *Between Ourselves: Letters between Mothers and Daughters*. Boston: Houghton Mifflin, 1983.

Penelope, Julia, and Susan J. Wolfe. *The Original Coming Out Stories*. Freedom, Calif.: The Crossing Press, 1989.

Quindlen, Anna. *Object Lessons*. New York: Random House, 1991.

Rhys, Jean. *Wide Sargasso Sea*. New York: Norton, 1982. (What happens before *Jane Eyre*—how the first wife became mad and got put in the attic)

Rose, Phyllis. *Parallel Lives: Five Victorian Marriages*. New York: Vintage Books, 1984.

Santiago, Esmeralda. *When I Was Puerto Rican*. Reading, Mass.: Addison-Wesley, 1993.

Saxton, Marsha, and Florence Howe, eds. *With Wings: An Anthology of Literature by and about Women with Disabilities*. New York: The Feminist Press, 1987.

Schoenfielder, Lisa, and Barb Wieser, eds. *Shadow on a Tightrope: Writings by Women on Fat Oppression*. San Francisco: Aunt Lute, 1983.

Slovo, Shawn. *A World Apart*. New York: Faber & Faber, 1988. (A white woman's activism against apartheid in South Africa told from her twelve-year-old daughter's perspective; also a great movie)

Smith, Barbara, ed. *Home Girls: A Black Feminist Anthology*. Latham, N.Y.: Kitchen Table/Women of Color Press, 1983. (Personal reflections and political analysis)

Tan, Amy. *The Joy Luck Club*. New York: Vintage Contemporaries, 1991. (Stories of four Chinese women and their Chinese-American daughters)

Vélez, Diana. *Reclaiming Medusa: Short Stories by Contemporary Puerto Rican Women*. San Francisco: Aunt Lute, 1988.

Walker, Alice. *Possessing the Secret of Joy*. New York: Harcourt Brace Jovanovich, 1992. Also by this author, *The Color Purple*, New York: Pocket Books, 1988.

Winterson, Jeanette. *Oranges Are Not the Only Fruit.* New York: Atlantic Monthly Press, 1987. (A young girl adopted by a zealous Christian discovers her love for women.) Also by this author, *The Passion,* New York: Vintage Books, 1987.

Yamamoto, Hisaye. *Seventeen Syllables and Other Stories.* Latham, N.Y.: Kitchen Table/Women of Color Press, 1988.

Zahava, Irene, ed. *My Mother's Daughter: Writings by Women.* Freedom, Calif.: The Crossing Press, 1991.

Zandy, Janet, ed. *Calling Home: Working-Class Women's Writings an Anthology.* New Brunswick, N.J.: Rutgers University Press, 1990.

PSYCHOLOGY AND RESEARCH ON GIRLS' AND WOMEN'S LIVES

Apter, Terri. *Altered Loves: Mothers and Daughters during Adolescence.* New York: St. Martin's, 1990.

Belenky, Mary Field, Blythe Clinchy McVicker, Nancy Rule Goldberger, and Jill Mattuck Tarule. *Women's Ways of Knowing: The Development of Self, Voice and Mind.* New York: Basic Books, 1986.

Brown, Lyn Mikel and Carol Gilligan. *Meeting at the Crossroads: Women's Psychology and Girls' Development.* Cambridge, Mass.: Harvard University Press, 1992.

Caplan, Paula. *Don't Blame Mother: Mending the Mother-Daughter Relationship.* New York: HarperCollins, 1989.

Eichenbaum, Luise, and Susie Orbach. *Understanding Women: A Feminist Psychoanalytic Approach.* New York: Basic Books, 1983.

Fine, Michelle. *Disruptive Voices: The Possibilities of Feminist Research.* Ann Arbor: University of Michigan Press, 1992.

Gilligan, Carol. *In a Different Voice: Psychological Theory and Women's Development.* Cambridge, Mass.: Harvard University Press, 1982.

Gilligan, Carol, Nona Lyons, and Trudy Hanmer, eds. *Making Connections: The Relational Worlds of Adolescent Girls at Emma Willard School.* Cambridge, Mass.: Harvard University Press, 1990.

Gilligan, Carol, Annie Rogers, and Deborah Tolman, eds. *Women, Girls & Psychotherapy: Reframing Resistance.* Binghamton, N.Y.: Haworth Press, 1991.

Goodrich, Thelma Jean, ed. *Women and Power: Perspectives for Family Therapy.* New York: Norton, 1991.

Herman, Judith. *Trauma and Recovery.* New York: Basic Books, 1992.

———. *Father-Daughter Incest.* Cambridge, Mass.: Harvard University Press, 1981.

Heyn, Dalma. *The Erotic Silence of the American Wife.* New York: Signet/Penguin Books, 1993.

Holland, Dorothy, and Margaret Eisenhart. *Educated in Romance: Women, Achievement and College Culture.* Chicago: University of Chicago Press, 1990.

hooks, bell. *Sisters of the Yam: Black Women and Self-Recovery.* Boston: South End Press, 1993.

Jack, Dana Crowley. *Silencing the Self: Women and Depression.* Cambridge, Mass.: Harvard University Press, 1991.

Jordan, Judith, Jean Baker Miller, Irene Stiver, and Janet Surrey. *Women's Growth in Connection: Writings from the Stone Center.* New York: Guilford Press, 1991.

Josselson, Ruthellen. *The Space between Us: Exploring the Dimensions of Human Relationships.* San Francisco: Jossey-Bass, 1992.

Levy, Barrie, ed. *Dating Violence: Young Women in Danger.* Seattle: Seal Press, 1991.

Marone, Nicky. *How to Father a Successful Daughter.* New York: McGraw-Hill, 1988.

Miller, Alice. *Banished Knowledge: Facing Childhood Injuries.* New York: Anchor Books/Doubleday, 1990.

Miller, Jean Baker. *Toward a New Psychology of Women.* Boston: Beacon Press, 1976.

Minnesota Women's Fund. *Reflections on Risk: Growing Up Female in Minnesota.* Minneapolis: Author, February 1990.

Orbach, Susie. *Fat Is a Feminist Issue: A Self-Help Guide for Compulsive Eaters.* New York· Berkley Books, 1980.

Sadker, Myra, and David Sadker. *Failing at Fairness: How America's Schools Cheat Girls.* New York: Scribners, 1994.

Schaef, Anne Wilson. *Women's Reality: An Emerging Female System in the White Male Society.* Minneapolis: Winston Press, 1981.

349

Steinem, Gloria. *Revolution from Within: A Book of Self-Esteem.* Boston: Little, Brown, 1992.

Tannen, Deborah. *You Just Don't Understand: Women and Men in Conversation.* New York: Ballantine Books, 1991.

Terr, Lenore. *Too Scared to Cry: Psychic Trauma in Childhood.* New York: HarperCollins, 1990.

CRITICAL THINKERS

Albert, Michael, Leslie Cagan, Noam Chomsky, Robin Hannet, Mel King, Lydia Sargent, and Holly Sklar. *Liberating Theory.* Boston: South End Press, 1986.

Albrecht, Lisa, and Rose M. Brewer. *Bridges of Power: Women's Multicultural Alliances.* Philadelphia: New Society Publishers, 1990.

Alexander, Jacqui, Lisa Albrecht, Sharon Day, Mab Segrest, and Norma Alarcón. *The Third Wave: Feminist Perspectives on Racism.* Latham, N.Y.: Kitchen Table/ Women of Color Press, 1993.

Ascher, Carol, Louise DeSalvo, and Sara Ruddick. *Between Women: Biographers, Novelists, Critics, Teachers and Artists Write about Their Work on Women.* Boston: Beacon Press, 1984.

Bateson, Mary Catherine. *Composing a Life.* New York: NAL-Dutton, 1990.

Bellah, Robert, Richard Madsen, William M. Sullivan, Ann Swidler, and Steven M. Tipton. *Habits of the Heart: Individualism and Commitment in American Life.* New York: HarperCollins, 1986.

Bell-Scott, Patricia, Beverly Guy-Sheftalle, Jacqueline Jones Royster, Janet Sims-Wood, Miriam DeCosta-Willis, and Lucille P. Fultz. *Double Stitch: Black Women Write about Mothers and Daughters.* New York: HarperPerennial, 1991.

Brandt, Barbara. *Whole Life Economics: Revaluing Daily Life.* Philadelphia: New Society Publishers, 1993.

Brownmiller, Susan. *Femininity.* New York: Fawcett, 1985.

Brumberg, Joan Jacobs. *Fasting Girls: The Emergence of Anorexia Nervosa as a Modern Disease.* New York: New American Library, 1988.

Chapkis, Wendy. *Beauty Secrets: Women and the Politics of Appearance.* Boston: South End Press, 1986.

Cleage, Pearl. *Mad at Miles: A Blackwoman's Guide to Truth*. Southfield, Mich.: Cleage Group, 1990.

Davis, Angela. *Women, Race, and Class*. New York: Random, 1983.

Dinnerstein, Dorothy. *The Mermaid and the Minotaur: Sexual Arrangements and Human Malaise*. New York: Harper & Row, 1976.

Ehrenreich, Barbara, and Deirdre English. *For Her Own Good: 150 Years of the Experts' Advice to Women*. New York: Anchor/Doubleday, 1978.

Faludi, Susan. *Backlash: The Undeclared War against American Women*. New York: Crown, 1991.

Fink, Rus Ervin. *Stopping Rape: A Challenge for Men*. Philadelphia: New Society Publishers, 1988.

Harris, Maria. *Women and Teaching*. New York: Paulist Press, 1988.

Heilbrun, Carolyn. *Writing a Woman's Life*. New York: Ballantine, 1989.

Hine, Darlene Clark, ed. *Black Women in America: An Historical Encyclopedia*. Two vols. Brooklyn, N.Y.: Carlson Publishing, 1993.

hooks, bell. *Feminist Theory: From Margin to Center*. Boston: South End Press, 1984. (All of this author's works are important and available through South End Press)

Janeway, Elizabeth. *The Powers of the Weak*. New York: Knopf, 1980. (out of print)

Joseph, G. and J. Lewis. *Common Differences: Conflicts in Black and White Feminist Perspectives*. Boston: South End Press, 1981.

Lorde, Audre. *Sister Outsider*. Freedom, Calif.: Crossing Press, 1984.

McAllister, Pam. *This River of Courage: Generations of Women's Resistance and Action*. Philadelphia: New Society Publishers, 1991.

Miedzian, Myriam. *Boys Will Be Boys: Breaking the Link between Masculinity and Violence*. New York: Doubleday, 1991.

Olsen, Tillie. *Silences*. New York: Laurel/Seymour Lawrence, 1978.

Omolade, Barbara. *It's a Family Affair: The Real Lives of Black Single Mothers*. Latham, N.Y.: Kitchen Table/Women of Color Press, 1987.

Pharr, Suzanne. *Homophobia: A Weapon of Sexism*. Inverness, Calif.: Chardon Press, 1988.

Pogrebin, Letty Cottin. *Family Politics: Love and Power on an Intimate Frontier*. New York: McGraw-Hill, 1984.

Rich, Adrienne. *Of Woman Born: Motherhood as Experience and Institution.* New York: Norton, 1986. (Also, her other books of essays: *Blood, Bread and Poetry,* New York: Norton, 1986, and *On Lies, Secrets and Silences,* New York: Norton, 1979)

Ruddick, Sara, and Pamela Daniels, eds. *Working It Out: 23 Women Writers, Artists, Scientists and Scholars Talk about Their Lives and Work.* New York: Pantheon Books, 1977.

Schor, Juliet. *The Overworked American: The Unexpected Decline of Leisure.* New York: Basic Books, 1991.

Spender, Dale. *Women of Ideas and What Men Have Done to Them.* London: Pandora Press, 1982.

Steinem, Gloria. *Outrageous Acts and Everyday Rebellions.* New York: NAL-Dutton, 1986.

Walker, Alice. *In Search of Our Mother's Gardens: Womanist Prose.* New York: Harcourt Brace Jovanovich, 1983.

Wolf, Naomi. *The Beauty Myth: How Images of Beauty Are Used against Women.* New York: Morrow, 1991.

Woolf, Virginia. *Three Guineas.* New York: Harcourt Brace Jovanovich, 1966. (Powerful essay about women's education and ending of war) Also by this author, *A Room of One's Own,* New York: Harcourt Brace Jovanovich, 1991.

GRAB BAG OF BOOKS AND TOOLS FOR GREAT GIRLS (AND THEIR MOTHERS)

Capacchione, Lucia. *The Creative Journal: The Art of Finding Yourself.* North Hollywood, Calif.: New Castle, 1989.

Chelsea House Publishers, New York, has two series of biographies for preadolescents and adolescents. One is the "American Women of Achievement" series of fifty women, from Georgia O'Keeffe to Gloria Steinem. The other is the "Black Americans of Achievement" series, which has many biographies of women such as Alice Walker, Angela Davis, and Rosa Parks.

Dorris, Michael. *Morning Girl.* New York: Hyperion Books for Children, 1992.

Griffin, Lynne, and Kelly McCann. *The Book of Women: 300 Notable Women*

History Passed By. Holbrook, Mass.: Bob Adams, 1992. (Stories of women rodeo stars, daredevils, "women who looked death in the face and lived to tell the tale," and other wild women)

Hart, Carol, Letty Cottin Pogrebin, Mary Rodgers, and Marlo Thomas, eds. *Free to Be . . . You and Me.* New York: Bantam Books, 1987.

Heard, Georgia. *For the Good of the Earth and the Sun—Teaching Poetry.* Portsmouth, N.H.: Heinemann Educational Books, 1989. (Ways of facilitating a child's voice in creative writing)

Hunter, Latoya. *The Diary of Latoya Hunter.* (Real diary of a seventh-grader)

New Moon: The Magazine for Girls and Their Dreams and *New Moon Parenting: For Adults Who Care About Girls.* Published by Nancy Gruver and Joe Kelly with an editorial board of girls. The magazine is as girl-run as possible. Available from P.O. Box 3587, Duluth, MN 55803 or call 218-788-5507. Also available in select bookstores.

Rainer, Tristine. *The New Diary: How to Use a Journal for Self-Guidance and Expanded Creativity.* Los Angeles: Tarcher, 1978.

Starck, Marcia. *Women's Medicine Ways: Cross-Cultural Rites of Passage.* Freedom, Calif.: The Crossing Press, 1993. (Ideas for creating celebrations at puberty)

ORGANIZING AND TAKING ACTION

Bingham, Mindy, Lari Quinn, and William P. Sheehan. *Mother Daughter Choices: A Handbook for the Coordinator.* Santa Barbara, Calif.: Advocacy Press, 1990. Facilitators guide to doing six-week-long mother-run programs for mothers and daughters about life-planning. Targeted for sixth-grade girls, the program can also be used for girls from ages 10 to 14. It uses the companion workbooks/journals *Choices* and *Changes,* which are great in their own right (from the same publisher). This is an excellent program for mothers to begin creating a community of support for their daughters.

Coover, Virginia, Ellen Deacon, Charles Esser, and Christopher Moore. *Resource Manual for a Living Revolution: A Handbook of Skills and Tools for Social Change Activists.* Philadelphia: New Society, 1985.

Haug, Frigga, ed. *Female Sexualization: A Collective Work of Memory.* (Trans. Erica

Carter.) New York: Routledge, Chapman & Hall, 1987. (Describes and defines a process of reclaiming for women to do in groups)

The National Association of Mother's Centers operates a national network of over 200 mother-run support centers, primarily for mothers of young children. Call 1-800-645-3828 to obtain information on starting or joining a group.

National Organization for Women, *NOW Guidelines for Feminist Consciousness-Raising*, 1982. Can be purchased for $10 through NOW, 1000 16th Street, N.W., Suite 700, Washington, D.C. 20036. 202-331-0066. A detailed guide for creating groups to explore women's experiences of being female in this culture. The rules provide for a minimum of flexibility in order to create maximum safety. This can be a good place to begin while a group's members find their way together.

Sarachild, Kathie. "A Program for Feminist Consciousness-raising." In *Women Together,* Judith Papachristou, ed. New York: Knopf, 1976.

Steinem, Gloria. "Afterword" to paperback version of *Revolution from Within,* Boston: Little, Brown, 1992.

Index

abortion, 303–4

abuse. *See* sexual abuse

academic performance, decline of, 10, 19, 88

achievement, beauty equals, 236–37

acknowledgment and recognition, 89, 133, 148, 151

action, taking, 196–201
  on behalf of daughters, 196
  and building autonomy, 200
  mothers' groups, 286–93
  at school, 197–98
  and solidarity, 234

adjusting to changes in daughters, 149

Adolescent Health Program (Minneapolis), 123

African-American
  communities, and sharing mothering, 281–82
  families, 267, 268

African-American girls
  assertive mothers and, 156
  assessment of future roles, 68–69, 89
  and authoritarian mothers, 156
  and desire for acknowledgment and recognition, 89
  and discrimination 17–18
  double vision of, 18
  and eating disorders, 251–52
  and fighting, 164
  and independence, 70
  and individuality vs. community, 59
  and mother daughter relationships, 25, 67–68
  othermothers and, 281–82
  and racelessness, 59
  resistance and, 16–17, 117
  romance stories and, 89
  in sports, 193
  and struggle during adolescence, 64
  survival strategies of, 117, 184
  voice and, 16–17

AIDS, 210

Aladdin, 83

alienation and "women's work," 28

American Association of University Women (AAUW), xxi, 288
  on self-esteem, 190
  on self-perception, 10–11, 13

anger, 113–15, 163–68
  boys', 81
  and connection, 97, 163–64
  expression, 113–14, 168
  and fear of abandonment, 167, 1687
  and inclusion/exclusion, 52
  and loss, 107–108
  male, 164
  toward mother, 30–31
  between mother and daughter, 68–69
  purpose of, 113
  and self-control, 164
  suppressing, 164–65

Acknowledgments

We would like to acknowledge our mothers and sisters in revolution —Gloria Steinem and Carol Gilligan. They have encouraged and guided us through their vision, voice, and support. The mothers who joined us to share their struggles and successes as mothers of daughters and as daughters of mothers have inspired our writing. Their candor and generosity, their love for their daughters, made this book possible. We are also deeply grateful to the researchers at the Harvard Project on Women's Psychology and Girls' Development and to the board and staff of the Ms. Foundation for Women.

ELIZABETH:

My understanding of girls' development has grown through endless hours of conversation with my colleagues and friends at the Harvard Project. I am grateful for their generosity, love, insight, and passion. Special thanks to Lyn Brown, Judy Dorney, and Barb Miller from the Laurel team; to Deb Tolman for her boundless desire, and to Martina Verba, Annie Blais, and Amanda Federman for their perceptive analysis of interviews. Extra special thanks to my students and to the girls and their families who have been part of our work. I would like to acknowledge my debt to Sarah Hanson for her calm, her intelligence, and her great heart. Thanks to all the feminist researchers, such as Michelle Fine and Judith Herman, who are revisioning the human world.

I would also like to thank the othermothers and allies in my own life.

Not only did Henry Duda and Jan Mellinger give me new life, but Kay Miller, Adriana D'Amico, Shyam Bhatnagar, Sara Andrews, and Asma Hamdani helped me to find my way and my voice. I owe deep thanks to my friends and family for not getting fed up with me as I dropped out of sight to write. Special thanks to Emily, Barb, Deb, Sara, Alison, Maria, Sharon, Hila, Flora, Karen, Nancy, Jennifer, Buzzy, Catherine, Lisa, Kathleen, and all the others with whom I have lived and learned while writing. Thanks to my brother, Richard, the computer wizard, and to Michael and Amy for their faith in me. I am especially grateful to Esti and Gaby for sharing their home and their mother for months. And, finally, thank you, Peter Martynowych; without your insight, intelligence, humor, and love I might not have made it through this project (let alone had fun). You have taught me so much.

MARIE:

My voice in this book and in life has been nurtured by being joined with women in mutually strengthening relationships. First by Nancy Lee who, against all odds, kept her voice and helps me keep mine. Lois Braverman, Laurisa Sellers, and Kitty Kolbert taught me what it means to live your life in a community of women. The entire family of the Ms. Foundation for Women who Idelisse names below provided the environment where work with girls could grow; their commitment to the daughters of this country provided daily sustenance during the book's writing. (Please read the list of names twice for my personal thanks, too.) Wendy Purifoy reinforced my decision to pursue the implications of the Harvard Project research; Catlin Fullwood and Ann Roberts generously shared their own experiences with girls; and Jungian analyst Jean Shinoda Bolen consistently called and told me the right story at the most essential time.

Othermothers to this book included several old and new friends. Nancy Meyer's interview was inspiring, but beyond that her consistent enthusiasm about the book's importance was boundless. Dan Hunter, my political campaign manager, also campaigned for me to write for a decade. Paula Pressley was my original teacher about the value of othermothers for our daughters as well as our sons. I learned an enormous amount from Thelma Jean Goodrich, Judith Musick, Anne St. Germaine, and Michael Resnick, who were gracious with their expertise about girls and adolescence. Nell Merlino's creative work on *Take Our Daughters to Work* paved the way for a new public consciousness about girls. Judith Stern Peck helped me begin, and Joan Stein helped me finish. Finally, my father: thanks for being proud of me throughout life.

IDELISSE:

My relationship with my daughter Esti has made its way into this book in ways that are obvious to any reader. What is less obvious, but no less profound, are the ways in which this book has been shaped by my relationship with my fifteen-year–old son, Gabriel. I am truly graced to have them both in my life. I am also graced by loving and unconditionally supportive parents who nurtured me and my children whenever and however we needed while this book was being written. *Gracias, Mami y Papi.* My friends, the kids' othermothers, Judy Katz, Laura Norman, Anne Mendel McCormack, Adele Marano, and Aurea Nieves, showered us with their love, attention, and care. They took the kids out when I was working and spent hours and hours with me on the phone. I thank them and all my friends for their generosity and thoughtfulness, and for the ideas they enthusiastically shared with me. Thinking with you all is one of the great pleasures of my life. Extra special thanks to Sandra Garcia, Elba Montalvo, Barbara Keleman, Myra La Joie, Marion Kaplan, and my niece, Melissa Malavé.

I offer my personal thanks to all the women I work with—and learn from—at the Ms. Foundation for Women: Susan, Jean, Martha, Kristen, Sara, Hana, Susie, Catherine, Nell, Patty, Marianna, Yvette, Kalima,

Robin, Joanne, Therese, Tani, Bette, and Carol. You are a very wonderful group of women.

This book has been in the best of hands since it was no more than an idea. Katinka Matson and John Brockman, our agents, gave us enthusiastic and savvy support. Liz Perle McKenna, our editor, has provided unflagging support and endless wisdom. Liz shared our vision and helped us to refine it so that we could share it with others. We owe her a great deal of thanks for standing by through the long nights at the end. The team at Addison-Wesley has been a pleasure to work with. Wendy Hickok Robinson gave up her nights and weekends to make final changes in the uncopyedited manuscript. Beth Burleigh, the production editor, Sharon Sharp, the copy-editor, and Carol Woolverton, the compositor, pulled out all the stops to keep this book on schedule. Our team at Bantam has also been great. Thanks particularly to Toni Burbank for her vision and commitment and to Alison Rivers for her intelligent support. Authors couldn't want for more support from publishers; we thank you all.

About the Authors

Elizabeth Debold has been a member of the Harvard Project on Women's Psychology and Girls' Development since 1986. She has consulted to a variety of organizations, such as the Ms. Foundation for Women and Children's Television Workshop.

Idelisse Malavé joined the Ms. Foundation for Women as Vice President in 1990, where she worked closely with Marie Wilson to develop the National Girls Initiative. A graduate of Columbia Law School, she was previously a civil rights litigator with the Puerto Rican Legal Defense and Education Fund and practiced family law. She has two children, one of whom is an eleven-year-old girl.

Marie C. Wilson has been President of the Ms. Foundation for Women in New York City for ten years. While at Ms. she founded the National Girls Initiative, a grant-making and public education campaign for pre-adolescent and adolescent girls, and sponsored the Annual "Take Our Daughters to Work" Day in which 25 million people participated in 1994. She is the mother of two grown daughters and three sons.